Grounded in God's Word

Grounded in God's Word

A Daily Devotional Based on the
Westminster Shorter Catechism

Dennis D. Hustedt

PUBLISHING WITH A MISSION

**PUBLISHING WITH A MISSION**

EVANGELICAL PRESS
Faverdale North Industrial Estate, Darlington, DL3 0PH England
email: sales@evangelicalpress.org

EVANGELICAL PRESS USA
PO Box 825, Webster, NY 14580 USA
email: usa.sales@evangelicalpress.org

www.evangelicalpress.org

Printed in the United States of America

Scripture references, unless otherwise noted, are from the New International Version of the Bible.

Set in Segoe Script and Sabon Monotype

British Library Cataloguing in Publication Data available

ISBN-10 0 8523 4683 2
ISBN-13 978 0 85234 683 9

Contents

INTRODUCTION

The book you hold in your hands is both a devotional and a concise overview of Christian theology. These readings will introduce you to the basic doctrines of the Christian faith, grounded in Scripture, while providing a guide for your daily devotional time.

Each week focuses on one catechism question and answer from the *Westminster Shorter Catechism*. A catechism is simply a series of questions and answers which explain established doctrinal truths from the Bible. Catechism questions and answers help us understand what the Bible teaches, and what we believe as Christians.

The *Westminster Shorter Catechism* was developed in England in 1647 by a group of Christian ministers who were concerned about the lack of sound teaching of the Word of God in their communities. In response, they wrote both a confession of faith and a larger and shorter catechism. For hundreds of years people in churches in English-speaking countries all over the world have memorized the catechism as part of their training in the Christian faith.

The shorter catechism contains 107 catechism questions and answers, but only 52 (62 if you include the Ten Commandments themselves — they are your theme verses for weeks 28-37!) are included in this devotional — one for each week of the year. I have found deep comfort and spiritual growth from these centuries-old lessons. A friend in England, a prolific writer, testifies that of all her instruction in the Christian faith, she harkens back to her catechetical instruction as the most valuable asset she now possesses, both for daily living and for clear thinking when she writes on Christian themes.

The devotional will take you through a year of meditative reading. The catechism questions and answers are taken sequentially from the Westminster Shorter Catechism. Of the 107 catechisms in the Westminster I have chosen for this devotional the following fifty-two which can be logically divided into four sections:

Section One: *Christian Basics*: 1-10, 13, 14;
Section Two: *Jesus is Lord*: 21, 23-29; 33-35, 37, 39;
Section Three: *The Moral Law*: 42, 46, 50, 54, 58, 64, 68, 71, 74, 77, 80, 82, 84;
Section Four: *The Means of Grace*: 86, 87, 89, 90, 93, 98, 100-107.

Each day for an entire week one catechism question and answer will be considered, with Bible references and comments to reinforce the doctrine under consideration. The questions and comments in each day's devotional reading will enhance your understanding of the catechism question, deepen your grasp of Christian doctrine, and provide you with a guide for personal reflection.

Christians everywhere are seeing the necessity of being grounded in these substantial doctrines that have been faithfully passed down through the generations. I believe that if the truths of these catechism questions are studied and learned you will emerge well-grounded in the essential truths of the Christian faith. If you are investigating the Christian faith I hope this study of Christian doctrine leads you to surrender to Jesus Christ in repentance and faith. And if you already know and love the Lord Jesus, my prayer is that the following devotional deepens your growth in knowledge and love and joy of him who died for you.

Dennis D. Hustedt

PART 1:

CHRISTIAN BASICS

January 1
DESIGNED FOR WORSHIP
(WEEK 1: DAY 1)

The chief end of man

Westminster Catechism Question #1:

What is the chief end of man? *Answer*: The chief end of man is
to glorify God and to enjoy him forever.

Theme Verse: 'So whether you eat or drink or whatever you do,
do it all for the glory of God' (1 Cor. 10:31).

The Westminster Shorter Catechism opens with a somewhat surprising question and answer. Why do humans exist? Why are we
here? For those unfamiliar with the teaching of Scripture the answer is a surprising one: 'to glorify God and to enjoy Him forever.'
The catechism answer boldly confesses that we were created for
praise and that our worship should be directed exclusively towards
the Father, Son and Holy Spirit. We are made for God's pleasure
and our highest joy is tied up in loving and honouring and glorifying our Creator. How do we glorify God? 1 Corinthians 10:31, the
theme verse for this week, declares that we should glorify God all
the time, even while doing mundane tasks like eating a sandwich
or sipping a coca-cola. It may seem strange, and even uncomfortable, to think about worshiping God with all of our selves and
our actions all of the time. However, the Bible teaches that God's
eye is always upon us and he is to be the 'Great Centre' in all the
decisions we make no matter how trivial they may seem to us. In
light of 1 Corinthians 10:31, today is a good day for self-examination, having a closer look at how our lives reflect glory back to the
Lord. What are the activities, both mundane and significant, that
will be opportunities for bringing honour to Christ Jesus, both
today and throughout the year?

SCRIPTURE READING: 1 CORINTHIANS 10:23 – 11:1

January 2
Enjoying God
(WEEK 1: DAY 2)

The chief end of man

Westminster Catechism Question #1:

What is the chief end of man? *Answer:* The chief end of man is
to glorify God and to enjoy him forever.

Theme Verse: 'So whether you eat or drink or whatever you do,
do it all for the glory of God' (1 Cor. 10:31).

A sincere, vital relationship with the Lord brings great joy to the
believer. All healthy relationships, whether human or divine, are
designed for this purpose. God said: 'It is not good for man to
be alone' (Gen. 2:18). We were never designed to be autonomous
creatures, but to have deep relationships. This is particularly true
when relating to the One who created us. Sin separates us from
God, but joy comes when drawing near to the Source of Joy, our
Lord Jesus Christ. 'Though you have not seen him, you love him;
and even though you do not see him now, you believe in him and
are filled with an inexpressible and glorious joy, for you are receiving the goal of your faith, the salvation of your souls' (1 Peter
1:8-9). That's it! The goal of our relationship with Jesus is his
glory and our joy in salvation. One way to respond to the joy that
Christ's salvation brings is simply to thank him. 'Be joyful always;
pray continually; give thanks in all circumstances, for this is God's
will for you in Christ Jesus' (1 Thess. 5:16-18). When so many circumstances in life could rob our joy the Apostle Paul commands
fellow believers to give thanks in all circumstances. What circumstances will arise today where this command will need to remembered and practised?

SCRIPTURE READING: 1 THESSALONIANS 5:16-28

January 3

The chief end of man

Westminster Catechism Question #1:

What is the chief end of man? *Answer:* The chief end of man is to glorify God and to enjoy him forever.

Theme Verse: 'So whether you eat or drink or whatever you do, do it all for the glory of God' (1 Cor. 10:31).

If our 'chief end' or purpose for living is to glorify God does that mean that God enjoys being glorified? No one knows the Father like the Lord Jesus and no one knows the Son like the Father. There, in the Garden of Gethsemane, Jesus prayed. What is on the Savior's heart and mind during those dark hours before his crucifixion? John 17:24 records his thoughts: 'Father, I want those you have given me to be with me where I am, and to see my glory, the glory you have given me because you loved me before the creation of the world.' It is his glory — glory given to him by his Father from before time. He wants 'his children', his disciples and all those who will come after them, to behold him in all his beauty, in all his glory. We should not be stingy toward God in this area since Jesus is infinitely worthy of our praise. It is the Saviour's great desire to take his followers to heaven for this very purpose, that they might behold his glory — 'the glory of the One and Only, who came from the Father, full of grace and truth' (John 1:14). The psalmist was effusive in praising God. Psalms 149 and 150 are particularly noteworthy in this respect. If we reflect on the Lord's longing that we praise him, for his glory and our good, we will experience a natural outpouring of desire to join the Psalmist in enthusiastic praise of the Lord.

SCRIPTURE READING: PSALM 150

January 4
EXPRESSING APPRECIATION
(WEEK 1: DAY 4)

The chief end of man

Westminster Catechism Question #1:

What is the chief end of man? *Answer*: The chief end of man is to glorify God and to enjoy him forever.

Theme Verse: 'So whether you eat or drink or whatever you do, do it all for the glory of God' (1 Cor. 10:31).

When you enjoy something how do you show it? We cheer at basketball games, give standing ovations at music concerts, and ask our hostess for the recipe when the dessert is too delicious for words. Think of the spontaneity, the unrepressed joy of children who clap their hands at things that delight them. When you enjoy something, whether it's your favourite meal, striving for a great athletic achievement, or receiving a bonus for a job well done, you talk about it to those who are close to you. The psalmist found praising God an enjoyable exercise and called each of us to join in. 'Give thanks to the Lord, call on his name; make known among the nations what he has done. Sing to him, sing praise to him; tell of all his wonderful acts. Glory in his holy name; let the hearts of those who seek the Lord rejoice' (Ps. 105:1-3). 'Praise the Lord. How good it is to sing praises to our God, how pleasant and fitting to praise him' (Ps. 147:1). Those who refuse to praise the Lord must repress this God-given urge: 'For although they knew God, they neither glorified him as God nor gave thanks to him, but their thinking became futile and their foolish hearts were darkened' (Rom. 1:21). But we will join the psalmist in praising our God today, for he has made us and given us all good things to enjoy.

SCRIPTURE READING: PSALM 105:1-7

January 5

The chief end of man

Westminster Catechism Question #1:

What is the chief end of man? *Answer*: The chief end of man is to glorify God and to enjoy him forever.

Theme Verse: 'So whether you eat or drink or whatever you do, do it all for the glory of God' (1 Cor. 10:31).

Do you find it more enjoyable to worship God in private or with other believers? While believers can and do enjoy times of reading and prayer alone with the Saviour (he enjoyed praying in solitary places; see Matthew 14:23 and Mark 1:35), the Lord's people are best able to enjoy him and bring glory to him in fellowship with other believers. Most people do not enjoy attending a sports or musical event alone because most of the fun is in the sharing of the experience. That is the way God intended it to be when it comes to glorifying him. Most of the enjoyment is sharing with others the greatness of our God! 'Let the word of Christ dwell in you richly as you teach and admonish one another with all wisdom, and as you sing psalms, hymns, and spiritual songs with gratitude in your hearts to God. And whatever you do, whether in word or deed, do it all in the name of the Lord Jesus, giving thanks to God the Father through him' (Col. 3:16-17). Our times of worship with fellow believers are to bring inner joy, growth and spiritual blessing. Wise followers of Christ look for opportunities to join other believers for the purpose of worship, whether it is in small groups, or in larger, gathered assemblies. 'How good and pleasant it is when brothers live together in unity!' (Ps. 133:1).

SCRIPTURE READING: COLOSSIANS 3:12-17

January 6
OUR HAPPY GOD
(WEEK 1: DAY 6)

The chief end of man

Westminster Catechism Question #1:

What is the chief end of man? *Answer*: The chief end of man is to glorify God and to enjoy him forever.

Theme Verse: 'So whether you eat or drink or whatever you do, do it all for the glory of God' (1 Cor. 10:31).

Do you think God is happy? The Apostle Paul refers to God as 'the blessed God' (1 Tim. 1:11). Of course, this isn't the 'ha-ha' short-lived happiness of the town drunk. This is the happiness of the eternally contented God who is complete in himself and satisfied in all his words, all his creation and all that he purposes to do. Christians can be content, first and foremost, because the God they love and serve is himself content and happy being God. 'At that time Jesus, full of joy through the Holy Spirit, said: "I praise you, Father, Lord of heaven and earth, because you have hidden these things from the wise and learned, and revealed them to little children"' (Luke 10:21). Jesus was full of joy because it was his Father's will to reveal the truth about his kingdom and give salvation to the humble. That is the kind of joy that would be foreign to people who are unfamiliar with the interests and purposes of God. God is interested in making himself known and bringing salvation to sinners. God glories in his own gospel and seeing the good news expanding into our world. What makes God joyful should make us joyful as well. So if you want to be blessed, like your Father in heaven is blessed, seek the things that make him joyful, that which 'conforms to the glorious gospel of the blessed God' (1 Tim. 1:11).

SCRIPTURE READING: LUKE 10:17-24

January 7

(WEEK 1: DAY 7)

The chief end of man

Westminster Catechism Question #1:

What is the chief end of man? *Answer*: The chief end of man is to glorify God and to enjoy him forever.

Theme Verse: 'So whether you eat or drink or whatever you do, do it all for the glory of God' (1 Cor. 10:31).

Do you think God wants you to be happy? The eminent Puritan Jeremy Taylor once proclaimed in a sermon: 'The Lord threatens terrible things if you will not be happy!' A happy heart honours the Lord. In fact, no matter what our circumstances, God commands us to worship him with gladness. Psalm 100 gives us clear commands. We are commanded to 'shout for joy'; 'worship the Lord with gladness'; 'come before him with joyful songs'; 'enter his gates with thanksgiving and his courts with praise'; and 'give thanks to him and praise his name'. These aren't optional extras or commands reserved for 'super-saints'. All followers of Christ are called to a life of praise. And why shouldn't we? 'For the Lord is good and his love endures forever'! Think about how you enjoy and glorify God. Can you say that you enjoy God? Can you say that you love to praise and glorify him? The whole purpose of Christ's life and death, his words and ministry, the intent of the Bible's exhortations, and the promptings of the Holy Spirit, are all to move us in this direction. Even in the hard times, God strengthens his children so that we can maintain a lifestyle of praise and joy in the midst of difficulty. Remember, it is your primary calling in life 'to glorify God and to enjoy him forever'.

SCRIPTURE READING: PSALM 100

January 8

The Scriptures

Westminster Catechism Question #2:

What book has God given to direct us how we may glorify and enjoy him? *Answer*: The Word of God, which is contained in the Old and New Testaments, is the only authority by which we are directed how we may glorify and enjoy him.

Theme verse: 'All Scripture is God-breathed and is useful for teaching, rebuking, correcting and training in righteousness' (2 Tim. 3:16).

If we want to glorify and enjoy God forever how should we go about doing it? Some religions ask their devotees to physically harm themselves in order to show their commitment to their faith. Should Christians do that? Others may ask their followers to make a great trek or pilgrimage to a far-off land. Should followers of Christ do the same thing, perhaps to their favourite shrine or holy site? Thankfully, the Lord has given us his Word, and in it we discover what we need for life and godliness. It is the Christian's handbook, providing us with directions for living that, when followed, lead us to Christ-likeness. 'All Scripture is God-breathed and is useful for teaching, rebuking, correcting and training in righteousness, so that the man of God may be thoroughly equipped for every good work' (2 Tim. 3:16-17). The Bible teaches us so that we understand who God is and his desire for us, it rebukes us when we rebel against the Lord's instruction, it corrects us so that we get it right the next time, and it trains us so that we become firm in the faith we hold dear. As you approach your reading of the Bible, make it your intention for the Word of God to accomplish its purpose in your life: to teach you, rebuke you, correct you, and train you in righteousness.

SCRIPTURE READING: 2 TIMOTHY 3:10-17

January 9
A 'GOD-BREATHED' BIBLE
(WEEK 2: DAY 2)

The Scriptures

Westminster Catechism Question #2:

What book has God given to direct us how we may glorify and enjoy him? *Answer*: The Word of God, which is contained in the Old and New Testaments, is the only authority by which we are directed how we may glorify and enjoy him.

Theme verse: 'All Scripture is God-breathed and is useful for teaching, rebuking, correcting and training in righteousness' (2 Tim. 3:16).

Sometimes a person is described as an 'inspired' runner, or 'inspired' singer. Is that the same thing as an 'inspired' Bible? Inspiration is a word that has been borrowed from Christian doctrine and diluted. The root meaning of 'inspired' means having the 'Spirit in' us. True inspiration is a work of the Holy Spirit. Our theme verse tells us that all Scripture is 'God-breathed', that is, written with the Holy Spirit's imprint on every thought and every word. 2 Peter 1:20-21 carries this idea further when Peter declares that 'no prophecy of Scripture came about by the prophet's own interpretation. For prophecy never had its origin in the will of man, but men spoke from God as they were carried along by the Holy Spirit.' These verses inform us that both God and humans were involved in the production of Scripture, but that only God was the source of the content of Scripture, so that what it says is what God has said. Today, as you open up your Bible, thank the Lord that you can trust every word and thought it contains. Count on the Bible to always tell you the truth. It is completely reliable since God saw to it that the Bible writers wrote under divine inspiration and were given the very words of God. That is why you can trust the Bible to 'teach, rebuke, correct and train' you.

SCRIPTURE READING: 2 PETER 1:16-21

January 10
THOROUGHLY EQUIPPED
(WEEK 2: DAY 3)

The Scriptures

Westminster Catechism Question #2:

What book has God given to direct us how we may glorify and enjoy him? *Answer*: The Word of God, which is contained in the Old and New Testaments, is the only authority by which we are directed how we may glorify and enjoy him.

Theme verse: 'All Scripture is God-breathed and is useful for teaching, rebuking, correcting and training in righteousness' (2 Tim. 3:16).

The theme verse for this week is 2 Timothy 3:16. It is such a powerful verse, stating clearly what the God-breathed Scriptures intend to accomplish in our lives. But the following verse, 2 Timothy 3:17 explains why the Holy Spirit uses the Bible to teach, rebuke, correct and train us. Here it is: 'that the man of God may be thoroughly equipped for every good work'. That's it. We become thoroughly equipped to do what pleases the Lord. For example, the fruit of the Spirit (Christ-like character) becomes evident in our lives. The Bible 'teaches us to say "No" to ungodliness and worldly passions, and to live self-controlled, upright and godly lives in this present age' (Titus 2:12). The Holy Spirit explains and applies the Word of God so that we avoid the activities and resist the temptations that would kill joy and quench the Holy Spirit's work in us. The Word of God begins to shape our thinking so that we use the resources God gives us for kingdom purposes, in service to others, perhaps in missionary endeavours or in directly witnessing of our love for Christ in word and deed. Knowledge of the Word of God and hiding its truths in our hearts make us useful in the hands of the Master. Include the words 'make me useful, Lord' as part of your prayers today.

SCRIPTURE READING: TITUS 2:1-15

January 11

The Scriptures

Westminster Catechism Question #2:

What book has God given to direct us how we may glorify and enjoy him? *Answer*: The Word of God, which is contained in the Old and New Testaments, is the only authority by which we are directed how we may glorify and enjoy him.

Theme verse: 'All Scripture is God-breathed and is useful for teaching, rebuking, correcting and training in righteousness' (2 Tim. 3:16).

If you were stranded on an island and could possess only one of the sixty-six books of the Bible which one would you choose? Would it be the Gospel of John or the book of Romans? How could you live without the Psalms? Fortunately, most if not all of us will never have to make such a decision. We have the complete Word of God to enjoy. It is a good thing, too, since God gave us a Bible that is fully inspired as well as cohesive and harmonious. Think of it, a book that has more than fifteen authors who wrote at different times over a two-thousand year period, who wrote from different countries covering unique circumstances amidst differing cultures. Yet the authors complement one another perfectly! In fact, they complement one another so perfectly that Old Testament events foretell the greater fulfilment of those events in the New Testament through the Lord Jesus and his Church. 'And beginning with Moses and all the Prophets, Jesus explained to them what was said in all the Scriptures concerning himself' (Luke 24:27). Give thanks to the Holy Spirit for giving us a living, breathing, harmonious, cohesive Word that is true to history but ever contemporary and relevant to our lives today. 'I remember your ancient laws, O Lord, and I find comfort in them' (Ps. 119:52).

SCRIPTURE READING: PSALM 119:49-56

January 12
A LIFELESS BOOK?
(WEEK 2: DAY 5)

The Scriptures

Westminster Catechism Question #2:

What book has God given to direct us how we may glorify and enjoy him? *Answer*: The Word of God, which is contained in the Old and New Testaments, is the only authority by which we are directed how we may glorify and enjoy him.

Theme verse: 'All Scripture is God-breathed and is useful for teaching, rebuking, correcting and training in righteousness' (2 Tim. 3:16).

This week we have been noting how majestic the Bible is. We have described the Bible as 'inspired', 'harmonious', 'cohesive' and 'God-breathed'. So why do we so often find the Bible boring and lifeless? Why is it that we can leave it on the shelf for days or weeks at a time? Although the Bible is inexhaustible and perfect, it often seems dull and lifeless to us because there is coldness in our own hearts towards spiritual things. It becomes a living book, however, when we are guided and directed by the Holy Spirit who gives us understanding of its contents and applies its truths to our daily lives. Ephesians 6:17 says: 'take the helmet of salvation and the sword of the Spirit, which is the Word of God'. To be fully armoured, to be equipped for the day, we need the Bible as our resource. Then it is the Holy Spirit's work to shape our mind and heart by using the power, majesty and truth of the Scriptures. The Apostle Paul could write to Timothy: 'But as for you, continue in what you have learned and have become convinced of … and how from infancy you have known the Holy Scriptures, which are able to make you wise for salvation through faith in Christ Jesus' (2 Tim. 3:14-15). Ask the Lord to give you his Spirit to understand, love, and be enraptured by the God-breathed Word today.

SCRIPTURE READING: PSALM 119:129-136

January 13
THE BIBLE'S AUTHORITY
(WEEK 2: DAY 6)

The Scriptures

Westminster Catechism Question #2:

What book has God given to direct us how we may glorify and enjoy him? *Answer*: The Word of God, which is contained in the Old and New Testaments, is the only authority by which we are directed how we may glorify and enjoy him.

Theme verse: 'All Scripture is God-breathed and is useful for teaching, rebuking, correcting and training in righteousness' (2 Tim. 3:16).

For the Bible to rule over our thinking it must be inspired, true and reliable. Did Jesus think it was accurate? Since the New Testament had not been written, did Jesus believe the Old Testament was fully reliable, accurate and true? Here is what the Saviour says in Matthew 5:18: 'I tell you the truth, until heaven and earth disappear, not the smallest letter, not the least stroke of a pen, will by any means disappear from the Law until everything is accomplished.' When Jesus spoke about the smallest letter, he was referring to a tiny Hebrew letter, the *yodh*, which is about the size of an English comma. He then spoke about 'the least stroke of a pen', the slight embellishment on certain Hebrew letters that gave them a certain flair and distinctiveness. What Jesus was saying is that he did not come into our world to change the unchangeable, authoritative Word of God in even the slightest way. He came, rather, to fulfil in his own life, death and resurrection all that the Old Testament was pointing towards. The prophets spoke of him and the ancient believers waited in anticipation for him. When he arrived on planet earth Christ's intention was to live by every word that proceeded from the mouth of God and to fulfil all that his Father had commissioned him to do. Our calling is to do the same.

SCRIPTURE READING: MATTHEW 5:17-20

January 14

The Scriptures

Westminster Catechism Question #2:

What book has God given to direct us how we may glorify and enjoy him? *Answer*: The Word of God, which is contained in the Old and New Testaments, is the only authority by which we are directed how we may glorify and enjoy him.

Theme verse: 'All Scripture is God-breathed and is useful for teaching, rebuking, correcting and training in righteousness' (2 Tim. 3:16).

Many Christians prefer reading the New Testament rather than the Old Testament. 'Just give me Jesus' is often the thought behind such a preference. But Jesus believed the Old Testament was all about himself as well. After his resurrection Jesus suddenly appeared to his disciples (Luke 24:36-49). They were startled, thinking they were seeing a ghost. But Jesus calmed their fears, showed them his hands and feet and welcomed them to touch him. Then Jesus said to them, 'This is what I told you while I was still with you: Everything must be fulfilled that is written about me in the Law of Moses, the Prophets and the Psalms' (Luke 24:44). Jesus was saying that all of the Old Testament is about him. And we know that he fulfils everything in the New Testament as well through his life, death and resurrection. Luke 24 goes on to say: 'Then he opened their minds so they could understand the Scriptures' (Luke 24:45). The disciples were then able to see how Jesus fulfilled everything spoken in the Old Testament. 'Were not our hearts burning within us while he talked with us on the road and opened the Scriptures to us?' (Luke 24:32). Ask the Holy Spirit to fill your mind with both the Old and New Testaments, that you might see Jesus in the Word and be directed how best to glorify and enjoy him today.

SCRIPTURE READING: LUKE 24:13-49

January 15
THE BIBLE'S PURPOSE
(WEEK 3: DAY 1)

The primary teaching of Scripture

Westminster Catechism Question #3:

What do the Scriptures primarily teach? *Answer*: The Scriptures primarily teach what we are to believe about God, and what duty God requires of us.

Theme verse: 'Fear God and keep his commandments, for this is the whole duty of man' (Eccles. 12:13).

Do you ever wonder why the book of Ecclesiastes is even in the Bible? The book rarely refers to God, and the writer, King Solomon, seems so cynical about life. But then we catch the punch-line which is our theme verse for the week. Since all our pursuits and aspirations are merely 'a chasing after the wind' unless we have a relationship with God, Solomon's wise conclusion was: 'Fear God and keep his commandments, for this is the whole duty of man.' The Scriptures teach us many things but have two main purposes. One is to teach us about God; his nature, his attributes, his names, and his purposes for the church and the world he has made. In the Bible we have a description of God's plan of salvation and the way by which our sins can be forgiven. The Bible's other focus was Solomon's conclusion, that is, our responsibility to our Creator. How should I live in order to please my Saviour, the One who made me and died for me? How do I relate to God's commands? The Bible shows us the way that leads to heaven. It teaches us everything we need to know, points out everything we need to believe, and explains everything we need to do in order to be spiritually wise. It is also the only book that can comfort us at death. 'Oh, how I love your law! I meditate on it all day long' (Ps. 119:97).

SCRIPTURE READING: ECCLESIASTES 12:9-14; JOHN 17:13-19

January 16
THE FEAR OF GOD
(WEEK 3: DAY 2)

The primary teaching of Scripture

Westminster Catechism Question #3:

What do the Scriptures primarily teach? *Answer*: The Scriptures primarily teach what we are to believe about God, and what duty God requires of us.

Theme verse: 'Fear God and keep his commandments, for this is the whole duty of man' (Eccles. 12:13).

Some people love scary movies. Others of us will never understand why people would pay to be frightened out of their minds. Regardless, horror movies are big business. When our theme verse instructs us to 'fear God', however, it is not urging us to cower in his presence. Instead, Solomon is exhorting us to possess a reverential trust and loving respect for God. True, Solomon is exhorting us to be afraid to disobey God — the Lord is angered by sin in our lives and he promises to deal with rebels who refuse to obey his commands. In this regard Jesus solemnly warned us, 'Do not be afraid of those who kill the body but cannot kill the soul. Rather, be afraid of the One who can destroy both soul and body in hell' (Matt. 10:28). Such healthy fear should drive us to the Saviour. But the emphasis of Solomon's exhortation is that true 'fear' of God should be prompted by gratitude and reverence for our compassionate and holy Saviour who first loved us and gave himself for us. Jesus cleared up our thinking on this subject when he said: 'God did not send his Son into the world to condemn the world, but to save the world through him' (John 3:17). Jesus did not enter our world to frighten us away; rather, he bids us to draw near in reverence and faith to find rest for our souls and comfort for the journey.

SCRIPTURE READING: JOHN 3:16-21

January 17
DEMONSTRATING LOVE TO GOD
(WEEK 3: DAY 3)

The primary teaching of Scripture

Westminster Catechism Question #3:

What do the Scriptures primarily teach? *Answer*: The Scriptures primarily teach what we are to believe about God, and what duty God requires of us.

Theme verse: 'Fear God and keep his commandments, for this is the whole duty of man' (Eccles. 12:13).

The catechism answer informs us that God has expectations that he wants his children to fulfil. He has laid down laws that are referred to in the Bible as commands or statutes. You also find Jesus exhorting his followers to live as he lived, to follow him; not just being hearers but also doers of his word. Why all the emphasis on rules, laws, commands and statutes? Every parent knows the answer: 'If you love me, you will obey what I command', Jesus said (John 14:15). Here is how it is stated in the Old Testament: 'The Lord commanded us to obey all these decrees and to fear the Lord our God, so that we might always prosper and be kept alive, as is the case today. And if we are careful to obey all this law before the Lord our God, as he has commanded us, that will be our righteousness' (Deut. 6:24-25). Our righteousness and our expression that we have a vital, personal relationship with Jesus will be seen in our daily lives as we obey what he commands us. The commands Jesus lays down for us are not burdensome; they are clearly reasonable. Jesus said, 'Take my yoke upon you and learn from me ... For my yoke is easy and my burden is light' (Matt. 11:29). For those who are trained by them, the Lord's commands are never a burden; they are a joy and delight.

SCRIPTURE READING: DEUTERONOMY 6:20-25

January 18

God's early intention to bless
(week 3: day 4)

The primary teaching of Scripture

Westminster Catechism Question #3:

What do the Scriptures primarily teach? *Answer*: The Scriptures primarily teach what we are to believe about God, and what duty God requires of us.

Theme verse: 'Fear God and keep his commandments, for this is the whole duty of man' (Eccles. 12:13).

The Bible does not waste any time teaching us what we are to believe about God. In Genesis, the very first chapter, God is revealed as our Creator. He delights in creating light, plants and animals, water, galaxies and our blue sky. We learn how extravagant God is, for the waters teem with living creatures and the birds are commanded to multiply rapidly. Genesis 1 informs us that God made men and women in order to have a relationship with us, placing within us a 'living soul'. We learn that God is not selfish: he gives substantial responsibility for caring for the world he has made to our first parents and progressively on to us. Happily, we learn in the very first chapter of the Bible that God is gracious, kind and loving towards us. When he finished making Adam and Eve he blessed them. And it has been God's intention to bless us ever since. The Apostle John wrote: 'From the fullness of his grace we have all received one blessing after another' (John 1:16). We might be tempted to think that God's blessing and grace is more evident in the New Testament than in the Old. But it was God's intention to bless us right from the start. How do we respond to such a God as the One revealed from the very outset of the Bible as gracious, kind and resolute in doing us good?

SCRIPTURE READING: GENESIS 1:1-31

29

January 19
SQUASHING MISCONCEPTIONS
(WEEK 3: DAY 5)

The primary teaching of Scripture

Westminster Catechism Question #3:

What do the Scriptures primarily teach? *Answer*: The Scriptures primarily teach what we are to believe about God, and what duty God requires of us.

Theme verse: 'Fear God and keep his commandments, for this is the whole duty of man' (Eccles. 12:13).

People have often shied away from involvement in a local church because of a perception that the Christian life is essentially a list of rules and regulations. Perhaps it is merely an excuse, but none the less, the perception is there. These concerns are not new. Even when Jesus was on earth people were asking if they really had to follow the rules. One day an expert in the Old Testament tested Jesus by asking: 'Teacher, which is the greatest commandment in the Law?' (Matt. 22:36). In other words, if I have to keep to the rules and regulations, at least tell me which one is at the top of the heap! Another time a different expert in the Old Testament law asked Jesus a similar question: 'What should I do to inherit eternal life?' That question is also presuming that we have to keep a list to see if our good deeds outweigh our bad. Jesus squashed such thinking. He informed these teachers that what God required was to love the Lord with all our heart, soul and mind and to love our neighbour as much as we love ourselves (Matt. 23:37-39). It is not about rules or trying to get the Lord to notice our efforts at being nice. It is all about a heart of love to Christ and those he has made. When Jesus told us of our 'duty', he freed us from the tyranny of rules, regulations and human effort. But at the same time, he made us dependent on his grace and power.

SCRIPTURE READING: MATTHEW 23:34-46

January 20
POWER TO OBEY
(WEEK 3: DAY 6)

The primary teaching of Scripture

Westminster Catechism Question #3:

What do the Scriptures primarily teach?

Answer: The Scriptures primarily teach what we are to believe about God, and what duty God requires of us.

Theme verse: 'Fear God and keep his commandments, for this is the whole duty of man' (Eccles. 12:13).

Jesus taught that the Christian life is not about rules and regulations, but about living in the power of God's grace and forgiveness. The Saviour explained that the evidence of a changed life is demonstrated by the way Christians live their lives: 'If you love me, you will obey what I command' (John 14:15). However, we are told in Romans 8 that the sinful mind is hostile to God. It refuses to submit to God's Law. In fact, left to ourselves we don't have the ability to obey God. Only when our lives are controlled by the Holy Spirit, causing us to obey the Word of God, is there clear evidence and assurance that we really are children of God. So where does the power come from to keep the Lord's commands? 'If you live according to the sinful nature, you will die; but if by the Spirit you put to death the misdeeds of the body, you will live' (Rom. 8:13). The Apostle Paul states the same truth in another way: 'The mind of sinful man is death, but the mind controlled by the Spirit is life and peace' (Rom. 8:6). People become children of God through faith in Jesus Christ, and being led by the Spirit of God is the hallmark of this new relationship. Ask your heavenly Father to fill you with the Holy Spirit in order that you might reverence God and willingly obey him today.

SCRIPTURE READING: ROMANS 8:1-11

January 21
DISCUSSING GOD'S COMMANDS
(WEEK 3: DAY 7)

The primary teaching of Scripture

Westminster Catechism Question #3:

What do the Scriptures primarily teach? *Answer*: The Scriptures primarily teach what we are to believe about God, and what duty God requires of us.

Theme verse: 'Fear God and keep his commandments, for this is the whole duty of man' (Eccles. 12:13).

In Deuteronomy 5 Moses rehearses the Ten Commandments with the people of Israel. Then in Deuteronomy 6:6-7 he admonishes that 'these commandments that I give you today are to be upon your hearts. Impress them on your children. Talk about them when you sit at home and when you walk along the road, when you lie down and when you get up.' God's warning through Moses in chapter 6 is that we have a tendency to forget what God has commanded us. We even have a tendency to forget God himself! To keep us from becoming sluggish in the Christian life we are challenged to talk about the Lord at every opportunity, to discuss his Word, to memorize Scripture, and even to learn and memorize catechisms! In fact, God commands that we talk about his commands! In John Bunyan's *Pilgrim's Progress* the two believers, 'Christian' and 'Hopeful', make a conscious decision to enter into 'goodly conversation'. They discuss the things of God as they are walking along the road and their spirits are elevated. Practise the same in your life today as you discuss with others the gracious commands of God. 'I rejoice in following your statutes as one rejoices in great riches. I meditate on your precepts and consider your ways' (Ps. 119:14-15).

SCRIPTURE READING: DEUTERONOMY 6:1-9

January 22

WORSHIPING IN SPIRIT AND TRUTH

(WEEK 4: DAY 1)

Who is God?

Westminster Catechism Question #4:

Who is God? *Answer*: God is a Spirit, infinite, eternal and unchangeable, in his being, wisdom, power, holiness, justice, goodness and truth.

Theme verse: 'God is Spirit, and his worshipers must worship in spirit and in truth' (John 4:24).

In the book of Revelation the Apostle John is given a heavenly vision of unbridled, sinless angelic worship of the Lord Jesus: 'Worthy is the Lamb, who was slain, to receive power and wealth and wisdom and strength and honor and glory and praise!' (Rev. 5:12). If you are a Christian then one day soon you will join the angels 'lost in wonder, love and praise' at the greatness of God. Even now, while we live in this world, we are at our best when we join the hosts of heaven in worshiping the Lord. To worship the Lord correctly, as our theme verse informs us, we must worship God in spirit and truth. In order to worship God in spirit, our spirits must be in communion with Christ and the Holy Spirit must have taken up residence in our lives. To worship in truth, we need to know who God is and what the Bible teaches about him. We can never worship correctly without having both the truth about God as it is revealed in his Word and the Holy Spirit dwelling in us, guiding us into the truth. When we possess both, we are able to offer true worship to the Lord. Can you say with assurance you have both the Holy Spirit within you and a solid grasp of what the Scriptures teach about the true God? There is no more important question to be answered this side of heaven.

SCRIPTURE READING: JOHN 4:7-26

January 23

THE GLORY OF GOD
(WEEK 4: DAY 2)

Who is God?

Westminster Catechism Question #4:

Who is God? *Answer*: God is a Spirit, infinite, eternal and unchangeable, in his being, wisdom, power, holiness, justice, goodness and truth.

Theme verse: 'God is Spirit, and his worshipers must worship in spirit and in truth' (John 4:24).

Our catechism answer defines God as possessing attributes that are eternal and unchangeable. That is important for us. It tells us that God is the same 'yesterday, today, and forever' (Heb. 13:8). His character will never alter. He is the one great constant in a world of change. 'The Glory of Israel does not lie or change his mind; for he is not a man, that he should change his mind' (1 Sam. 15:29). '(The earth and the heavens) will perish, but you remain; they will all wear out ... but you remain the same' (Ps. 102:26). God's 'glory' is that his attributes are infinite, eternal and unchangeable. When we praise God we are telling him what we think of him; that he is excellent beyond description in his being, wisdom, power, holiness, justice, goodness and truth. When you add it all up we are praising God's glory, all that he is in his unchanging character. Focusing our thoughts on God is a lofty exercise because the Lord is 'high and lifted up'. A good goal today is to have loftier thoughts of our Saviour, to meditate on the perfections of his divine, unchanging character. 'Your righteousness reaches to the skies, O God, you who have done great things. Who, O God, is like you?' (Ps. 71:19). 'Your ways, O God, are holy. What god is so great as our God?' (Ps. 77:13).

SCRIPTURE READING: PSALM 102:18-28

34

January 24
Contemplating God's Character
(WEEK 4: DAY 3)

Who is God?

Westminster Catechism Question #4:

Who is God? *Answer*: God is a Spirit, infinite, eternal and unchangeable, in his being, wisdom, power, holiness, justice, goodness and truth.

Theme verse: 'God is Spirit, and his worshipers must worship in spirit and in truth' (John 4:24).

God's glory is the sum total of all of his attributes, all of his perfect character. However, God is glorified whether we are contemplating just one of his divine attributes or attempting to stretch our brain to consider many of them at the same time. For instance, the psalmist writes: 'The heavens declare the glory of God' (Ps. 19:1). That verse is concentrating on the majesty, wisdom, and power of the Lord. 'Holy, holy, holy, the whole earth is full of his glory' (Isa. 6:3). In Isaiah's vision the angels are declaring that God's majestic holiness is present and displayed throughout the whole earth. In the sentence 'all have sinned and fall short of the glory of God', the Apostle Paul is referring to God's perfect righteousness. In the verse 'Christ was raised from the dead through the glory of the Father' (Rom. 6:4), Paul is focusing on God's power and his love and faithfulness to his Son. It is a good exercise for us to notice when different attributes of God are being described to us in Scripture. We can become unbalanced in our conception of who God is if we concentrate too much on one attribute while neglecting another. Our God is a God of wrath *and* mercy, of justice *and* grace. 'O Lord my God, you are very great; you are clothed with splendor *and* majesty' (Ps. 104:1).

Scripture reading: Isaiah 6

January 25

THE GLORY OF GOD IN THE PSALMS
(WEEK 4: DAY 4)

Who is God?

Westminster Catechism Question #4:

Who is God? *Answer*: God is a Spirit, infinite, eternal and unchangeable, in his being, wisdom, power, holiness, justice, goodness and truth.

Theme verse: 'God is Spirit, and his worshipers must worship in spirit and in truth' (John 4:24).

The Book of Psalms is universally loved by Christians. One reason why we love the psalms so much is because of their capacity to comfort us during times of affliction. But another good reason to love this book is that within the 150 psalms are perpetual declarations of the glory of God, his greatness and worthiness to be praised. It is more than a day's meditation to reflect on the attributes of God on display in Psalm 147 alone. 'He determines the number of the stars and calls them each by name' (Ps. 147:4) is a proclamation of awe-inspiring wonder by itself. He gives names to the billions of stars within the billions of galaxies. 'Great is the Lord and mighty in power; his understanding has no limit' (Ps. 147:5) speaks to the Lord's omniscience. God knows all things with ease and has no difficulty governing the activities of six billion plus people on planet earth as well as all other living things. 'The Lord sustains the humble but casts the wicked to the ground' (Ps. 147:6). He not only controls the universe with limitless power, but he also deciphers the thoughts and intentions of each heart. He shows kindness to the humble and repentant, his anger and wrath against the rebel. What hymn or praise song will help you join the psalmist in glorifying the Lord today?

SCRIPTURE READING: PSALM 147

January 26
THE GREAT 'I AM'
(WEEK 4: DAY 5)

Who is God?

Westminster Catechism Question #4:

Who is God? *Answer*: God is a Spirit, infinite, eternal and unchangeable, in his being, wisdom, power, holiness, justice, goodness and truth.

Theme verse: 'God is Spirit, and his worshipers must worship in spirit and in truth' (John 4:24).

When we ask the question: 'Who is God?' we must remember that we are not talking only about the Father, but the triune God; that is, Father, Son and Holy Spirit. At the burning bush Moses asked God: 'who are you, what is your name, what shall I tell the people of Israel about you?' God said to Moses: 'I AM WHO I AM'. Tell the Israelites: 'I AM has sent me to you.' This was the name that expressed God's character as the dependable and faithful God who is to be fully trusted. In John 8:53 Jesus was asked a similar question by the people of his day: 'Who do you think you are?' they angrily inquired. A few verses later, in John 8:58-59 Jesus replied: 'I AM!' In so doing he applied the name of God to himself. Jesus was expressing that he was infinite, eternal and unchangeable in his being, wisdom, power, holiness, justice, goodness and truth. He was also expressing that he and his Father were one and the same God. When we read of the holy character and mighty deeds of God in the Old Testament as well as the New Testament, we are beholding the person of Jesus. Who is God? He is God the Father, God the Son, and God the Holy Spirit; and these three are one God, the same in substance, equal in power and glory.

SCRIPTURE READING: JOHN 8:48-59

January 27

Who is God?

Westminster Catechism Question #4:

Who is God? Answer: God is a Spirit, infinite, eternal and unchangeable, in his being, wisdom, power, holiness, justice, goodness and truth.

Theme verse: 'God is Spirit, and his worshipers must worship in spirit and in truth' (John 4:24).

We are all religious by nature. God has made us that way. But we would grope around in the dark, searching for the 'unknown God', if the Lord didn't tell us about himself. However, the Bible wasn't written simply to fill our heads with correct information about God. It was written so that we can respond back to the Lord in love. In Exodus 34:6-7 we have God proclaiming that he is the great 'I AM'. But what is also worthy of our attention is the response of Moses a few verses later. 'Moses bowed to the ground at once and worshiped' (Exod. 34:8). To know God and see him for who he really is will cause us to worship, praise and adore him. The response of our hearts is to feel affection, joy and adoration for our mighty Saviour. The Bible testifies that God's wonderful purpose in sending his Son was to take rebellious sinners and to turn them into worshipers of the King of kings and Lord of lords. To capture a glimpse of the greatness of God will cause us to do what Moses did when he beheld the glory of Jehovah. So open our eyes, Lord, we want to see Jesus in all his beauty and holiness. 'They fell down on their faces before the throne and worshiped God, saying: Amen! Praise and glory and wisdom and thanks and honor and power and strength be to our God forever and ever. Amen!' (Rev. 7:11-12).

SCRIPTURE READING: EXODUS 34:1-9

January 28

Who is God?

Westminster Catechism Question #4:

Who is God? *Answer*: God is a Spirit, infinite, eternal and unchangeable, in his being, wisdom, power, holiness, justice, goodness and truth.

Theme verse: 'God is Spirit, and his worshipers must worship in spirit and in truth' (John 4:24).

There's a chorus that says: 'I was made to praise you, I was made to glorify your name'. However imperfectly, the purpose of life is the worship of Christ in spirit and in truth. We could even say that our lives in this world are simply a training ground for perfect worship in the next world. It is clear enough from the book of Revelation that the angels and living creatures in heaven worship God perfectly. They enjoy the blessing of beholding the Lord, and when they do their natural response to his majesty is overflowing worship and praise. Day and night there is unceasing exaltation of the holiness of the Lord God Almighty (Rev. 4:8). There is powerful singing by elders and millions of angels of a new song extolling the mighty victory of Jesus at the cross (Rev. 5:9-12). And everyone in heaven, absolutely everyone, sings 'To him who sits on the throne and to the Lamb be praise and honor and glory and power, for ever and ever!' (Rev. 5:13). If we want a solid purpose for living today it is to prepare ourselves for worship in heaven in the near future. Make worship in spirit and truth your lifetime vocation, that is, worship in the power of the Holy Spirit and with an ever-expanding understanding of the Lord in the fullness of his character as he is made known to you in the Bible.

SCRIPTURE READING: REVELATION 5:1-14

January 29
No other God
(WEEK 5: DAY 1)

There is one God

Westminster Catechism Question #5:

Are there more gods than one? *Answer*: There is but one only, the living and true God.

Theme verse: 'Hear, O Israel, the LORD our God, the LORD is one' (Deut. 6:4).

Perhaps the biggest question confronting the world today is which God is the true God. The great clashes in civilization today are essentially theological, that is, the collision of cultures with different belief systems about the nature of God: his purposes, his character and even his name. Terrorist acts are justified based on the reasoning that the victims of such violence are 'infidels', worshipers of a false god. The Lord Jesus did not send us into the world with a sword but with a gospel message that lovingly asserts that there is no other God than the One described to us in the Bible. He is known and loved through the pages of Holy Scripture. 'But the Lord is the true God; he is the living God, the everlasting King' (Jer. 10:10). The Bible's monotheistic (one-God) assertion is supported and assumed by both the Old and New Testaments. The Christian believes in no other god than the God of the Bible. All other gods are idolatrous creations by those who have 'exchanged the truth of God for a lie, and worshiped and served created things rather than the Creator' (Rom. 1:25). In our evangelism, we must not be callous towards people of other faiths, but we also must lovingly hold fast to the fundamental truth that there is 'no other name under heaven given to men by which we must be saved' (Acts 4:12).

SCRIPTURE READING: ROMANS 1:18-25

January 30
THE TRUE GOD RESISTED
(WEEK 5: DAY 2)

There is one God

Westminster Catechism Question #5:

Are there more gods than one? *Answer*: There is but one only, the living and true God.

Theme verse: 'Hear, O Israel, the LORD our God, the LORD is one' (Deut. 6:4).

When missionaries head off to regions of the world where the gospel has never been heard they never discover a religious vacuum. Missionaries always find a religion of some sort. The Apostle Paul discovered this when he entered Ephesus for the first time. Acts 19 records a great disturbance that took place when Paul and others began preaching the gospel in Ephesus. Demetrius and other local artisans made silver shrines to a false goddess named Artemis. They saw their business in grave danger if Paul's preaching about Christ was successful. A riot broke out as Demetrius stirred the crowd against Paul and the true faith. When we read such a story we recognize that the true gospel is resisted today for many reasons, not just the profit motive as in the case of Demetrius. Personal patterns of sinfulness or sinful traditions in the community, lust, power, etc., make people resistant to the gospel. Does this mean that we should stop evangelizing when it appears that people everywhere are antagonistic? No, we are reminded that we must bring all of our persuasive and Spirit-led powers to the missionary task. Pray for someone you know who is living and proclaiming the message of the true God in a region where there is great resistance to the gospel. And ask God to bless your witness for Christ as well.

SCRIPTURE READING: ACTS 19:23-41

January 31
The names of God
(week 5: day 3)

There is one God

Westminster Catechism Question #5:

Are there more gods than one? *Answer*: There is but one only, the living and true God.

Theme verse: 'Hear, O Israel, the LORD our God, the LORD is one' (Deut. 6:4).

In the Western mind very little significance is usually attached to the meaning of a child's name. We normally choose a name based on personal preference. But in the ancient Middle East a given name commemorated some great historical event or denoted the parent's aspiration for their child. God selected names for himself in keeping with Middle Eastern thinking: 'El' is used 217 times in the Old Testament for the true God and means 'Mighty One'. 'Elohim' is found 2,570 times in the Old Testament and means 'He who is to be feared'. 'El elyon' means 'most high' or 'most exalted'. 'Adonai' means 'Lord' or 'Master' and is often used to describe the Lord Jesus. 'Yahweh' occurs more than 6,000 times in the Hebrew Bible and may be thought of as God's proper name. It means 'self-existent, Sovereign One' and is a title given to Father, Son and Holy Spirit. Then there is simply the name 'God', which comes from the Greek *'theos'*. Finally, there is the name 'Lord' (*'kurios'* in Greek) to describe primarily our great Saviour as ruler of our lives. Meditating on the names of God elevates our prayers and our contemplation of the great Saviour. 'Within your temple, O God, we meditate on your unfailing love. Like your name, O God, your praise reaches to the end of the earth' (Ps. 48:10).

SCRIPTURE READING: PSALM 48:1-14

February 1
ELIJAH'S GOD
(WEEK 5: DAY 4)

There is one God

Westminster Catechism Question #5:

Are there more gods than one? *Answer:* There is but one only, the living and true God.

Theme verse: 'Hear, O Israel, the LORD our God, the LORD is one' (Deut. 6:4).

Approximately eight centuries before Christ, the prophet Elijah appeared out of nowhere as God's great representative. Elijah's calling was to prophesy against the people of Israel because of their shocking idolatry. Ahab and Jezebel were on the throne and the worship of Baal, a false deity imported from Jezebel's native country of Lebanon, had divided the people's loyalty to Jehovah. People were worshiping both the true God and the false god. This was reprehensible to God. 'Do not worship any other god, for the LORD, whose name is Jealous, is a jealous God' (Exod. 34:14). He will not share his glory with another. In the contest between Elijah and the false prophets of Baal on Mount Carmel the Lord passionately consumed Elijah's animal sacrifice while the prophets of Baal were powerless to call upon a god who didn't exist. God demonstrated his existence and showed his great power when put to the test. 'When all the people saw this, they fell prostrate and cried, "The Lord — he is God! The Lord — he is God!"' (1 Kings 18:39). Today we are still constantly tempted to form idols that compete for worship that is due the Lord alone; whether it is money, sport, music, a job, or a relationship. Are there any idols that are rivalling Christ for pre-eminence in your life today?

SCRIPTURE READING: 1 KINGS 18:16-40

February 2
THE TEMPTATION OF JESUS
(WEEK 5: DAY 5)

There is one God

Westminster Catechism Question #5:

Are there more gods than one? *Answer*: There is but one only, the living and true God.

Theme verse: 'Hear, O Israel, the LORD our God, the LORD is one' (Deut. 6:4).

In Matthew 4 and Luke 4 we read about the Messiah's encounter with the devil. The meeting was no accident. It was divinely intended at the outset of the Saviour's ministry to show that he alone is the true representative of his people. In Genesis we read how Adam yielded to Satan's temptation, rejecting the Lord's command not to eat from the tree of life, and in so doing, plunged the whole world into sin. But Jesus, despite having fasted forty days and nights, successfully thwarted the devil's most cunning efforts to solicit worship from him. Jesus was victorious because he lived 'on every word that comes from the mouth of God' (Matt. 4:4). Jesus, therefore, demonstrated his right to be our substitute, our 'merciful and faithful high priest' (Heb. 2:17). He is now 'able to help those who are being tempted' (Heb. 2:18). When the devil sought the Saviour's worship Jesus responded by quoting from Deuteronomy 6:13: 'It is written: "Worship the Lord your God, and serve him only"' (Luke 4:8). When we are tempted, we have someone who is able to help us overcome idolatry. The Lord relied on his knowledge of God's Word and the abiding presence of his Father and the Holy Spirit to overcome false worship. What will you rely on when temptation arises?

SCRIPTURE READING: LUKE 4:1-13

February 3
THE GOD OF MATERIALISM
(WEEK 5: DAY 6)

There is one God

Westminster Catechism Question #5:

Are there more gods than one? *Answer*: There is but one only, the living and true God.

Theme verse: 'Hear, O Israel, the LORD our God, the LORD is one' (Deut. 6:4).

If the Lord has given you taste buds that are working then you are like everyone else: you love good food. Go without a good meal for a day and you begin to fantasize about a medium-rare steak or another favourite food. However, when the Apostle Paul wrote that some people make a god out of their stomach, he wasn't just addressing the problem of overeating (Phil. 3:19). He was speaking about the idol called 'self', about people who live deeply self-centred lives, whose desires and appetite for worldly possessions are foremost in their thinking. These are people we meet daily who have made a false god out of pleasing themselves, living for status, money, power and prestige. 'Their mind is on earthly things' (Phil. 3:19) and what this world can offer them. This is an insidious idol because it takes our mind off of eternity. 'But our citizenship is in heaven' (Phil. 3:19), Paul reminds us. This false god called 'materialism' is an idol that every Christian must fight against every single day. Possessions can weigh us down and consume our time and energy. If Christ is to be the unrivalled Lord of our lives we must work hard to overcome materialism. 'For the love of money is a root of all kinds of evil. Some people, eager for money, have wandered from the faith' (1 Tim. 6:10).

SCRIPTURE READING: PHILIPPIANS 3:12-21

February 4

THE GOD OF MONEY
(WEEK 5: DAY 7)

There is one God

Westminster Catechism Question #5:

Are there more gods than one? *Answer*: There is but one only, the living and true God.

Theme verse: 'Hear, O Israel, the LORD our God, the LORD is one' (Deut. 6:4).

The most profound message ever preached was the Saviour's 'Sermon on the Mount' found in Matthew 5-7. One of his strongest warnings in that discourse is: 'Do not store up for yourselves treasures on earth ... but store up for yourselves treasures in heaven' (Matt. 6:19-20). A few verses later Jesus is even more direct: 'No one can serve two masters. Either he will hate the one and love the other, or he will be devoted to the one and despise the other. You cannot serve both God and Money' (Matt. 6:24). The capital 'M' in money is not a misprint. It denotes a false god, a powerful rival to Christ's supremacy in our hearts. This false god demands our time and energy, our emotion and will. A consuming desire to have more money and a passionate chasing after it is sin. Although money is a necessity of life for all people, including Christians, it is far too easy to fall into the trap of focusing all of life on pursuing money and the pleasures it can bring. Christians are not to make money their god. Jesus loved the rich young ruler of Mark 10. But there was no way to break through to offer a better, more joyous way of living until the young man was willing to renounce his idolatrous grip on the Money-god. As our catechism reminds us, there is but one God only, the living and true God.

SCRIPTURE READING: MARK 10:17-31

February 5
THREE PERSONS, EQUALLY DIVINE
(WEEK 6: DAY 1)

The Trinity

Westminster Catechism Question #6:

How many persons are there in the Godhead? *Answer*: There are
three persons in the Godhead; the Father, the Son, and the Holy
Spirit; and these three are one God, the same in substance, equal
in power and glory.

Theme verse: 'Therefore go and make disciples of all nations,
baptizing them in the name of the Father and of the Son, and of
the Holy Spirit' (Matt. 28:19).

Our minds cannot fully understand what it means for God to be
only one God yet at the same time three distinct persons. However, the Bible consistently and purposefully reveals God as triune.
Each of the persons of the Trinity is divine. The Father thunders
from Mount Sinai: 'I AM the Lord your God' (Exod. 20:2). Jesus
claimed to be God many times, including his use of 'I AM' (John
8:58) as a proclamation of his deity and eternal oneness with the
Father (see also John 8:24,28; 17:21-22). Hebrews 1:1-3 declares
powerfully that Jesus is the 'exact representation' of the Father's
being. The Holy Spirit is referred to as divine throughout the
Scriptures (see Genesis 1:2; Psalm 106:33; Romans 8:9-11). Each
member of the Godhead (Father, Son and Spirit) is equally divine,
but serves a different function. Look upon the Father, Son and
Holy Spirit in their distinctive roles as Creator, Redeemer, and
Sustainer. Our Heavenly Father creates us, tenderly cares for us
and is sovereign over all things. Christ is our Redeemer and Mediator who will one day judge the world. The Holy Spirit sustains
us, dwells within us and comforts us as he carries out the will
of both Father and Son. The Spirit also shows us our need for a
Saviour, the Lord Jesus Christ. Has the Spirit made Jesus known
to you?

SCRIPTURE READING: HEBREWS 1:1-14

February 6
THE TRINITY WITH US
(WEEK 6: DAY 2)

The Trinity

Westminster Catechism Question #6:

How many persons are there in the Godhead? *Answer*: There are three persons in the Godhead; the Father, the Son, and the Holy Spirit; and these three are one God, the same in substance, equal in power and glory.

Theme verse: 'Therefore go and make disciples of all nations, baptizing them in the name of the Father and of the Son, and of the Holy Spirit' (Matt. 28:19).

Consider how the Trinity was present at the Saviour's baptism. The Holy Spirit was there. As soon as Jesus was baptized, he went up out of the water. 'At that moment heaven was opened, and he saw the Spirit of God descending like a dove and lighting upon him' (Matt. 3:16). The Heavenly Father was also there. 'And a voice from heaven said, "This is my Son, whom I love; with him I am well pleased"' (Matt. 3:17). From the start of Christ's ministry he enjoyed the assurance that he was not alone. His Father, who loved him, and the Holy Spirit, who encouraged him, abided with the great Redeemer. At the end of Jesus' earthly ministry he gave a commission to his disciples and to all of us who are his followers. 'Go and make disciples, baptizing them in the name of the Father and of the Son and of the Holy Spirit, and teaching them to obey everything I have commanded you' (Matt. 28:19-20). We, too, enjoy the presence of the Trinity at our baptisms and in our daily lives. We have the assurance that Father, Son and Holy Spirit will never leave or forsake us. This is another aspect of the greatness of our God — he ministers to his needy children in his tri-unity. Thank him that he has shepherded you in his capacities as your Creator, Redeemer, and Sustainer.

SCRIPTURE READING: MATTHEW 3:13-17

February 7
The Trinity at Christmas
(WEEK 6: DAY 3)

The Trinity

Westminster Catechism Question #6:

How many persons are there in the Godhead? *Answer*: There are three persons in the Godhead; the Father, the Son, and the Holy Spirit; and these three are one God, the same in substance, equal in power and glory.

Theme verse: 'Therefore go and make disciples of all nations, baptizing them in the name of the Father and of the Son, and of the Holy Spirit' (Matt. 28:19).

A portion of the Christmas story is found in Luke 1:39-45. In it, Mary is heading off to the hill country to spend some needed time with her relative, Elizabeth. Elizabeth is perfectly qualified to understand Mary's unique situation, for she too is carrying in her womb a miracle child, John, the forerunner of the coming Messiah. Notice the Trinity in this Christmas story. Upon her arrival Elizabeth is filled with the *Holy Spirit* (v. 41) and the unborn John is leaping in her womb for joy. It is a testimony of the powerful presence of the Holy Spirit and the happiness that comes upon a home bursting with good news. Elizabeth describes Mary's unborn baby Jesus as 'my Lord', (v. 43) a declaration that this Old Testament woman understands the New Testament paradigm shift: God is coming into the world in human form. And of course, *God the Father* is also declared to be Elizabeth's 'Lord' (v. 45). God the Father is the one who has prophesied that the Messiah is coming 'who will reign on David's throne and over his kingdom, establishing it with justice and righteousness from that time on and forever. The zeal of the Lord Almighty will accomplish this' (Isa. 9:7). Godly 'Old Testament' Jews had no difficulty embracing the idea that God existed in three persons.

SCRIPTURE READING: LUKE 1:39-45

The Trinity

Westminster Catechism Question #6:

How many persons are there in the Godhead? *Answer*: There are three persons in the Godhead; the Father, the Son, and the Holy Spirit; and these three are one God, the same in substance, equal in power and glory.

Theme verse: 'Therefore go and make disciples of all nations, baptizing them in the name of the Father and of the Son, and of the Holy Spirit' (Matt. 28:19).

Elizabeth wasn't the only member of her home who understood the Trinity. Her faithful husband, Zechariah, was also a believer. In his praise-song (Luke 1:67-79) Zechariah prophesies in the power of the *Holy Spirit* about both *Jesus* and his own son, John the Baptist (v. 67). He thanks the *Father*, the God of Israel, (v. 68) for sending the Lord Jesus to be 'the horn of salvation' for his people (v. 69). In Zechariah's mind there was no lessening of the power or majesty of any of the three persons of the Trinity. The Holy Spirit empowered and filled him to prophesy about Christ and the Father as equally divine. He understood that the Lord Jesus was sent by the Father at the Father's express command. And the Lord Jesus came to this world to redeem people from their sins, to be our Saviour, to be our 'horn of salvation'. Zechariah was given prophetic insight and was wondrously filled to sing his song. And that song had the distinctive roles of the Trinity weaving throughout it. Zechariah was a priest living in an 'Old Testament' world, yet his understanding of the Old Testament drew him to this truth: God has made himself known in three persons. Now, with both Old and New Testaments before us, we can see even more clearly the revelation that our God is triune: Father, Son and Spirit.

SCRIPTURE READING: LUKE 1:67-79

THE DIVINE CLAIM
(WEEK 6: DAY 5)

The Trinity

Westminster Catechism Question #6:

How many persons are there in the Godhead? *Answer*: There are three persons in the Godhead; the Father, the Son, and the Holy Spirit; and these three are one God, the same in substance, equal in power and glory.

Theme verse: 'Therefore go and make disciples of all nations, baptizing them in the name of the Father and of the Son, and of the Holy Spirit' (Matt. 28:19).

Jesus is declared to be the 'Son of God' in Scripture. Jesus often referred to himself as 'the Son of Man', to designate his brotherly love towards us. Such titles can easily confuse us. We may be tempted to think that a son is not equal to a father because of his subordinate role. However, the people listening to Jesus never doubted that he claimed to be God. The passage in John 10:22-33 is just one example of this. The religious leaders of his day asked Jesus if he was the Messiah. 'If you are the Christ, tell us plainly' (John 10:24). He replied forthrightly, that indeed he was the Christ. In fact, Jesus declared that you could not separate him from the Father. They were one and the same God (v. 30). The religious leaders listening to Jesus picked up stones to kill him. 'We are not stoning you for any of these [miracles]', replied the Jews, 'but for blasphemy, because you, a mere man, claim to be God' (John 10:33). Our faith stands or falls on this decisive issue. Either Jesus is God, as he claimed to be, or else he is a fraud. To reject Christ as Lord and God is to deny his very essence. We lower him whom the Father has raised above every other name. Raise Jesus to the level he deserves: King, Lord of the Universe, Son of God, and second person of the Trinity.

SCRIPTURE READING: JOHN 10:22-33

February 10
THE FELLOWSHIP OF THE TRIUNE GOD
(WEEK 6: DAY 6)

The Trinity

Westminster Catechism Question #6:

How many persons are there in the Godhead? *Answer*: There are three persons in the Godhead; the Father, the Son, and the Holy Spirit; and these three are one God, the same in substance, equal in power and glory.

Theme verse: 'Therefore go and make disciples of all nations, baptizing them in the name of the Father and of the Son, and of the Holy Spirit' (Matt. 28:19).

There are other major religions that teach there is only one God. However, unlike Christianity, these other monotheistic (one-God) religions do not believe that God is known in three persons. But consider a few things we believe about God because he is triune. The Bible speaks of our God being altogether happy within himself (1 Tim. 1:11; John 17:24-25). There is fellowship in the Godhead among the three persons. They communicate perfectly. There is great love expressed between the Father and the Son (John 17:1-5). Our God is a God of communication not only between the three persons of the Trinity but also with us who love him and are loved by him. God is not lonely. He is not distant. The Scriptures speak of a God who loves relationship. He draws near to us, loves us, dies for us and abides with us. Because God draws near we need never be lonely. Turn God into what theologians call a 'monad', that is, a one-person entity and God becomes immediately distant, reclusive, a stranger to fellowship and non-communicative. When God made us he declared: 'It is not good for man to be alone'. The same can be said about God. He is willing to fellowship with you. The triune God has said: 'Let *us* make man in *our* own image, in *our* likeness' (Gen. 1:26).

SCRIPTURE READING: JOHN 17:1-5

February 11

The full deity of Jesus

(week 6: day 7)

The Trinity

Westminster Catechism Question #6:

How many persons are there in the Godhead? *Answer*: There are three persons in the Godhead; the Father, the Son, and the Holy Spirit; and these three are one God, the same in substance, equal in power and glory.

Theme verse: 'Therefore go and make disciples of all nations, baptizing them in the name of the Father and of the Son, and of the Holy Spirit' (Matt. 28:19).

It would be difficult to find any passage in the Bible that more forthrightly affirms the full deity of Jesus Christ than Colossians 1:15-20. It spells out in cosmic proportions Christ's role in creating and preserving the universe. In this passage Paul declares that Jesus, as the Son of God, existed with the Father before the world was made. We are told that Jesus was God the Father's agent in creation and by his appearance on earth made the invisible God suddenly visible. This passage also states that Jesus is Lord not only of the natural creation but also the spiritual creation. He is the Head of the church because the Father wanted that for his Son. And Jesus, our Saviour, so desired to be the Head of the redeemed people of God that he died for us, making it possible for sinners to have relationship with the Trinity. The bottom line is that Paul is saying God has been made known to his people through Jesus Christ. This is the invisible God made visible. The Apostle John says in John 1:18: 'No one has ever seen God (the Father), but God the One and Only (Jesus), who is at the Father's side, has made him known.' When giving thanks to the Lord, if you haven't already done so, add this truth: that because of Christ's passion you now can know the Father, through the Son, by the Holy Spirit.

SCRIPTURE READING: COLOSSIANS 1:15-20

February 12

THE CHIEF END OF GOD
(WEEK 7: DAY 1)

The decrees of God

Westminster Catechism Question #7:

What are the decrees of God? *Answer*: The decrees of God are his eternal purpose, by which, for his own glory, he has ordained whatever comes to pass.

Theme verse: 'He does as he pleases with the powers of heaven and the peoples of the earth. No one can hold back his hand or say to him: "What have you done?"' (Dan. 4:35).

Our first catechism question was: 'What is the chief end of man?' And the answer was: 'The chief end of man is to glorify God and to enjoy him forever.' But what about God? What is the chief end of God? The answer must be the same. The chief end of God is to glorify and enjoy himself forever. It would be false for God to share his glory with anyone else. The Scriptures teach that God loves himself with his whole heart, strength and mind. What motivates God is to display his almighty power and perfect attributes before the principalities and powers in heavenly places. His choosing of Israel in the Old Testament was in order to display his awesome power among them. Time after time he delivered the people even when they rebelled against the Lord. Christ came into the world to glorify God by doing his Father's will to perfection. When Jesus returns, it is 'to be glorified in his holy people and to be marveled at among all those who have believed' (2 Thess. 1:9-10). What God decrees will certainly happen. Nothing can change it. We can thank the Lord for this wonderful reality. The sun will rise tomorrow at the precise moment God has ordained and God's purpose for your life, including today's activities, by divine decree, are fixed in heaven as well.

SCRIPTURE READING: EXODUS 5:22 – 6:8

54

February 13
THE SOVEREIGNTY OF GOD
(WEEK 7: DAY 2)

The decrees of God

Westminster Catechism Question #7:

What are the decrees of God? *Answer*: The decrees of God are his eternal purpose, by which, for his own glory, he has ordained whatever comes to pass.

Theme verse: 'He does as he pleases with the powers of heaven and the peoples of the earth. No one can hold back his hand or say to him: "What have you done?"' (Dan. 4:35).

Much of the book of Daniel is the recounting of the interwoven lives of Daniel and Nebuchadnezzar, the king of Babylon. In Daniel 4, Nebuchadnezzar has a dream and Daniel is given insight to explain its meaning. 'This is the interpretation, O king, and this is the decree the Most High has issued against my lord the king: You will be driven away from people and will live with the wild animals ... until you acknowledge that the Most High is sovereign over the kingdoms of men and gives them to anyone he wishes' (Dan. 4:24-25). Nebuchadnezzar's problem was intense pride. Such egotism is indeed crazy. Nebuchadnezzar thought that Babylon's greatness was due to his own personality and political shrewdness. The Lord humbled him by removing his rational powers. He became insane. However, this humbling experience had the positive effect of making the king recognize God's sovereignty. The trial the king endured restored him to correct thinking. He realized that he was not sovereign, that there was a power far greater than himself. Nebuchadnezzar now understood that God alone is sovereign and 'does as he pleases with the powers of heaven and the peoples of the earth'. The only sane response to the Supreme Ruler of the universe is humble adoration and surrender. Is the Lord sovereign in your life?

SCRIPTURE READING: DANIEL 4:28-37

February 14
GOD'S INTEREST IN ALL THINGS
(WEEK 7: DAY 3)

The decrees of God

Westminster Catechism Question #7:

What are the decrees of God? *Answer*: The decrees of God are his eternal purpose, by which, for his own glory, he has ordained whatever comes to pass.

Theme verse: 'He does as he pleases with the powers of heaven and the peoples of the earth. No one can hold back his hand or say to him: "What have you done?"' (Dan. 4:35).

Most people have little difficulty believing that God is involved in the 'big' things of life. God takes note, we assume, if we are changing jobs. If we are going to be missionaries God must be involved in that. If we are injured in a car accident God will get to the mishap ahead of the ambulance. But is God interested in the seemingly insignificant? The Scriptures make clear that God deposes earthly kings but also sees the tiny sparrow fall (Dan. 4:31-32; Matt. 10:29). God sets the boundaries for oceans and lands as well as numbers the hairs on our heads (Acts 17:26; Matt. 10:30). The Scriptures are filled with illustrations of God's absolute sovereignty over all that he has made. Whether we view events as major or minor, the Lord 'works *all* things after the counsel of his will' (Eph. 1:11). 'From him and through him and to him are *all* things' (Rom. 11:36; 1 Cor. 8:6). Such an understanding of God's eternal decrees, where God ordains whatever happens, encourages us to pray for what we consider are 'small' matters. We should never think we are somehow bothering God to spread before him the 'little issues' of life. Take everything to God in prayer. Whether the concerns of our lives seem great or small, place them at the feet of him who fashioned the worlds.

SCRIPTURE READING: ACTS 17:24-34

February 15

The decrees of God

Westminster Catechism Question #7:

What are the decrees of God? *Answer*: The decrees of God are his eternal purpose, by which, for his own glory, he has ordained whatever comes to pass.

Theme verse: 'He does as he pleases with the powers of heaven and the peoples of the earth. No one can hold back his hand or say to him: "What have you done?"' (Dan. 4:35).

Perhaps you live in a democratic country. You are free to vote and may voice your opinion about your government's policies. This is not the way it is in many countries. The story is told that King Heile Selassie, the king of Ethiopia in the mid-twentieth century, would demand that his subjects fall prostrate on the ground, not daring to look up, as his motorcade passed by in the streets of Addis Ababa. His kingship was unquestioned, his authority absolute. It is probably easier to understand God's decrees and appreciate God's sovereignty under such circumstances. Our calling is unquestioned obedience to the absolute sovereign God, whose dominion and power and majesty dwarf King Selassie's short-lived dictatorship. King David understood the absolute sovereignty of God. 'Yours, O Lord, is the greatness and the power and the glory and the majesty and the splendor, for everything in heaven and earth is yours. Yours, O Lord, is the kingdom; and you are exalted as head over all' (1 Chr. 29:11-12). Many of today's dictators lord their temporary power over their people, but our God's sovereign pleasure is to bless us. He uses his unrivalled power to accomplish his eternal purpose which is to do good to his people and all for his own glory.

SCRIPTURE READING: 1 CHRONICLES 29:10-20

February 16
God's will and our will
(week 7: day 5)

The decrees of God

Westminster Catechism Question #7:

What are the decrees of God? *Answer*: The decrees of God are his eternal purpose, by which, for his own glory, he has ordained whatever comes to pass.

Theme verse: 'He does as he pleases with the powers of heaven and the peoples of the earth. No one can hold back his hand or say to him: "What have you done?"' (Dan. 4:35).

An obvious question comes to mind when trying to understand God's decrees and absolute sovereignty. That question, simply put, is: 'Where do I fit into all this?' If God does whatever he pleases and he is in complete charge of everything, does that make all of us nothing more than robots? The answer is that we do have free will, but that will is either demonstrating its opposition to God or gladly submitting to the Lord's will. This does not change God's sovereignty. The teacher in the book of Proverbs states the combination of God's decreed purposes and our freedom in an interesting way: 'Many are the plans in a man's heart, but it is the Lord's purpose that prevails' (Prov. 19:21). 'A man's steps are directed by the Lord. How then can anyone understand his own way?' (Prov. 20:24). 'In his heart a man plans his course, but the Lord determines his steps' (Prov. 16:9). 'There is no wisdom, no insight, no plan that can succeed against the Lord' (Prov. 21:30). Solomon, the likely writer of Proverbs, understood that God's purposes cannot be thwarted or impeded in any way. No person, angel or demon can oppose what God has decreed will come to pass. We are at our best when we can say as did Jesus from the cross: 'Not my will, but yours be done'.

SCRIPTURE READING: PROVERBS 16:1-9

February 17
JOB'S FRESH UNDERSTANDING
(WEEK 7: DAY 6)

The decrees of God

Westminster Catechism Question #7:

What are the decrees of God? *Answer*: The decrees of God are his eternal purpose, by which, for his own glory, he has ordained whatever comes to pass.

Theme verse: 'He does as he pleases with the powers of heaven and the peoples of the earth. No one can hold back his hand or say to him: "What have you done?"' (Dan. 4:35).

The book of Job does not skirt around the tough issues. Job was put through severe trials in his lifetime, and as a consequence wrestled with questions about God's will for his life. Job struggled to figure out how to respond to God when it seemed like God's anger was directed straight at him. When Job raised these questions his friends were miserable counsellors. Rather than offering comfort they focused on trying to discern what Job might have done wrong to deserve such tribulation. Job ignored their advice. Instead, he continued to seek an answer from God through prayer. And God did answer (Job 38 – 41). God said that he was sovereign over every sphere of Job's life and that it was his supreme right to do what he willed with his children. What was Job's response? 'I know that you can do all things; no plan of yours can be thwarted' (Job 42:1-2). At the end of the book God blessed Job with more than he had before his trials. Job found comfort in his new understanding that God 'does as he pleases with the powers of heaven and the peoples of the earth'. God uses trials to test his children. They are the means God uses to grow us into Christ-likeness. What trials has God sent to you for the very purpose of doing you good? How have you responded to his fatherly discipline?

SCRIPTURE READING: JOB 12:10-23

February 18
SOVEREIGN IN SALVATION
(WEEK 7: DAY 7)

The decrees of God

Westminster Catechism Question #7:

What are the decrees of God? *Answer*: The decrees of God are his eternal purpose, by which, for his own glory, he has ordained whatever comes to pass.

Theme verse: 'He does as he pleases with the powers of heaven and the peoples of the earth. No one can hold back his hand or say to him: "What have you done?"' (Dan. 4:35).

The Lord Jesus was very emphatic that he is sovereign over our lives. He said that sparrows do not fall to the ground apart from his will, the hairs of our head are all numbered, and the Father hides eternal truths from the wise and reveals them to little children since it is his pleasure to do so. Jesus was very direct about this with regards to our salvation: 'No one can come to me unless the Father has enabled him' (John 6:65). 'I am not praying for the world, but for those you have given me, for they are yours' (John 17:9). 'You did not choose me, but I chose you to go and bear fruit — fruit that will last' (John 15:16). The early church affirmed God's sovereignty over all of life, pointing out that the Lord was crucified by evil men only because 'they did what your power and will had decided beforehand should happen' (Acts 4:28). One can only become a Christian 'by the power of God, who has saved us and called us to a holy life — not because of anything we have done but because of his own purpose and grace. This grace was given us in Christ Jesus before the beginning of time' (2 Tim. 1:9). If you are not a believer, God extends his arms to you and invites you to trust him with your life. He alone has the power to cleanse you from your sins and call you into a life of holy living.

SCRIPTURE READING: ROMANS 9:10-26

February 19
GOD'S BLUEPRINT IN ACTION
(WEEK 8: DAY 1)

God's Control

Westminster Catechism Question #8:

How does God execute his decrees? *Answer*: God executes his decrees in the works of creation and providence.

Theme verse: 'I make known the end from the beginning, from ancient times, what is still to come. I say: My purpose will stand, and I will do all that I please' (Isa. 46:10).

God's decrees are the blueprint that guides the world. God made his decree in eternity past, has guided the course of history, and will continue to guide the future. God's decrees are revealed in his work of creation and the daily activities of the world he has made: people, historical events, nature, and particularly, in his care and love for his Church. In our theme verse above from the book of Isaiah, God makes his plan and purpose known: 'I make known the end from the beginning'. The Apostle Paul wrote that the most important decree of God is that Jesus is the focus of history: 'In him we were also chosen, having been predestined according to the plan of him who works out everything in conformity with the purpose of his will in order that we who were the first to hope in Christ, might be for the praise of his glory' (Eph. 1:11-12). Whether we are talking about the world God has made, the church he has died for, or each of us individually, God's purpose was to reveal his Son Jesus Christ as the centrepiece of all his plans and purposes. God has made known the mystery of his decreed will. It is 'to bring all things in heaven and on earth together under one head, even Christ' (Eph. 1:10). The call in our lives is to get in line with God's great purpose by living for Christ's glory.

SCRIPTURE READING: EPHESIANS 1:1-14

February 20

GOD OF THE INSIGNIFICANT
(WEEK 8: DAY 2)

God's Control

Westminster Catechism Question #8:

How does God execute his decrees? *Answer*: God executes his decrees in the works of creation and providence.

Theme verse: 'I make known the end from the beginning, from ancient times, what is still to come. I say: My purpose will stand, and I will do all that I please' (Isa. 46:10).

Some assume that God has removed his daily control over insignificant matters. What does it matter if a few hundred locusts are busy eating the leaves from several trees in an African village? However, if those same locusts multiply rapidly, as occurs from time to time, they can wipe out thousands of fields of ripened grain, leaving millions without food. The point, of course, is that God, who is infinite in power and wisdom, not only creates all things; he also upholds, directs, controls and governs all things. This includes both animate and inanimate objects, great or small, by his supremely wise purpose. It seems impossible that God can be overseeing everything at the same time — the weather, the flight of birds, the dolphin's destination, the activity of the bee or the ant, and your personal journey. But God asks Jeremiah: 'I am the Lord, the God of all mankind. Is anything too hard for me?' (Jer. 32:27). It is a comforting thought that God has decreed exactly when the sun will rise and set and the pathway of the planets every single day. This same God daily attends to the care of his children: 'Look at the birds of the air; they do not sow or reap or store away in barns, and yet your heavenly Father feeds them. Are you not much more valuable than they?' (Matt. 6:26).

SCRIPTURE READING: GENESIS 18:1-15

February 21
Sin and God's sovereignty
(week 8: day 3)

God's Control

Westminster Catechism Question #8:

How does God execute his decrees? *Answer*: God executes his decrees in the works of creation and providence.

Theme verse: 'I make known the end from the beginning, from ancient times, what is still to come. I say: My purpose will stand, and I will do all that I please' (Isa. 46:10).

If God is in control of everything, why doesn't he put a stop to all the sin, evil and violence in our world? We could even personalize the question: 'If God cares about us as individuals, why doesn't he keep us from sinning?' One answer to these questions is that God will do that very thing. One day Jesus will return to judge the earth and bring an end to unrighteousness in our world. He will establish a new heaven and new earth and believers will be for ever changed into his likeness. There will be no mourning, crying or pain, no more violence and no more sin (Rev. 21:4). But God will also, in a most wise and righteous way, allow his very own children to fall for a time into a variety of temptations in order to experience the sinfulness of their own hearts. He does this in order for us to see our great need of him, to recognize our weakness in order to make us stronger in Christ. Seeing ourselves for what we are humbles us because it reveals to us the hidden strength of evil still dwelling in us and the deceitfulness of our hearts. Such experiences help us to guard against sin in the future. Even when it comes to the ugliness of our own sin, 'we know that in all things God works for the good of those who love him, who have been called according to his purpose' (Rom. 8:28).

SCRIPTURE READING: ROMANS 8:28-39

February 22
OVERRULING STUBBORN SERVANTS
(WEEK 8: DAY 4)

God's Control

Westminster Catechism Question #8:

How does God execute his decrees? Answer: God executes his
decrees in the works of creation and providence.

Theme verse: 'I make known the end from the beginning, from
ancient times, what is still to come. I say: My purpose will stand,
and I will do all that I please' (Isa. 46:10).

Jonah had no intention of doing God's will. God ordered him to
preach to the great city of Nineveh but he despised the Ninevites
and had no interest in fulfilling his divinely appointed task. He
found a ship going in the opposite direction from Nineveh and got
on it. We know the story. The Lord sent a great wind on the sea,
a violent storm arose, and Jonah, blamed for the storm, was cast
overboard. Rather than drowning, Jonah was swallowed by a great
whale that spat him out onto dry land. This time, Jonah obeyed
the Lord, went to Nineveh and called the great city to repent of
its wickedness. A mighty revival broke out; the city entered into
a time of repentance and fasting, putting on sackcloth as a sign
of their contrition. When God saw the people of Nineveh turning from their evil ways he had compassion on them. Jonah was
displeased with all of this: 'I knew that you are a gracious and
compassionate God, slow to anger and abounding in love, a God
who relents from sending calamity' (Jonah 4:2). But God replied:
'Should I not be concerned about that great city?' (Jonah 4:11).
Here is a story of God's grace, his concern for people and animals, and his special care over Jonah and the world he has made.
God even overrules in the lives of his stubborn, sinful servants in
order to accomplish his divine purposes.

SCRIPTURE READING: THE BOOK OF JONAH

February 23
GOD'S SPECIAL CARE
(WEEK 8: DAY 5)

God's Control

Westminster Catechism Question #8:

How does God execute his decrees? Answer: God executes his decrees in the works of creation and providence.

Theme verse: 'I make known the end from the beginning, from ancient times, what is still to come. I say: My purpose will stand, and I will do all that I please' (Isa. 46:10).

One night, in a time of great crisis in the life of the Apostle Paul, the Lord Jesus drew near to him and said: 'Take courage! As you have testified about me in Jerusalem, so you must also testify in Rome' (Acts 23:11). 'The next morning a group of Jewish leaders formed a conspiracy and bound themselves with an oath not to eat or drink until they had killed Paul' (Acts 23:12). What do you think was the chance that their plot to kill Paul would succeed? Later in the book of Acts we read about one of Paul's journeys by ship to Rome. A violent storm arose and after many days of being violently tossed by the raging waves even the veteran sailors 'gave up all hope of being saved' (Acts 27:20). Unsurprisingly, Paul was the only person on board who was unafraid. How could that be? 'Last night an angel of the God whose I am and whom I serve stood beside me and said, "Do not be afraid, Paul. You must stand trial before Caesar; and God has graciously given you the lives of all who sail with you"' (Acts 27:23-24). Even though outward circumstances looked completely hopeless, God had other plans for Paul. Today we also have confidence that even when circumstances look bleak, God's providential care reaches all the way to our concerns and meets us in a special way. Such is God's love for his children.

SCRIPTURE READING: ACTS 23:11-22

February 24
WHO KILLED THE LORD?
(WEEK 8: DAY 6)

God's Control

Westminster Catechism Question #8:

How does God execute his decrees? *Answer*: God executes his decrees in the works of creation and providence.

Theme verse: 'I make known the end from the beginning, from ancient times, what is still to come. I say: My purpose will stand, and I will do all that I please' (Isa. 46:10).

Who was responsible for death of the Lord Jesus? Was it Pilate that should be primarily blamed, or Judas? The answer is that Jesus had to die to fulfil God's purpose and providence. The Father and the Lord Jesus entered into a covenant in eternity and that decree was then fulfilled in time and space: 'But when the time had fully come, God sent his Son' (Gal. 4:4). At the appointed time Jesus took upon himself a human nature, with all its essential characteristics and its common difficulties except for our sinful nature. In fulfilling the Father's decreed will Jesus lived out his earthly life under the providential care of his Father, acting only in accordance with his Father's pleasure and will. At the end of his earthly life he voluntarily underwent the punishment that was due to us, dying in our place. Those who participated in the crucifixion of Christ acted according to their own nature. Pilate did what was politically expedient. The religious leaders were fiercely jealous of Christ. Judas was disappointed that Jesus refused to be a political king. But regardless of the personalities involved, 'it was the Lord's will to crush him and cause him to suffer' (Isa. 53:10); executing his will perfectly through his Son, establishing his kingdom, and making reconciliation between God and his people possible.

SCRIPTURE READING: ISAIAH 53:1-12

February 25

God's Control

Westminster Catechism Question #8:

How does God execute his decrees? *Answer*: God executes his decrees in the works of creation and providence.

Theme verse: 'I make known the end from the beginning, from ancient times, what is still to come. I say: My purpose will stand, and I will do all that I please' (Isa. 46:10).

'He is before all things, and in him all things hold together' (Col. 1:17). We cannot understand how Jesus is 'sustaining all things by his powerful word' (Heb. 1:3), but the Bible is clear that the Lord preserves and upholds all things in order to keep the world from collapse. When an architect builds a house the structure can stand on its own without his assistance. But this is not how the world can operate, independent of its Architect. A builder must use materials that are already in existence, and his whole work consists of changing their form, combining them in a new order. But the very substance, as well as the form, of all created things, comes from the hand of God, and the withdrawal of God's hand would leave the universe unsupported. God's control over all events is taught throughout the Scriptures, whether it is the heart of the Pharaoh of Egypt, wind or rain, plagues, birds of the air, or hairs of our head. The question for us is whether we are interested in being under God's control or demanding to live independently of his love and care. Unconverted men and women are, by nature, unable and unwilling to submit to God's providential leading in their lives. But those who love the Lord gladly surrender to his providential leadership, seeking to walk according to his will.

SCRIPTURE READING: COLOSSIANS 1:15-23

February 26

Creation

Westminster Catechism Question #9:

What is the work of creation? *Answer*: The work of creation is God, by his mighty power, making all things from nothing, in the space of six days, and all very good.

Theme verse: 'By faith we understand that the universe was formed at God's command, so that what is seen was not made out of what was visible' (Heb. 11:3).

This week we are studying and meditating on creation and our God as Creator. The theme verse for this week (Heb. 11:3) teaches several wonderful truths: first of all, to believe in God as Creator is an act of faith. Individuals who believe we are here by chance rather than an intentional act of God exhibit a misplaced faith. Secondly, Hebrews 11:3 tells us that creation occurred by divine command. 'And God said "Let there be light," and there was light' (Gen. 1:3). Thirdly, our theme verse teaches that what we see around us has not always been in existence. Life forms and matter did not exist in some previous state in some far flung part of the universe; rather, the Lord made them all and brought them into existence at the proper time. The Latin term is *'ex nihilo'*, which means 'out of nothing'. God did not form the world by using chemicals or substances that were conveniently floating about in the universe. Instead, he used only his own sovereign power to make visible what was not there before. The catechism answer states that what God made was all very good. Even for a person with misplaced faith the existence of the universe is an incredible miracle. The difference for us who believe Jesus Christ is the Creator of the universe is that we know who to thank.

SCRIPTURE READING: HEBREWS 11:1-6

February 27
THE HEAVENS DECLARE GOD'S GLORY
(WEEK 9: DAY 2)

Creation

Westminster Catechism Question #9:

What is the work of creation? *Answer*: The work of creation is God, by his mighty power, making all things from nothing, in the space of six days, and all very good.

Theme verse: 'By faith we understand that the universe was formed at God's command, so that what is seen was not made out of what was visible' (Heb. 11:3).

The created universe exists as an amazing witness to the glory of God and his mighty power. King David proclaimed: 'The heavens declare the glory of God; the skies proclaim the work of his hands. Day after day they pour forth speech; night after night they display knowledge. There is no speech or language where their voice is not heard. Their voice goes out into all the earth, their words to the ends of the world' (Ps. 19:1-4). When we communicate it is through voice or pen and paper. But David is stating that the universe has a language of its own which is perpetually and eternally proclaiming the immense greatness of the glory of God. What is the message the universe is declaring? 'Since the creation of the world God's invisible qualities — his eternal power and divine nature — have been clearly seen, being understood from what has been made, so that men are without excuse' (Rom. 1:20). God's attributes: his power, majesty, sovereignty, goodness, orderliness, beauty, omniscience and splendour are unmistakable characteristics that we cannot miss if we simply look around us and take in all that he has made. Our calling is to join the universe in declaring the glory of God. 'Praise him, sun and moon, praise him, all you shining stars … young men and maidens, old men and children' (Ps. 148:3,12).

SCRIPTURE READING: PSALM 148

February 28

Creation

Westminster Catechism Question #9:

What is the work of creation? *Answer*: The work of creation is God, by his mighty power, making all things from nothing, in the space of six days, and all very good.

Theme verse: 'By faith we understand that the universe was formed at God's command, so that what is seen was not made out of what was visible' (Heb. 11:3).

There is a wonderful orderliness to God's creation activity. On day one of creation God created light (Gen. 1:1-5). Corresponding to day one is day four where God created 'lights'; that is, the sun, moon, and stars (Gen. 1:14-19). On day two God created water above and below the sky (Gen. 1:6-8). Correspondingly, on day five God created the birds to fill the sky and fish to fill the waters (Gen. 1:20-23). On day three God created dry ground and vegetation. So on day six God created livestock, creatures that move along the ground, and wild animals, giving them every green plant for food (Gen. 1:24-31). And, of course, also on day six God created mankind, both male and female (Gen. 1:26). God gave us dominion over all that he had made in order to populate the earth, care for it and use its resources wisely. Especially for the Christian, our care and love of what God has made is a reflection of our love for him who made it. Protecting the environment is not the sole task of political action groups and government agencies. It is the response of a believer who understands that the world is a display of God's glory, creativity and love of beauty. The more beautifully it is preserved the more clearly it shows forth the attributes of a gracious, powerful and majestic God.

SCRIPTURE READING: GENESIS 1:1-28

February 29
THE DANGER OF FORMAL RELIGION
(LEAP YEAR)

'To those who through the righteousness of our God and Savior
Jesus Christ have received a faith as precious as ours'
(2 Peter 1:1).

'How shall we escape if we ignore such a great salvation?'
(Heb. 2:3).

Believers are able to rejoice in their faith because Jesus has reconciled us to God. Persons who have nothing more than a formal religion cannot understand how we can possess such confidence knowing that all our sins are forgiven us. Be sure you are not busily serving your local church, perhaps involved in service ministries, even prayer gatherings, but find yourself experiencing a sense of unease about the safety of your own soul. There is no comfort in our religious activities in and of themselves. What is important is not to neglect this great salvation, seeking somehow to be approved by God without looking exclusively to the blood-offering Jesus poured out for you. Jesus spoke directly to the religious leadership of his day about this delusion, 'Woe to you, teachers of the law and Pharisees, you hypocrites! You travel over land and sea to win a single convert, and when he becomes one, you make him twice as much a son of hell as you are' (Matt. 23:15). Jesus was not condemning their evangelical zeal. Rather, the priests of his day relied on their religious duties and pious actions as proof that they were approved by God. Only Jesus can bring peace between you and God in his double role as Mediator and High Priest. He offers his own lifeblood to make reconciliation possible.

SCRIPTURE READING: MATTHEW 23:13-26

Creation

Westminster Catechism Question #9:

What is the work of creation? *Answer*: The work of creation is God, by his mighty power, making all things from nothing, in the space of six days, and all very good.

Theme verse: 'By faith we understand that the universe was formed at God's command, so that what is seen was not made out of what was visible' (Heb. 11:3).

'The day of the Lord will come like a thief. The heavens will disappear with a roar; the elements will be destroyed by fire, and the earth and everything in it will be laid bare' (2 Peter 3:10). There is no question that the Bible teaches one day God will make a new creation. He will replace what he first created with a new heaven and a new earth. 'That day will bring about the destruction of the heavens by fire, and the elements will melt in the heat. But in keeping with his promise we are looking forward to a new heaven and a new earth, the home of righteousness' (2 Peter 3:12-13). If that is the case, a person might be tempted to think that since God is going to destroy the earth anyway it doesn't matter if you treat it badly today. Importantly, the Apostle Peter did not reason that an attitude of sloppiness and irreverence towards God's creation should then prevail. Quite the contrary: 'Since everything will be destroyed in this way, what kind of people ought you to be? You ought to live holy and godly lives as you look forward to the day of God and speed its coming' (2 Peter 3:11-12). In view of the Lord's return, will godliness be our goal today? What will be of first importance in our lives? How will we treat what God has created and the people he has made?

SCRIPTURE READING: 2 PETER 3:8-14

March 2

Creation

Westminster Catechism Question #9:

What is the work of creation? *Answer*: The work of creation is God, by his mighty power, making all things from nothing, in the space of six days, and all very good.

Theme verse: 'By faith we understand that the universe was formed at God's command, so that what is seen was not made out of what was visible' (Heb. 11:3).

Who created the world? Was it God the Father or God the Son? Genesis 1:3 has the Father speaking: 'Let there be light'. And there was light. So it must be God the Father. But then in Colossians we are informed that Jesus created the *cosmos*. 'For by him (Jesus) all things were created; things in heaven and on earth, visible and invisible' (Col. 1:16). The answer is that when God the Father spoke activity occurred. The 'Word' went forth to create. Who was that 'Word'? It was the pre-incarnate Jesus. John describes Jesus this way: 'In the beginning was the Word, and the Word was with God, and the Word was God ... through him all things were made' (John 1:1,3). Today, the Father and the Son are still creating. 'For God, who said, "Let light shine out of darkness," made his light to shine in our hearts to give us the light of the knowledge of the glory of God in the face of Christ' (2 Cor. 4:6). Today, Jesus sends the Holy Spirit into human hearts to effect a 'new creation'. 'If anyone is in Christ, he is a new creation; the old has gone, the new has come!' (2 Cor. 5:17). The same heavenly Father who sent Jesus to create the universe now sends the Holy Spirit into human hearts to create a new person. Are you a new creation by the power of Christ at work in you?

SCRIPTURE READING: GENESIS 2:1-7

March 3
ENTERING GOD'S REST
(WEEK 9: DAY 6)

Creation

Westminster Catechism Question #9:

What is the work of creation? *Answer*: The work of creation is God, by his mighty power, making all things from nothing, in the space of six days, and all very good.

Theme verse: 'By faith we understand that the universe was formed at God's command, so that what is seen was not made out of what was visible' (Heb. 11:3).

On the seventh day of creation God rested. God was not tired. He rested because his work of creation was complete. 'His work has been finished since the creation of the world' (Heb. 4:3). This mighty work was perfect, fully effective and very good. It did not have to be repeated or changed in any way. So the Lord rested in order to commemorate his work. The author of the book of Hebrews saw a clear analogy between the rest that God enjoyed after creation and the Sabbath rest the people of God enjoy after salvation. This rest is ours when we stop striving to work our way to heaven and accept the finished work that Jesus accomplished for us at the cross. The writer of Hebrews lamented that many of his fellow Jews still had not entered that rest because they were trying to enter by their own efforts rather than believing by faith in Jesus. 'The message they heard was of no value to them, because those who heard did not combine it with faith. Now we who believe enter that rest' (Heb. 4:2-3). This rest is the assurance that we belong to God and that one day we will enter 'eternal rest' where we will live forever with the Lord Jesus. 'Let us, therefore, make every effort to enter that rest, so that no one will fall by following their example of disobedience' (Heb. 4:11).

SCRIPTURE READING: HEBREWS 4:1-13

March 4
GOD'S RE-CREATION
(WEEK 9: DAY 7)

Creation

Westminster Catechism Question #9:

What is the work of creation? *Answer*: The work of creation is God, by his mighty power, making all things from nothing, in the space of six days, and all very good.

Theme verse: 'By faith we understand that the universe was formed at God's command, so that what is seen was not made out of what was visible' (Heb. 11:3).

God's creation is complete and perfect, yet it is God's will to re-create. 'Then I saw a new heaven and a new earth, for the first heaven and the first earth had passed away' (Rev. 21:1). 'He who was seated on the throne said, "I am making everything new!"' (Rev. 21:5). There will be one great difference between the old heaven and earth and the new heaven and earth. It is Christ. In the new heaven and earth Jesus will always be physically present with us. 'I saw the Holy City, the new Jerusalem, coming down out of heaven from God, prepared as a bride beautifully dressed for her husband. And I heard a loud voice from the throne saying, "Now the dwelling of God is with men, and he will live with them. They will be his people, and God himself will be with them and he will be their God"' (Rev. 21:2-4). This is the Garden of Eden, only better. Paradise lost is paradise re-gained, only with greater blessing and more resplendent joys. Christ will be the centre, the light of heaven and everyone living there will offer grateful worship and joyful praise to him who redeemed them. 'He who overcomes will inherit all this, and I will be his God and he will be my son' (Rev. 21:7). 'No eye has seen, no ear has heard, no mind has conceived what God has prepared for those who love him' (1 Cor. 2:9).

SCRIPTURE READING: REVELATION 21:1-8

March 5

THE CREATION OF MAN
(WEEK 10: DAY 1)

The image of God

Westminster Catechism Question #10:

How did God create man? *Answer*: God created man male and
female, after his own image, in knowledge, righteousness and
holiness, with dominion over the creatures.

Theme verse: 'So God created man in his own image, in the image of God he created him; male and female he created them'
(Gen. 1:27).

In Genesis 1 we have an overview of the creation story. But in
Genesis 2:5-25 we read a more specific account of the creation of
man. Adam was not just one more created thing. Eve was not an
afterthought. They were the final, crowning achievement of God's
creative activity. On the sixth day, after everything else was made,
God created man. Everything else prior to the creation of humans
was preparatory. The earth and seas, sky and stars, and plants
and animals, were all groundwork for the noble creature God
would fashion from the dust of the earth. God would make man
who would rule and care for all that God had made. As God was
about to make man there was contemplation in heaven of what
was about to occur: 'Let us make man in our image'. This was the
Trinity of God agreeing to make us supremely noble, righteous,
holy and able to understand what he has done in creation. 'Let
us make a creature', God was saying, 'who will relate to us and
be like us. Let us give this new creature dominion to care for everything we have made. Let us give him the capacity to speak, to
pray to us, to commune with us, to enjoy us, and to give glory and
praise to the God who made him'. This was God's intention when
he made US. His intention has never changed.

SCRIPTURE READING: GENESIS 2:5-25

March 6

IMAGE-BEARERS
(WEEK 10: DAY 2)

The image of God

Westminster Catechism Question #10:

How did God create man? *Answer*: God created man male and female, after his own image, in knowledge, righteousness and holiness, with dominion over the creatures.

Theme verse: 'So God created man in his own image, in the image of God he created him; male and female he created them' (Gen. 1:27).

When God made us he created something unique and indeed special. God created us male and female. He placed within us the ability to reason and gave us souls that were designed to last forever. He gave us inside knowledge about himself and the world he had made. He made us righteous and truly holy. He wrote his own laws upon our hearts and gave us the power to fulfil his laws' requirements. These characteristics are what distinguish us as being made in God's image and likeness. In this regard, we are infinitely different from the animals God created. Any theory of evolution automatically reduces us since it minimizes the essential 'image of God' characteristics, focusing instead on our likeness to the animals. But the Bible teaches that man is the crowning achievement of God's creation. We are uniquely 'image-bearers' of God. The calling of the Christian is 'to put off your old self, which is being corrupted by its deceitful desires, to be made new in the attitude of your minds; and to put on the new self, created to be like God in true righteousness and holiness' (Eph. 4:22-24). There is our vocation today: To 'put off the old' and to 'put on the new self' in order to bear the image of God, making a solid advance in Christ-likeness.

SCRIPTURE READING: EPHESIANS 4:17-24

The image of God

Westminster Catechism Question #10:

How did God create man? *Answer*: God created man male and female, after his own image, in knowledge, righteousness and holiness, with dominion over the creatures.

Theme verse: 'So God created man in his own image, in the image of God he created him; male and female he created them' (Gen. 1:27).

In Genesis 2:7 mankind is given the 'breath of life' and 'man became a living being'. This is more than just the ability to breathe; it is spiritual comprehension to know God and to understand and act upon his commands. When God made us he wrote his Law on our hearts. The Apostle Paul wrote about this when talking about the Gentiles (non-Jews) of his day who understood right from wrong even though they didn't possess the Ten Commandments or Old Testament Scriptures. 'Indeed, when Gentiles, who do not have the law, do by nature things required by the law, they are a law for themselves, even though they do not have the law, since they show that the requirements of the law are written on their hearts' (Rom. 2:14-15). We all know what is right and wrong even when the Bible is not there in front of us pointing things out. The little child sneaking cookies from the cookie jar or the thief breaking into someone's home both know that they are doing wrong because God has given each one of us a conscience that has imprinted on it God's moral laws. The Christian is called to keep his conscience tender and sensitive to God's commands and to the laws 'written upon his heart'. It is all part of what it means to bear the image of God.

SCRIPTURE READING: ROMANS 2:5-16

March 8

The image of God

Westminster Catechism Question #10:

How did God create man? *Answer*: God created man male and
female, after his own image, in knowledge, righteousness and
holiness, with dominion over the creatures.

Theme verse: 'So God created man in his own image, in the image of God he created him; male and female he created them'
(Gen. 1:27).

When King David wrote Psalm 8 he was likely out on the flat roof-
top of his palace. Perhaps he was looking up at the night's sky, reflecting on the galaxy-filled vastness of the universe and the greatness of God's power in creation. Here are his thoughts: 'When I
consider your heavens, the work of your fingers, the moon and
the stars, which you have set in place, what is man that you are
mindful of him, the son of man that you care for him?' (Ps. 8:3-4).
David was not comparing our insignificance to the magnificence
of God's universe. In fact, he was stating just the opposite. David
was scratching his head as to why God had made men and women
so significant, making us his most glorious achievement in all creation. 'You made him [only] a little lower than the heavenly beings
and crowned him with glory and honor. You made him ruler over
the works of your hands; you put everything under his feet' (Ps.
8:5-6). David does not try to answer the impossible as to why God
made the world as he did, crowning men and women with 'glory
and honor'. But David did know how to sing to God as he con-
templated such lofty thoughts: 'O LORD, our Lord, how majestic
is your name in all the earth!' (Ps. 8:9). King David sang of the
amazing kindness and plan of God to make us significant, give us
meaning, and give us a relationship with the living God.

SCRIPTURE READING: PSALM 8

March 9

RESTORING THE IMAGE OF GOD
(WEEK 10: DAY 5)

The image of God

Westminster Catechism Question #10:

How did God create man? *Answer*: God created man male and female, after his own image, in knowledge, righteousness and holiness, with dominion over the creatures.

Theme verse: 'So God created man in his own image, in the image of God he created him; male and female he created them' (Gen. 1:27).

The catechism answer states that God created mankind male and female, after his own image, in knowledge, righteousness and holiness. This means that to be image-bearers is not to physically look like God; rather, it is to possess a correct understanding of God, to be perfectly righteous and holy as God is perfectly righteous and holy. Of course, we all know that we fall far short of that. When Adam fell into sin in the Garden of Eden by disobeying God, the image of God was corrupted and his sin was passed on to all succeeding generations. Jesus came into the world to 'seek and to save that which was lost'. What was lost was the pure image of God in us. We became polluted. The greater the sin in us, the greater is the loss of the image of God. Jesus came to restore that image. 'Do not lie to each other, since you have taken off your old self with its practices and have put on the new self, which is being renewed in knowledge in the image of its Creator' (Col. 3:10). This verse takes us back to Genesis 1:27. Christ, by his cleansing work at the cross, restores the corrupted image of God and renews that image in us. We are renewed when true knowledge of God, greater righteousness and holiness increasingly are the hallmarks of our Christian lives.

SCRIPTURE READING: COLOSSIANS 3:1-11

80

March 10
WORK IN THE GARDEN
(WEEK 10: DAY 6)

The image of God

Westminster Catechism Question #10:

How did God create man? *Answer*: God created man male and female, after his own image, in knowledge, righteousness and holiness, with dominion over the creatures.

Theme verse: 'So God created man in his own image, in the image of God he created him; male and female he created them' (Gen. 1:27).

Adam was our first image-bearer. In Genesis 2:15 we read that God took Adam and placed him in the Garden of Eden. Interestingly, the Lord placed him there for the purpose of working it and taking care of it. Adam most likely was called upon to be a gardener, a horticulturalist of the vast variety of plants that God had made. More than likely, he would have cultivated the ground for the production of food. Perhaps he also tended the animals that were in the Garden of Eden. He had responsibility. He had work to do. This occurred before sin entered the world. It says something significant about work itself. Work is a gift of God and through work we are able to display the image of God in us. This should help us to see our work in the home, our 'nine-to-five' job, or the service we render to our church family or community in a new light. Work is to be a fulfilling way to display the image of Christ to others. We are not to see work as drudgery where we reluctantly put in hours for the boss in order to receive a pay check. Instead, our work is to honour the Lord. In that light the 'sweat of our brow' is an act of worship. It does not matter where we are employed, who our employer is, or what we are employed in, but rather when we work to 'do it all for the glory of God' (1 Cor. 10:31).

SCRIPTURE READING: 2 THESSALONIANS 3:6-15

March 11
No surprises
(WEEK 10: DAY 7)

The image of God

Westminster Catechism Question #10:

How did God create man? *Answer*: God created man male and female, after his own image, in knowledge, righteousness and holiness, with dominion over the creatures.

Theme verse: 'So God created man in his own image, in the image of God he created him; male and female he created them' (Gen. 1:27).

God entered into an agreement, or covenant, with Adam. 'The Lord God commanded the man, "You are free to eat from any tree in the garden; but you must not eat from the tree of the knowledge of good and evil, for when you eat of it you will surely die"' (Gen. 2:16-17). This agreement God made with Adam was based on performance. If Adam obeyed God then God would bless him. However, Adam would be subject to God's punishment of death should he disobey. When Adam was put to the test he failed miserably. Some people think that perhaps God was caught by surprise. But Romans 5 makes clear that God's sovereign purposes were being worked out in Adam's transgression: 'For if, by the trespass of the one man (Adam), death reigned through that one man, how much more will those who receive God's abundant provision of grace and of the gift of righteousness reign in life through the one man, Jesus Christ' (Rom. 5:17). Through Adam we lost our perfect knowledge and righteousness. However, through Christ, there is an abundant provision of grace and the gift of righteousness is available to us. God was not caught by surprise. He had a Redeemer waiting in the wings. The Redeemer is capable of restoring the image of God in fallen people.

SCRIPTURE READING: ROMANS 5:12-21

March 12
GOD'S WORD QUESTIONED
(WEEK 11: DAY 1)

The Fall

Westminster Catechism Question #13:

Did Adam and Eve remain in the condition in which they were created? *Answer*: Adam and Eve, being left to the freedom of their own will, fell from the condition in which they were created by sinning against God.

Theme verse: 'For as in Adam all die, so in Christ all will be made alive' (1 Cor. 15:22).

Adam and Eve had enjoyed God's divine favour under his benevolent care. When Eve was approached by the serpent in the Garden of Eden both she and Adam were in a warm and secure relationship with the living God. Satan's crafty attack was to question the fairness of that relationship. 'Did God really say, "You must not eat from any tree in the garden?"' (Gen. 3:1). Eve was called upon to defend what God had said to her and to Adam and she did so faithfully. However, for the first time, she had to mull over in her mind the fact that God had restricted Adam's and her freedom. Eve actually put words in God's mouth, declaring that God would not let them eat of the tree '*and you must not touch it*' (Gen. 3:3). Then Satan accused God of being unfair, wanting the superior position and keeping Adam and Eve 'in their place', a position of inferiority. Both Adam and Eve concluded that Satan was telling the truth and moved accordingly. Their actions that followed were simply consistent with their new understanding of the situation. There were many errors in their thinking, but one sin stands out: Adam and Eve questioned the *authority* of God's Word and made themselves the new authorities. Autonomy or independence from God has been the mark of Adam's descendants ever since.

SCRIPTURE READING: GENESIS 3:1-5

March 13
TWO KINGDOMS, TWO PATHS
(WEEK 11: DAY 2)

The Fall

Westminster Catechism Question #13:

Did Adam and Eve remain in the condition in which they were created? *Answer*: Adam and Eve, being left to the freedom of their own will, fell from the condition in which they were created by sinning against God.

Theme verse: 'For as in Adam all die, so in Christ all will be made alive' (1 Cor. 15:22).

Satan's initial question to Eve was subtle, asking what appeared to be a harmless question: 'Did God really say, "You must not eat from any tree in the garden?"' (Gen. 3:1). But after Eve's answer his attack was bold and challenging: 'You will not surely die', the serpent said to the woman. 'For God knows that when you eat of it your eyes will be opened, and you will be like God, knowing good and evil' (Gen. 3:4-5). The devil insinuated that God was cruelly frightening Adam and Eve to keep them in their subservient position. Satan suggested that the Lord was threatened by Adam and Eve's potential. God simply didn't want them to enjoy equality with him, and therefore, the idea of disobedience bringing death was nothing more than an idle threat. With the fear of death removed, and the allure of wisdom and equality ahead of them, both Adam and Eve moved towards the tree and defiantly and proudly rejected God's command and dire warning. At the end of the day, there are really only two types of religion in our world. There is religion based on doing God's will and religion based on doing our own will. There are only two kingdoms. There is the Kingdom of Christ and the Kingdom of Self. There are only two paths. One path leads to life; the other leads to death.

SCRIPTURE READING: GENESIS 3:1-7

LEADERSHIP IN THE HOME
(WEEK 11: DAY 3)

The Fall

Westminster Catechism Question #13:

Did Adam and Eve remain in the condition in which they were created? *Answer*: Adam and Eve, being left to the freedom of their own will, fell from the condition in which they were created by sinning against God.

Theme verse: 'For as in Adam all die, so in Christ all will be made alive' (1 Cor. 15:22).

Some have conjectured that Eve was probably more to blame than Adam for this debacle. She seems to be the prominent person in the discussion with Satan. However, a phrase in the story about the fall into sin is significant. 'When the woman saw that the fruit of the tree was good for food and pleasing to the eye, and also desirable for gaining wisdom, she took some and ate it. She also gave some to her husband, *who was with her*, and he ate it' (Gen. 3:6). What that phrase reveals is that Adam was present with his wife throughout the entire conversation with Satan and that he had abdicated his leadership in the home. Although he kept quiet throughout the conversation he was no less guilty than his wife. It is clear from the biblical account that Eve led and he willingly followed. No attempt was made by Adam to defend the Lord's integrity, to clarify the command of God, or to rebuff Satan for his attack on the Lord's authority. One more sin in the long list of sins that occurred in the garden is this: Adam abdicated his role as spiritual leader, defender and protector of his home. The Apostle Paul, in addressing the issue of male headship, writes: 'For Adam was formed first, then Eve' (1 Tim. 2:13). The apostle was reaffirming the creation order that men are to lovingly lead in their homes.

SCRIPTURE READING: 1 TIMOTHY 2:8-15

March 15

The Fall

Westminster Catechism Question #13:

Did Adam and Eve remain in the condition in which they were created? *Answer*: Adam and Eve, being left to the freedom of their own will, fell from the condition in which they were created by sinning against God.

Theme verse: 'For as in Adam all die, so in Christ all will be made alive' (1 Cor. 15:22).

When Adam and Eve's 'eyes were opened' (Gen. 3:6) to see their nakedness the two of them realized their former righteousness and holiness was a fading memory. What they now knew as a daily experience was the sense of inner guilt due to disobedience towards God. The physical nakedness was just the outer manifestation of their guilty consciences before the Lord. Trying to cover themselves (Gen. 3:7) was a pitiful attempt to relieve their shame and remove their guilt. Formerly Adam and Eve had enjoyed sweet fellowship with the Lord. Now they were in hiding. The Lord confronted Adam: 'Where are you?' (Gen. 3:9). Adam informed the Lord that he was hiding because he was physically naked. That was literally just another cover-up. The Lord told him otherwise: 'Have you eaten from the tree I told you not to eat from?' (Gen. 3:11). Adam's problem was a guilty conscience for having sinned against the Lord. Through Adam we have inherited this natural tendency to cover up our guilt and excuse our sin. Like a young boy hiding from a father's stern discipline, we are experts at hiding from the perfectly righteous Judge of all the earth. Fear of the consequences for sin always repels. Lonely and alienated, where will help come from?

SCRIPTURE READING: GENESIS 3:1-11

March 16
THE BLAME GAME
(WEEK 11: DAY 5)

The Fall

Westminster Catechism Question #13:

Did Adam and Eve remain in the condition in which they were created? *Answer*: Adam and Eve, being left to the freedom of their own will, fell from the condition in which they were created by sinning against God.

Theme verse: 'For as in Adam all die, so in Christ all will be made alive' (1 Cor. 15:22).

Someone has described hell as a place where people fall and continue falling forever. The first moments in hell one can still see light above but continued descent soon means the light diminishes until it vanishes from view. This concept gains support from the continuing distance between God and our first parents, Adam and Eve, as they descended into a pattern of unchecked sinfulness. After their disobedience came the blame game. First, Adam blamed God for his sin and then, secondarily, he blamed Eve: 'The woman *you* put here with me — she gave me some fruit from the tree, and I ate it' (Gen. 3:12). Eve blamed the devil: 'The serpent deceived me, and I ate' (Gen. 3:13). The original sin in the garden had now become habitual commandment-breaking. The Lord's response was to punish them for their sin. They would die, both physically and spiritually. They were banished from the garden and the tree of life. The good news is that one day this judgement will be lifted. 'Then the angel showed me the river of the water of life, clear as crystal, flowing from the throne of God and of the Lamb … On each side of the river stood the tree of life … No longer will there be any curse' (Rev. 22:1-3). One day followers of the Lamb will to return to the garden. Pray for a speedy return.

SCRIPTURE READING: GENESIS 3:8-20

March 17

The Fall

Westminster Catechism Question #13:

Did Adam and Eve remain in the condition in which they were created? *Answer*: Adam and Eve, being left to the freedom of their own will, fell from the condition in which they were created by sinning against God.

Theme verse: 'For as in Adam all die, so in Christ all will be made alive' (1 Cor. 15:22).

As catastrophic as the fall was for men and women, consider what it cost God. Surely the greatest loss was the image of God in man. God had made us to fellowship with him, to glorify him, and to enjoy him. But because of sin God lost that reflection of himself. We were to be the characterization of God's attributes in the world he had made. His love, joy, holiness, wisdom and truthfulness were to be on display through us to an observing universe. 'The Lord saw how great man's wickedness on the earth had become, and that every inclination of the thoughts of his heart was only evil all the time. The Lord was grieved that he had made man on the earth, and his heart was filled with pain' (Gen. 3:5-6). How Satan must have taunted the Lord about his creating us! From Genesis 3 onwards, the Scriptures unfold what the Father would do to correct this sorry state of affairs. In Genesis 3:21 God clothed Adam and Eve, caring for them. God's love towards sinners is evident throughout the centuries of biblical history. But the love of God towards us would be costly. To redeem us would be very expensive. The Apostle Paul understood this when he wrote: 'You were bought at a price' (1 Cor. 6:20). That price for our redemption was very high and very bloody.

SCRIPTURE READING: GENESIS 6:5-22

March 18

The Fall

Westminster Catechism Question #13:

Did Adam and Eve remain in the condition in which they were created? *Answer*: Adam and Eve, being left to the freedom of their own will, fell from the condition in which they were created by sinning against God.

Theme verse: 'For as in Adam all die, so in Christ all will be made alive' (1 Cor. 15:22).

'After he drove the man out, God placed on the east of the Garden of Eden cherubim and a flaming sword flashing back and forth to guard the way to the tree of life' (Gen. 3:24). Those cherubim were powerful security guards to keep Adam and Eve and their successors from returning to defile the garden in their sinful state. The flaming sword was a sword of judgement standing between God's garden and fallen humanity. The Lord was separating the holy from the profane, keeping sinners from the tree of life. However, the Lord never intended that we should live forever in a world of hopeless separation from God. He had something much better planned for us. To the church at Ephesus Jesus would say: 'To him who overcomes, I will give the right to eat from the tree of life, which is in the paradise of God' (Rev. 2:7). Our Saviour's purpose in dying was to remove that flaming sword which keeps us out of the garden. Incredibly, the Father wielded that sword against his own Son in order that his judgement would not fall on us. Christ's triumph means that cherubim no longer stand guard at the Garden of Eden. Entrance is once again possible. And one day there will be perfectly restored fellowship with Jesus in the garden of God to all who overcome through the sacrifice of Christ at Calvary.

SCRIPTURE READING: GENESIS 3:21-24

March 19

Sin

Westminster Catechism Question #14:

What is sin? *Answer*: Sin is not conforming to, or any breaking of, the law of God.

Theme verse: 'Everyone who sins breaks the law; in fact, sin is lawlessness' (1 John 3:4).

'If you really keep the royal law found in Scripture, "Love your neighbor as yourself," you are doing right. But if you show favoritism, you sin and are convicted by the law as lawbreakers. For whoever keeps the whole law and yet stumbles at just one point is guilty of breaking all of it' (James 2:8-10). We only need to break the Law of God in one point to be classified as sinners and to be guilty of breaking all of God's commandments. But as we discovered with Adam and Eve, we are never guilty of just breaking one of God's laws. If we covet someone's coat we open our minds to the idea of stealing it, or our hearts are filled with jealousy. If we steal the coat we demonstrate no love towards our neighbour, our family is dishonoured and we must lie about how we came to possess it. Another example of this is King David who did not just commit adultery with Bathsheba, but in an attempt to cover his tracks, had her husband killed. Lack of love towards God and his neighbour, covetousness, theft, dishonouring his family, lying — David's list of sins goes on and on. The good news about David is that when he was confronted by the prophet Nathan he repented of his sin. 'Have mercy on me, O God. Against you, you only, have I sinned and done what is evil in your sight' (Ps. 51:1,4).

SCRIPTURE READING: JAMES 2:8-13

March 20
Delighting in the Law
(WEEK 12: DAY 2)

Sin

Westminster Catechism Question #14:

What is sin? *Answer*: Sin is not conforming to, or any breaking of, the law of God.

Theme verse: 'Everyone who sins breaks the law; in fact, sin is lawlessness' (1 John 3:4).

One of the purposes of the Ten Commandments is to show us that we are sinners. 'Therefore no one will be declared righteous in his sight by observing the law; rather, through the law we become conscious of sin' (Rom. 3:20). The Law is meant to drive us to Christ because he alone has the power to break the stranglehold sin has on us. 'What shall we say, then? Is the law sin? Certainly not! Indeed I would not have known what sin was except through the law. For I would not have known what coveting really was if the law had not said, "Do not covet"' (Rom. 7:7). Before we become believers in Jesus the Law of God is like a hammer, knocking us down, pointing out our rebellion and showing us what we are really like. But after conversion to Christ the Law is something for which we can thank God. It guides us and shows us the way to live in order to please God. It is a standard that will not vary and a moral compass to keep us on a straight path. 'Walk in all the way that the Lord your God has commanded you' (Deut. 5:33). When we fail to do so, rather than having hopeless dejection, it should prompt us to once again look to him who has power to overcome sin and say: 'Lord, cleanse me from sin'. 'Direct me in the path of your commands, for there I find delight' (Ps. 119:35).

Scripture reading: Psalm 119:33-40

March 21

Sin

Westminster Catechism Question #14:

What is sin? *Answer*: Sin is not conforming to, or any breaking of, the law of God.

Theme verse: 'Everyone who sins breaks the law; in fact, sin is lawlessness' (1 John 3:4).

According to the Bible we have a serious problem. In fact, the problem is so big, it is truly overwhelming. The difficulty is not, first of all, sin itself. The greater issue is the sinful *nature* inherited from Adam. Our fallen nature, stemming from Adam's original sin, has corrupted and polluted us to such an extent that even when we want to avoid evil and do what is right, we have no power to resist our sinful nature's addiction to sin. 'The sinful mind is hostile to God. It does not submit to God's law, nor can it do so. Those controlled by the sinful nature cannot please God' (Rom. 8:7-8). Paul drives home the helplessness of our condition by describing us as 'slaves to sin'. 'We know that the law is spiritual; but I am unspiritual, sold as a slave to sin' (Rom. 7:14). Anyone who cares about pleasing God will be discouraged by this predicament. We feel hemmed in on all sides. The Apostle Paul felt that way, too. 'What a wretched man I am! Who will rescue me from this body of death?' (Rom. 7:24). Paul wanted to live for Christ. But he had no power in himself to overcome his sinful nature. Thankfully, Christ became a sin offering, conquering sin in order that 'the requirements of the law might be fully met in us, who do not live according to the sinful nature but according to the Spirit' (Rom. 8:4).

SCRIPTURE READING: ROMANS 7:21 – 8:11

March 22

Sin

Westminster Catechism Question #14:

What is sin? *Answer*: Sin is not conforming to, or any breaking of, the law of God.

Theme verse: 'Everyone who sins breaks the law; in fact, sin is lawlessness' (1 John 3:4).

True believers in Jesus are engaged in a lifelong battle against sin. Even though Christ has conquered sin at the cross on behalf of the believer and sin's power has been broken, there remains the lure of sin and temptation to disobey the Lord resulting in sinful practices. Because Christians live under God's grace and loving care, we should aim to please the Lord in practical ways. 'Count yourselves dead to sin but alive to God in Christ Jesus' (Rom. 6:11). A good first step in the battle against sinful actions is to recognize yourself as someone who, by the power of Christ mightily at work within you, no longer has to go on sinning. There is available power for sinful conduct to end. An important second step for the believer is to 'not let sin reign in your mortal body so that you obey its evil desires' (Rom. 6:12). This means that continuous sinful patterns of behaviour must be broken. Christians can be caught up in addictive sinful practices that are controlling. These practices must be confronted through much prayer, calling out to God for more grace and power. A third step is 'to offer yourselves to God, as those who have been brought from death to life' (Rom. 6:13). That is a powerful act of worship: each day, out of gratitude, bringing ourselves before God as our offering to him.

SCRIPTURE READING: ROMANS 6:8-14

March 23

Sin

Westminster Catechism Question #14:

What is sin? *Answer*: Sin is not conforming to, or any breaking of, the law of God.

Theme verse: 'Everyone who sins breaks the law; in fact, sin is lawlessness' (1 John 3:4).

A great discouragement to believers is that though we want to please Christ, our sinful actions continue anyway. Sinful actions like pride, lust, anger and lying all seem to get the better of us at times. The warning of Jesus to Peter: 'The spirit is willing, but the body is weak' (Matt. 26:41) might just as well have been directed at us. We want to walk in fellowship with the Lord, we want to do what is right, and we want our lives to differ radically from those who have no love for Christ, but we find ourselves so prone to wander from the God we love. If this is your experience take it as a source of comfort. You are making an honest confession that there is remaining sin in your life. Be glad that your sin is constantly being exposed by the light of Scripture. 'If we claim we have no sin, we deceive ourselves and the truth is not in us' (1 John 1:8). One mark of true faith in Jesus is an ongoing confession of sin and desire for pardon: 'If we confess our sins, he is faithful and just and will forgive us our sins and purify us from all unrighteousness' (1 John 1:9). This text is in the present tense. It is telling us that we should 'go on confessing our sins' since God will 'go on forgiving and cleansing us from our unrighteousness'. In your battle against sin, keep on confessing, and fight an honest fight.

SCRIPTURE READING: 1 JOHN 1:5-10

March 24

Sin

Westminster Catechism Question #14:

What is sin? *Answer*: Sin is not conforming to, or any breaking of, the law of God.

Theme verse: 'Everyone who sins breaks the law; in fact, sin is lawlessness' (1 John 3:4).

In the Sermon on the Mount, Jesus commanded us: 'Be perfect, therefore, as your heavenly Father is perfect' (Matt. 5:48). The Apostle Peter made the same declaration: 'As obedient children, do not conform to the evil desires you had when you lived in ignorance. But just as he who called you is holy, so be holy in all you do' (1 Peter 1:14-15). Is it possible to 'be perfect'? No, it is not. But it is the standard that we are called to strive for, to seek with all our hearts. No believer attains that standard during this life. Some Christians believe in all sincerity that they can attain perfection in this life. But the danger of this misunderstanding of Scripture is to fall into a legalistic, outward conformity to man-made rules and regulations, rather than facing the real depravity in our hearts. Because we all struggle with sins, doubts and fears we are given over to times of questioning whether we are really believers at all. But God does not want us to live wracked with guilt. We must not consider ourselves to be lesser Christians because of this struggle against sin. Instead we are to fight the good fight, pleading for strength during times of weakness, and pursuing holiness with all our heart, soul, strength and mind. At such times we call out to God for fresh grace and the gift of his nearness.

SCRIPTURE READING: I PETER 1:13-21

March 25
HOLY GOD, SINFUL MAN
(WEEK 12: DAY 7)

Sin

Westminster Catechism Question #14:

What is sin? *Answer*: Sin is not conforming to, or any breaking of, the law of God.

Theme verse: 'Everyone who sins breaks the law; in fact, sin is lawlessness' (1 John 3:4).

Before we leave this week's focus on personal sin and the transgression of the Law, let us remind ourselves of just how vast the gulf is between us and a holy God. The corruption that took place in the Garden of Eden was imputed to all of us and the Bible tells us flatly that we are 'conceived in sin'. 'For as in Adam all die' (1 Cor. 15:21) is the message of Scripture. We are 'by nature objects of wrath' (Eph. 2:3). If God is 'holy, holy, holy', then a description of the human race must be 'sinful, sinful, sinful'. When a man or woman is 'born again' it is impossible to overstate the magnificent transformation that takes place. The gulf separating us from God is closed. The Bible tells us that we are now 'reconciled' to God (Rom. 5:10), and 'we have peace with God through our Lord Jesus Christ' (Rom. 5:1). The Bible describes the transaction as going from darkness to light, from death to life. The Word of God goes so far as to say that the very same power that raised Jesus from the dead (Rom. 8:11) has been exerted in order to raise us from being 'dead in trespasses and sins' (Eph. 2:1). Martin Luther said that the essence of the Christian life is a thankful heart. It is easy to see why. We worship 'Jesus, who rescues us from the coming wrath' (1 Thess. 1:10).

SCRIPTURE READING: 1 THESSALONIANS 1:1-10

PART 2:

JESUS IS LORD

March 26

Christ the Redeemer

Westminster Catechism Question #21:

Who is the Redeemer of God's chosen people? *Answer*: The only Redeemer of God's chosen people is the Lord Jesus Christ, who, being the eternal Son of God, became man, and remains both God and man in one person for ever.

Theme verse: 'But when the time had fully come, God sent his Son, born of a woman, born under law, to redeem those under law, that we might receive the full rights of sons' (Gal. 4:4-5).

Jesus was sent into our world by his Father and submitted to the exacting requirements of the Law (the Law we could not keep), obeying God's Law and fulfilling it perfectly as our sinless Saviour. This made it possible for him to redeem us, pay the penalty for our sin and adopt us into God's family. Jesus came to bring two parties together who had been far apart. A holy God and a sinful people needed someone to represent both sides. Jesus is perfectly suited for such a role. He can represent his Father because Jesus is fully God. And he can represent us since he also is fully man, yet without sin. As a mediator between the two parties, Jesus is the only person who has ever lived who could accomplish redemption for us. He satisfied God the Father's demands who hates and condemns the sin that is within us. And Jesus meets the needs of his people, paying the price for our sin and dying in our place. 'For there is one God and one mediator between God and men, the man Christ Jesus, who gave himself as a ransom for all men' (1 Tim. 2:5-6). It is the amazing good news that prompts the inhabitants of heaven to sing: 'You are worthy ... because you were slain, and with your blood you purchased men for God from every tribe and language and people and nation' (Rev. 5:9).

SCRIPTURE READING: 1 TIMOTHY 2:1-7

March 27

Christ the Redeemer

Westminster Catechism Question #21:

Who is the Redeemer of God's chosen people? *Answer*: The only Redeemer of God's chosen people is the Lord Jesus Christ, who, being the eternal Son of God, became man, and remains both God and man in one person for ever.

Theme verse: 'But when the time had fully come, God sent his Son, born of a woman, born under law, to redeem those under law, that we might receive the full rights of sons' (Gal. 4:4-5).

What was Christ's purpose for coming into the world? There is probably no verse in Scripture more universally known and loved than John 3:16 and it, along with John 3:17, provides us the answer: 'For God so loved the world that he gave his one and only Son, that whoever believes in him shall not perish but have eternal life. For God did not send his Son into the world to condemn the world, but to save the world through him.' These words of Jesus speak of the deep love of God towards sinners and the invitation for us to come in simple trust, placing our confidence in Christ. They also inform us that the Saviour did not come into the world to point fingers at us and remind us that we are sinners. He did not come to tell us to shape up, to 'get our act together', only to return to heaven. He came to conquer sin, to wash us, cleanse us, to seek and to save us. The people of his day were shocked when Jesus invited himself to the home of Zacchaeus, a notorious sinner. But Jesus saw in Zacchaeus something that the people could not see. Zacchaeus was tired of his sinful ways and believed Jesus could redeem him. 'Today salvation has come to this house, because this man, too, is a son of Abraham. For the Son of Man came to seek and to save what was lost' (Luke 19:9-10).

SCRIPTURE READING: LUKE 19:1-10

March 28
THE CHRISTMAS MIRACLE
(WEEK 13: DAY 3)

Christ the Redeemer

Westminster Catechism Question #21:

Who is the Redeemer of God's chosen people? *Answer*: The only Redeemer of God's chosen people is the Lord Jesus Christ, who, being the eternal Son of God, became man, and remains both God and man in one person for ever.

Theme verse: 'But when the time had fully come, God sent his Son, born of a woman, born under law, to redeem those under law, that we might receive the full rights of sons' (Gal. 4:4-5).

The Bible records many great miracles that were done by Jesus. He raised people from the dead. He stilled a raging sea. He restored sight to the blind. But the greatest miracle of all is that Jesus came to this world in the first place in order to save us. The Christmas story is the wondrous miracle of all miracles. God came to earth, stepping out of eternity into time and taking on human flesh. Christ's birth was miraculous because no human father was involved in his conception. 'How can this be', Mary asked the angel, 'since I am a virgin?' The angel answered, 'The Holy Spirit will come upon you, and the power of the Most High will overshadow you. So the holy one to be born will be called the Son of God' (Luke 1:34-35). And he is fully human, having been born by a human mother, a virgin. 'For in Christ all the fullness of the Deity lives in bodily form' (Col. 2:9). Since Jesus possesses these two distinct natures, being both fully God and fully human, he is able to represent the Father to us and to represent us before the Father. Because he has a human nature Jesus is able to sympathize with our weaknesses. Here is love: 'Though he was rich, for your sakes he became poor, so that you through his poverty might become rich' (2 Cor. 8:9).

SCRIPTURE READING: LUKE 1:26-38

March 29

Christ the Redeemer

Westminster Catechism Question #21:

Who is the Redeemer of God's chosen people? *Answer*: The only Redeemer of God's chosen people is the Lord Jesus Christ, who, being the eternal Son of God, became man, and remains both God and man in one person for ever.

Theme verse: 'But when the time had fully come, God sent his Son, born of a woman, born under law, to redeem those under law, that we might receive the full rights of sons' (Gal. 4:4-5).

Our theme verse states that 'when the time had fully come, God sent his Son'. This means that God the Father had a very clear and direct plan of action. He sent his Son at exactly the time he had decreed and for the very purpose of seeking and saving that which was lost. Peter preached this truth in his Spirit-filled sermon: 'This man was handed over to you by God's *set purpose and foreknowledge*; and you, with the help of wicked men, put him to death by nailing him to the cross' (Acts 2:23). Here is clear evidence that Jesus came into the world for the purpose of dying for his children. The cross is central to the eternal plan of God. Even when the Bible names the wicked men who put Jesus to death we are told that 'they did what your power and will had decided beforehand should happen' (Acts 4:28). Christ's death was not a tragic mistake or the outcome of wicked men who conspired against the Saviour. Jesus said: 'the reason my Father loves me is that I lay down my life — only to take it up again. No one takes it from me, but I lay it down of my own accord' (John 10:17-18). Isaiah's prophecy records the same truth: 'yet it was the Lord's will to crush him and cause him to suffer' (Isa. 9:10). Here is cause for us to pause, wonder, and be amazed at the love of God for sinners.

SCRIPTURE READING: ACTS 4:23-31

March 30
THE NARROW DOOR
(WEEK 13: DAY 5)

Christ the Redeemer

Westminster Catechism Question #21:

Who is the Redeemer of God's chosen people? *Answer*: The only Redeemer of God's chosen people is the Lord Jesus Christ, who, being the eternal Son of God, became man, and remains both God and man in one person for ever.

Theme verse: 'But when the time had fully come, God sent his Son, born of a woman, born under law, to redeem those under law, that we might receive the full rights of sons' (Gal. 4:4-5).

When you consider all that God has done for us in sending his Son to be our Redeemer, you would think that everyone would long to receive the salvation that he offers. But Jesus was not surprised that so few received him. 'O Jerusalem, Jerusalem, you who kill the prophets and stone those sent to you, how often I have longed to gather your children together, as a hen gathers her chicks under her wings, but you were not willing!' (Luke 13:34-35). While there was a limited period of time that Jesus enjoyed public popularity, the crowd quickly were stirred against him, shouting 'Crucify him, crucify him' (Luke 23:21). Jesus was not surprised by this widespread rejection of his message and ministry: 'the Son of Man will be betrayed to the chief priests and teachers of the law. They will condemn him to death and will hand him over to the Gentiles, who will mock him and spit on him, flog him and kill him. Three days later he will rise' (Mark 10:33-34). His teaching so often spoke of his rejection by the people that someone asked him, 'Lord, are only a few people going to be saved?' (Luke 13:23). Jesus answered by saying, 'make every effort to enter by the narrow door' (Luke 13:24). He was declaring that there is only one Redeemer, and one way to life. Have you entered by the narrow door?

SCRIPTURE READING: LUKE 13:22-35

March 31
THE RESURRECTION OF THE REDEEMER
(WEEK 13: DAY 6)

Christ the Redeemer

Westminster Catechism Question #21:

Who is the Redeemer of God's chosen people? *Answer*: The only Redeemer of God's chosen people is the Lord Jesus Christ, who, being the eternal Son of God, became man, and remains both God and man in one person for ever.

Theme verse: 'But when the time had fully come, God sent his Son, born of a woman, born under law, to redeem those under law, that we might receive the full rights of sons' (Gal. 4:4-5).

Jesus cannot be our Redeemer if he did not rise from the grave. 'If Christ has not been raised our preaching is useless and so is your faith' (1 Cor. 15:14). But the resurrection is the best proof we have that Jesus is the Son of God, that our faith is not a bad joke, and that we have not been misled. 'But Christ has indeed been raised from the dead, the firstfruits of those who have fallen asleep' (1 Cor. 15:20). The Apostle Paul described Jesus as 'firstfruits'. The first sheaf of the harvest was given to the Lord and designated that the entire harvest belonged to God. Paul used it to declare that since Christ was raised from the dead all of God's redeemed people will rise as well. It is guaranteed and serves as a wonderful comfort for believers in Jesus. 'And God raised us up with Christ and seated us with him in the heavenly realms in Christ Jesus' (Eph. 2:6). Nothing less than the miraculous resurrection of Christ can explain the empty tomb or amazing conviction of the disciples that Jesus was God in the flesh. Their sadness and gloom at the death of Christ was turned to joy and willingness to die for their Redeemer. When Jesus died and was buried, we died and were buried with him (Col. 2:10-13). And because Jesus rose from the grave we too shall rise with him.

SCRIPTURE READING: 1 CORINTHIANS 15:12-19

April 1

Christ the Redeemer

Westminster Catechism Question #21:

Who is the Redeemer of God's chosen people? *Answer*: The only
Redeemer of God's chosen people is the Lord Jesus Christ, who,
being the eternal Son of God, became man, and remains both
God and man in one person for ever.

Theme verse: 'But when the time had fully come, God sent his
Son, born of a woman, born under law, to redeem those under
law, that we might receive the full rights of sons' (Gal. 4:4-5).

At his trial Jesus proclaimed, 'In the future you will see the Son of
Man sitting at the right hand of the Mighty One' (Matt. 26:64).
After his resurrection it was essential that Jesus return in triumph
to his Father if he was to be our Redeemer. The Father accepted
Christ's mighty work, for Jesus is now 'crowned with glory and
honor' (Heb. 2:9). Everything created has been put under his feet
(1 Cor. 15:26). Jesus has been given 'the highest place' (Phil. 2:9) of
honour in the entire universe. The ascension of Christ means that
everything that was necessary to accomplish and secure our salvation has been done. In the Garden of Gethsemane Jesus prayed: 'I
have brought you glory on earth by completing the work you gave
me to do. And now, Father, glorify me in your presence with the
glory I had with you before the world began' (John 17:4-5). The
work that the Father gave Jesus to do, of course, was to be 'born
of a woman, born under law, to redeem those under law, that we
might receive the full rights of sons' (Gal. 4:4-5). His longing now
is that we might join him in celebrating his triumph. 'Father, I
want those you have given me to be with me where I am, and to
see my glory' (John 17:24). What an amazing privilege awaits the
children of God.

SCRIPTURE READING: MATTHEW 26:57-68

April 2

Christ's Offices

Westminster Catechism Question #23:

What offices does Christ fulfill as our Redeemer? *Answer*:
Christ, as our Redeemer, fulfills the offices of a prophet, a priest,
and a king, both while he was on earth and now in heaven.

Theme verse: 'For to us a child is born, to us a son is given, and
the government will be on his shoulders. And he will be called
Wonderful Counselor, Mighty God, Everlasting Father, Prince of
Peace' (Isa. 9:6).

The catechism answer states that Jesus fulfils three Old Testament
offices: Prophet, Priest and King. These are more than just formal titles bequeathed on Jesus. They are positions he held while
he was on earth and he continues to fulfil these offices now that
he has returned to heaven. He will forever be our great Prophet,
Priest and King. Deuteronomy 18:14-22 describes the role of the
prophet: 'I will raise up for them a prophet like you from among
their brothers; I will put my words in his mouth, and he will tell
them everything I command him' (Deut. 18:18). A prophet was
to convey God's message to the people. A genuine prophet of the
Lord needed to speak the truth every single time he spoke. If one
of his prophecies failed then the prophet was to be considered a
false prophet. Jesus is our Great Prophet because his words are always reliable, always accurate and always true. Above all, they are
words given him by his Father to speak. 'When you have lifted up
the Son of Man, then you will know that I am the one I claim to
be, and that I do nothing on my own but speak just what the Father has taught me' (John 8:28). Here is another reason for trusting Christ. He never lies. He alone is our Great Prophet.

SCRIPTURE READING: DEUTERONOMY 18:14-22

April 3
PROPHETIC FULFILMENT
(WEEK 14: DAY 2)

Christ's Offices

Westminster Catechism Question #23:

What offices does Christ fulfill as our Redeemer? *Answer*:
Christ, as our Redeemer, fulfills the offices of a prophet, a priest,
and a king, both while he was on earth and now in heaven.

Theme verse: 'For to us a child is born, to us a son is given, and
the government will be on his shoulders. And he will be called
Wonderful Counselor, Mighty God, Everlasting Father, Prince of
Peace' (Isa. 9:6).

In Acts 3 we read how the Apostle Peter was given unusual power
to heal the crippled beggar. The miracle afforded Peter an audi-
ence and he seized the opportunity to speak powerfully of Christ.
One of his major emphases to his Jewish listeners was how Christ
fulfils prophecies made about Moses, David and Abraham. Moses
said, 'The Lord your God will raise up for you a prophet like me
from among your own people; you must listen to everything he
tells you. Anyone who does not listen to him will be completely
cut off from among his people' (Acts 3:22-23). Peter described Jesus as a prophet like Moses (vv. 22-23), the fulfilment of Samuel's
prophecy concerning David (v. 24), and the messenger of blessing
to all the nations promised to Abraham (vv. 25-26). He described
Jesus as God's servant, sent to bless us with the very words of
God. We cannot underestimate the importance of the prophetic
role of Christ. Repeatedly we are encouraged to heed the words
of Christ. 'Therefore everyone who hears these words of mine and
puts them into practice is like a wise man who built his house on
the rock' (Matt. 7:24). Jesus spoke with authority the very words
his Father had given him. A wise man or woman listens to the
Great Prophet and obeys.

SCRIPTURE READING: ACTS 3:17-26

April 4

Christ's Offices

Westminster Catechism Question #23:

What offices does Christ fulfill as our Redeemer? *Answer*:
Christ, as our Redeemer, fulfills the offices of a prophet, a priest,
and a king, both while he was on earth and now in heaven.

Theme verse: 'For to us a child is born, to us a son is given, and
the government will be on his shoulders. And he will be called
Wonderful Counselor, Mighty God, Everlasting Father, Prince of
Peace' (Isa. 9:6).

The role of an Old Testament priest is described in Hebrews 7.
He was responsible for offering sacrifices for the sins of the people
and also for his own sins. This was a daily routine, an endless
repetition throughout the year. Such sacrifices never were effective in atoning for the people's sins. Another problem with Old
Testament priests was that they died! 'Now there have been many
of those priests, since death prevented them from continuing in
office; but because Jesus lives forever, he has a permanent priesthood. Therefore he is able to save completely those who come to
God through him, because he always lives to intercede for them'
(Heb. 7:23-25). The importance of Christ's priesthood is that Jesus is a priest who will never die. He will never cease being our
great High Priest. He intercedes for us, representing us before our
heavenly Father. When we close a prayer by saying 'in Jesus' name'
or 'through Jesus Christ our Lord, Amen', we are recognizing the
priestly, intercessory role of Christ on our behalf. And Jesus is a
priest who has never sinned. He doesn't need to offer sacrifices
for himself. 'Such a high priest meets our need – one who is holy,
blameless, pure, set apart from sinners, exalted above the heavens'
(Heb. 7:26).

SCRIPTURE READING: HEBREWS 7:23-28

April 5
THE MOST HOLY PLACE
(WEEK 14: DAY 4)

Christ's Offices

Westminster Catechism Question #23:

What offices does Christ fulfill as our Redeemer? *Answer*:
Christ, as our Redeemer, fulfills the offices of a prophet, a priest,
and a king, both while he was on earth and now in heaven.

Theme verse: 'For to us a child is born, to us a son is given, and
the government will be on his shoulders. And he will be called
Wonderful Counselor, Mighty God, Everlasting Father, Prince of
Peace' (Isa. 9:6).

When the Jewish people were wandering in the desert after their
exodus from Egypt, God had the people build a temporary, move-
able temple known as the Tent of Meeting. Inside the Tent of
Meeting was an inner sanctuary, a room known as the Most Holy
Place. Inside was 'the gold-covered ark of the covenant. This ark
contained the gold jar of manna, Aaron's staff that had budded,
and the stone tablets of the covenant' (Heb. 9:4). 'Only the high
priest entered the inner room and that only once a year and never
without blood, which he offered for himself and for the sins the
people had committed in ignorance' (Heb. 9:7). The high priest
served as a mediator between God and the people and could represent the people before a holy God. But the system was hopelessly flawed. The high priest was a sinner right along with the people. The blood offerings he carried with him into the Most Holy
Place had no power to cleanse the people from their sin. But 'when
Christ came as high priest ... he entered the Most Holy Place once
for all by his own blood, having obtained eternal redemption ...
How much more, then, will the blood of Christ ... cleanse our
consciences from acts that lead to death' (Heb. 9:11,12,14). The
blood drawn from the Saviour's veins never loses its power.

SCRIPTURE READING: HEBREWS 9:11-15

April 6
WONDERFUL COUNSELLOR
(WEEK 14: DAY 5)

Christ's Offices

Westminster Catechism Question #23:

What offices does Christ fulfill as our Redeemer? *Answer*: Christ, as our Redeemer, fulfills the offices of a prophet, a priest, and a king, both while he was on earth and now in heaven.

Theme verse: 'For to us a child is born, to us a son is given, and the government will be on his shoulders. And he will be called Wonderful Counselor, Mighty God, Everlasting Father, Prince of Peace' (Isa. 9:6).

A king's task is to rule wisely, to protect his subjects from adversaries and to ensure their safety in all aspects of life. In our theme verse Isaiah prophesies about Jesus, describing his kingly rule in exemplary fashion. The government rests on Christ's shoulders, meaning that this Son of David will rule authoritatively and in complete, sovereign control. The title 'Wonderful Counselor' points to the coming Messiah as an extraordinary and exalted king. He will carry out the eternal purposes of his Father and all the world will be in awe of his wisdom. The title 'Mighty God' emphasizes his divine power to overthrow all of his and our enemies as a righteous king. The designation 'Everlasting Father' is comforting as it proclaims that Christ will be an enduring and loving protector of his people, providing us with everything we need for life and godliness. As 'Prince of Peace' his kingship will be marked by peace and calmness. The lives of his subjects will be characterized by inner tranquillity and security. He will rule as our king and will bring spiritual health to individuals and to the world. This kingly rule is already taking place in heaven and in the hearts of his servants. One day this king will overthrow the last of his enemies and fully establish his rule on earth.

SCRIPTURE READING: ISAIAH 9:1-7

April 7

Christ's Offices

Westminster Catechism Question #23:

What offices does Christ fulfill as our Redeemer? *Answer*:
Christ, as our Redeemer, fulfills the offices of a prophet, a priest,
and a king, both while he was on earth and now in heaven.

Theme verse: 'For to us a child is born, to us a son is given, and
the government will be on his shoulders. And he will be called
Wonderful Counselor, Mighty God, Everlasting Father, Prince of
Peace' (Isa. 9:6).

It seems amazing that anyone would oppose such a wonderful
king as King Jesus. His government is perfect, his counsel is wise,
his power is unequalled, his protection is eternal, and his rule is
peaceful and restorative. But Christ was rejected as a king. '"Here
is your king," Pilate said to the Jews. But they shouted, "Take him
away! Take him away! Crucify him!" "Shall I crucify your king?"
Pilate asked. "We have no king but Caesar," the chief priests answered. Finally Pilate handed him over to them to be crucified'
(John 19:14-16). It wasn't just his own Jewish people who rejected the Messiah's kingship. Wherever the gospel message spread
there was resistance. Psalm 2 is David's prophesy that Christ, the
Anointed One, would be rejected. 'The kings of the earth take
their stand and the rulers gather together against the Lord and
against his Anointed One. "Let us break their chains," they say,
"and throw off their fetters"' (Ps. 2:2). Most earthly rulers and
nations look upon Christ as king as nothing less than oppression
and enslavement. Adam's sin in the Garden of Eden was rebellion against the Lord's authority and a desire for independence.
His descendants have followed suit. But those who love Jesus have
discovered him to be a king of grace and peace.

SCRIPTURE READING: JOHN 19:1-16

April 8
THE CHOSEN SERVANT
(WEEK 14: DAY 7)

Christ's Offices

Westminster Catechism Question #23:

What offices does Christ fulfill as our Redeemer? *Answer*: Christ, as our Redeemer, fulfills the offices of a prophet, a priest, and a king, both while he was on earth and now in heaven.

Theme verse: 'For to us a child is born, to us a son is given, and the government will be on his shoulders. And he will be called Wonderful Counselor, Mighty God, Everlasting Father, Prince of Peace' (Isa. 9:6).

Without straining the text of Scripture it's possible to see all three offices that Christ holds in Matthew 12:15-21. God's chosen servant, the one he loves, 'will proclaim justice to the nations' (Matt. 12:18). This speaks of Christ's prophetic role in proclaiming justice, in preaching reconciliation between God and mankind. 'A bruised reed he will not break, and a smoldering wick he will not snuff out' (Matt. 12:20) refers to his priestly role of caring for and healing the broken, contrite spirit. The final phrases, 'He leads justice to victory. In his name the nations will put their hope' (Matt. 12:20-21) mentions Christ's kingly victory over the nations as he leads his church. This passage from Matthew is one of the servant songs about the Messiah. It is taken from Isaiah 42. In it we see the less obvious ways that Christ fulfils his three offices. He is not the Prophet pronouncing woes on the Pharisees as in Matthew 23. Instead, he is proclaiming reconciliation. This passage does not highlight Christ as the High Priest who offers up his life at Calvary for sinners. Rather, he tenderly heals the sensitive spirit. This is not the King who returns to earth in blazing fire, but the quiet, conquering hero of the church. Enjoy the Redeemer in the fulness of all his offices.

SCRIPTURE READING: MATTHEW 12:15-21

111

April 9
CHRIST'S PROPHETIC WORDS
(WEEK 15: DAY 1)

Christ the Prophet

Westminster Catechism Question #24:

How does Christ fulfill the office of a prophet? *Answer*: Christ fulfills the office of a prophet because he has revealed to us, by his Word and Spirit, the will of God for our salvation.

Theme verse: 'No one has ever seen God, but God the one and only, who is at the Father's side, has made him known' (John 1:18).

Our theme verse is an explicit declaration of Christ's deity. Jesus is God and is at the Father's side. It was his calling to enter our world, becoming fully human, in order to bring redemption and also to make the Father known to us. Christ has made the Father known both by his mighty deeds and his prophetic words. There were prophets in the Old Testament. Some represented the Lord well but some were false prophets. However, the Lord Jesus, who is at the Father's side, has perfectly represented his Father. At the transfiguration of Jesus the Father spoke from heaven: 'This is my Son, whom I love. Listen to him!' (Mark 9:7). Everything that Jesus has spoken, therefore, comes from the Father and is to be trusted and obeyed. The catechism answer addresses this, informing us that Christ is the greatest of all the prophets because he revealed perfectly, both in his teaching and by the power of the Holy Spirit, his Father's will concerning salvation. Because of his deep love for us Jesus imparted a heavenly message to his followers: 'I no longer call you servants, because a servant does not know his master's business. Instead, I have called you friends, for everything that I learned from my Father I have made known to you' (John 15:15). Good followers pass his Word along.

SCRIPTURE READING: JOHN 15:9-17

April 10

Christ the Prophet

Westminster Catechism Question #24:

How does Christ fulfill the office of a prophet? *Answer*: Christ fulfills the office of a prophet because he has revealed to us, by his Word and Spirit, the will of God for our salvation.

Theme verse: 'No one has ever seen God, but God the one and only, who is at the Father's side, has made him known' (John 1:18).

To believe in Jesus means trusting his every prophetic word. This is a larger step of faith than one may think. Consider the seemingly upside-down logic of the Beatitudes in Matthew 5:1-12. Jesus is saying that it is not the rich but the poor who are blessed. People that deserve to be congratulated are people who mourn, who hunger and thirst for righteousness, and who are persecuted. 'Blessed are you when people insult you, persecute you and falsely say all kinds of evil against you because of me' (Matt. 5:11). At times like that you should 'rejoice and be glad, because great is your reward in heaven, for in the same way they persecuted the prophets who were before you' (Matt. 5:12). One can only believe such words from the lips of our Saviour if you believe he is a prophet sent from God. He is telling us that true happiness comes from pursuing righteousness, not from the pleasures of this world. The world does not tell us to mourn over our sin, or to hunger and thirst for righteousness, or to rejoice when we face persecution. There was a marked contrast between Christ's prophetic teaching and the accepted beliefs of his day. The same is true today. To listen to the prophetic voice of Jesus will mean that we reject the false voices of contemporary advertising.

SCRIPTURE READING: MATTHEW 5:1-12

April 11

A QUESTION OF THE HEART
(WEEK 15: DAY 3)

Christ the Prophet

Westminster Catechism Question #24:

How does Christ fulfill the office of a prophet? *Answer*: Christ fulfills the office of a prophet because he has revealed to us, by his Word and Spirit, the will of God for our salvation.

Theme verse: 'No one has ever seen God, but God the one and only, who is at the Father's side, has made him known' (John 1:18).

'You have heard that it was said, "Do not commit adultery." But I tell you that anyone who looks at a woman lustfully has already committed adultery with her in his heart' (Matt. 5:27). In contrast to the teaching of the Pharisees ('You have heard that it was said …'), Christ's teaching demands not just outward conformity to the Ten Commandments, but an inward change of heart that can only be realized through faith in Christ. The Pharisees had reduced the seventh commandment, 'Do not commit adultery', to cover only the physical act of adultery itself. As long as they were not guilty of the physical act they considered themselves innocent of law-breaking. People who believe like the Pharisees did, that they can honour God and receive his salvation based on their own actions, fall into this error. Instead, Jesus points us to the fuller and true understanding of the law. The law is not fulfilled by an external keeping of it; rather, it is a question of the heart. Jesus is exposing our sinful hearts and revealing how impossible it is to keep the law perfectly. The lust of the flesh abides in every one of us. Thankfully, he is not only our Prophet; Jesus also is our Saviour who cleanses the hearts of sinners, empowering them by the Holy Spirit to keep the law's demands willingly and joyfully.

SCRIPTURE READING: MATTHEW 5:21-32

April 12
MEASURING OUR FAITH
(WEEK 15: DAY 4)

Christ the Prophet

Westminster Catechism Question #24:

How does Christ fulfill the office of a prophet? *Answer*: Christ
fulfills the office of a prophet because he has revealed to us, by
his Word and Spirit, the will of God for our salvation.

Theme verse: 'No one has ever seen God, but God the one and
only, who is at the Father's side, has made him known'
(John 1:18).

In Matthew 6:1-18 Christ is warning us about hypocritical religion. All religion turns to hypocrisy if Christ has not replaced our
proud hearts with humble, receptive hearts which seek first his
kingdom and his righteousness. 'Be careful not to do your "acts of
righteousness" before men, to be seen by them. If you do, you will
have no reward from your Father in heaven' (Matt. 6:1). Here is
a prophetic warning to serve the Lord out of love for him and his
people, not to be seen and praised by others. 'And when you pray,
do not be like the hypocrites, for they love to pray standing in the
synagogues and on the street corners to be seen by men' (Matt.
6:5). Again, our true Prophet's warning is to pray in secret, where
no person is able to see you. One measure of our love for Christ
is the amount of time we spend with him alone in prayer where
no one can see us 'being religious'. 'When you fast, do not look
somber as the hypocrites do, for they disfigure their faces to show
men they are fasting' (Matt. 6:16). The Lord's principle in all this
is to remember that we live out our faith ultimately before an au-
dience of just one, our Heavenly Father. Measure the genuineness
of your faith when you are alone, those times when there is no one
else but you and the Lord.

SCRIPTURE READING: MATTHEW 6:1-18

Christ the Prophet

Westminster Catechism Question #24:

How does Christ fulfill the office of a prophet? *Answer*: Christ fulfills the office of a prophet because he has revealed to us, by his Word and Spirit, the will of God for our salvation.

Theme verse: 'No one has ever seen God, but God the one and only, who is at the Father's side, has made him known' (John 1:18).

The Lord knows what a temptation it is for us to place our trust in the things we see — that is, in material possessions and money. What advice does our Great Prophet have for us? 'Do not store up for yourselves treasures on earth, where moth and rust destroy and where thieves break in and steal. But store up for yourselves treasures in heaven' (Matt. 6:19-20). The Lord is saying that our whole ethical outlook on life is controlled by where we place our treasure, and that ultimately determines our relationship with God. 'So do not worry, saying, "What shall we eat?" or "What shall we drink?" or "What shall we wear?" For the pagans run after all these things, and your heavenly Father knows that you need them' (Matt. 6:31-32). If we talk about God, attend worship regularly, and even fast and pray, yet we live for this world and cling to our possessions, Jesus is telling us that our devotion is misplaced. Indeed, we are nothing more than idolaters. 'But seek first his kingdom and his righteousness, and all these things will be given to you as well' (Matt. 6:33). This is the kind of hard statement from our Lord that requires self-examination. How are we doing in this area of life? Has this idol been smashed or are possessions a rival for our Lord's affection?

SCRIPTURE READING: MATTHEW 6:19-34

April 14

Christ the Prophet

Westminster Catechism Question #24:

How does Christ fulfill the office of a prophet? *Answer*: Christ
fulfills the office of a prophet because he has revealed to us, by
his Word and Spirit, the will of God for our salvation.

Theme verse: 'No one has ever seen God, but God the one and
only, who is at the Father's side, has made him known'
(John 1:18).

In the Sermon on the Mount Jesus also warned us about false
prophets. Although they talk and act like true prophets, they have
a hidden agenda. This is usually a desire for money, power or fame.
'Watch out for false prophets. They come to you in sheep's clothing, but inwardly they are ferocious wolves. By their fruit you will
recognize them' (Matt. 7:15-16). What makes them so ferocious?
It is because these false teachers will attempt to persuade you not
to follow the narrow way that leads to Christ. You may be considering what Jesus says in the Sermon on the Mount. You may want
to follow Christ. But just as Adam and Eve were tricked by Satan's
craftiness in the Garden of Eden, false prophets will steer you
away from salvation and discipleship. Often times they are hard
to discover (they come in sheep's clothing). 'They will secretly introduce destructive heresies ... many will follow their shameful
ways ... in their greed these people will exploit you with stories
they have made up' (2 Peter 2:1-3). Jesus is warning us about those
who will tell you that the Sermon on the Mount can be listened to
but not practised. Jesus is calling us to enter by the narrow gate
that leads to life. We are to shun a 'health-and-wealth' gospel and
cultic religions. It is the narrow path that leads us home.

SCRIPTURE READING: MATTHEW 7:15-23

April 15

Christ the Prophet

Westminster Catechism Question #24:

How does Christ fulfill the office of a prophet? *Answer*: Christ fulfills the office of a prophet because he has revealed to us, by his Word and Spirit, the will of God for our salvation.

Theme verse: 'No one has ever seen God, but God the one and only, who is at the Father's side, has made him known' (John 1:18).

At the end of the Sermon on the Mount we are told that 'when Jesus had finished saying these things the crowds were amazed at his teaching, because he taught as one who had authority and not as their teachers of the law' (Matt. 7:28-29). The Pharisees were hypocritical in their teachings because they twisted the law of God to suit their own purposes and enhance their own power and lifestyle. Jesus came as the true Prophet, sent from his Father, in order to teach us the will of God for our salvation. Jesus taught us that we must forget about ever thinking we can attain salvation on our own. Our best efforts fall far short of the glory of God. He taught us that human striving will never make us righteous or fit to stand in the presence of God. Yet the Christian's response to the Sermon on the Mount or any of Christ's teaching in the Gospels is to put Christ's words into practice. 'Why do you call me, "Lord, Lord," and do not do what I say?' (Luke 6:46), Jesus asked. The person who hears his words and puts them into practice, Jesus told us, 'is like a man building a house, who dug down deep and laid the foundation on rock' (Luke 6:48). The prophetic warning is clear. We are to listen to the inspired, authoritative voice of the Lord Jesus. We must trust his words and live by them.

SCRIPTURE READING: LUKE 6:43-49

April 16
A SYMPATHETIC HIGH PRIEST
(WEEK 16: DAY 1)

Christ the Priest

Westminster Catechism Question #25:

How does Christ fulfill the office of a priest? *Answer*: Christ fulfills the office of a priest by offering himself once as a sacrifice to satisfy the Father's righteous anger against sin, thereby reconciling us to God, and interceding for us now.

Theme verse: 'Such a high priest meets our need – one who is holy, blameless, pure, set apart from sinners, exalted above the heavens' (Heb. 7:26).

Hebrews tells us a great deal about Christ in his role as the great High Priest who died as the substitute for sinners, paying the penalty for sin and redeeming us from slavery to sin. As our High Priest, Jesus intercedes for us constantly before his Father in heaven. The Old Testament priest offered animal blood sacrifices before God that were powerless to cleanse us from sin. Christ's blood, which atoned for our sins, is the continual source of power for daily cleansing from sin. The theme verse states why Jesus is the perfect High Priest. He is perfectly holy, and the Father has accepted his sacrifice at Calvary. The writer to the Hebrews elaborates on Christ's excellence: 'Therefore, since we have a great high priest who has gone through the heavens, Jesus the Son of God, let us hold firmly to the faith we profess. For we do not have a high priest who is unable to sympathize with our weaknesses, but we have one who has been tempted in every way, just as we are – yet was without sin' (Heb. 4:14-15). Because our high priest has experienced human temptation he is able to sympathize with us when we are tempted. We can confidently approach this high priest in prayer with our every weakness and every concern 'that we may receive mercy and find grace to help us in our time of need' (Heb. 4:16).

SCRIPTURE READING: HEBREWS 4:14 – 5:10

Christ the Priest

Westminster Catechism Question #25:

How does Christ fulfill the office of a priest? *Answer*: Christ fulfills the office of a priest by offering himself once as a sacrifice to satisfy the Father's righteous anger against sin, thereby reconciling us to God, and interceding for us now.

Theme verse: 'Such a high priest meets our need — one who is holy, blameless, pure, set apart from sinners, exalted above the heavens' (Heb. 7:26).

When a priest in the Old Testament died he would have to be replaced by another priest who could perform the duties of the office. One of the reasons why Jesus is the more excellent High Priest is that his term of office is eternal. His office as high priest is a position he held while on earth and continues to hold now that he is in heaven. The amazing benefit for us, the writer to the Hebrews tells us, is that Jesus is able to continuously intercede for us. 'Now there have been many of those priests, since death prevented them from continuing in office; but because Jesus lives forever, he has a permanent priesthood. Therefore he is able to save completely those who come to God through him, because he always lives to intercede for them' (Heb. 7:23-25). Our Saviour not only saves us, but he also consistently defends our cause before the Father in heaven. It is as if the Father were daily asking, 'Why should I let this sinner into my heaven?' To this our Saviour might daily reply, 'Because I washed him in my blood and covered him in my righteousness.' Christ's intercession for us is a daily blessing, not a once-for-all-time event. Therefore, he bids us come daily to him to confess our sins, spread our needs before him, and plead for fresh grace to serve him.

SCRIPTURE READING: NUMBERS 20:22-29

April 18

Christ the Priest

Westminster Catechism Question #25:

How does Christ fulfill the office of a priest? *Answer*: Christ fulfills the office of a priest by offering himself once as a sacrifice to satisfy the Father's righteous anger against sin, thereby reconciling us to God, and interceding for us now.

Theme verse: 'Such a high priest meets our need — one who is holy, blameless, pure, set apart from sinners, exalted above the heavens' (Heb. 7:26).

The book of Exodus, chapters 25-40, is a lengthy list of instructions from God to Moses on how the Lord wanted the Tent of Meeting built. 'Then have them make a sanctuary for me, and I will dwell among them. Make this tabernacle and all its furnishings exactly like the pattern I will show you' (Exod. 25:8). The furnishings needed to be exact. The priests had to be from the tribe of Levi. Their clothing and the process of ordination had to meet God's standard. When it came to religious symbols within the Holy Place the Lord reminded Moses: 'See that you make them according to the pattern shown you on the mountain' (Exod. 25:40). Why all the fuss? It was because the manmade copy needed to resemble the perfect sanctuary in heaven and all that takes place there. Yet even the best efforts of Moses and the Aaronic priests still left us with an inadequate, imperfect system. The sacrifices and daily rituals of the tabernacle could never take away sin. But, 'When Christ came as high priest of the good things that are already here, he went through the greater and more perfect tabernacle (heaven) that is not man-made ... He did not enter by means of the blood of goats and calves; but he entered the Most Holy Place once for all by his own blood, having obtained eternal redemption' (Heb. 9:11-12).

SCRIPTURE READING: EXODUS 25:1-9

April 19

Christ the Priest

Westminster Catechism Question #25:

How does Christ fulfill the office of a priest? *Answer*: Christ fulfills the office of a priest by offering himself once as a sacrifice to satisfy the Father's righteous anger against sin, thereby reconciling us to God, and interceding for us now.

Theme verse: 'Such a high priest meets our need — one who is holy, blameless, pure, set apart from sinners, exalted above the heavens' (Heb. 7:26).

The Old Testament priest presented two kinds of offerings before the Lord. One was a thanksgiving offering, the other was an offering of atonement. 'Every high priest is selected from among men and is appointed to represent them in matters related to God, to offer gifts and sacrifices for sins' (Heb. 5:1). If you wanted to thank the Lord for a mercy received you gave one type of offering. If you wanted to confess sin you came with an offering of atonement. The sacrifices for sin were animal sacrifices unless a person was very poor, then a grain offering would suffice. If a person came with both a thank offering and a sin offering, then the sin offering was always offered first since sin had to be dealt with first. Then a person recommitted himself to God and expressed gratitude for the Lord's mercy through a thank offering. It reminds us of the words of Jesus, 'if you are offering your gift at the altar and there remember that your brother has something against you, leave your gift there in front of the altar. First go and be reconciled to your brother; then come and offer your gift' (Matt. 5:23-24). Praise God, we offer no sacrifice of atonement to God other than the perfect sacrifice of Jesus at Calvary. But the Lord does require a contrite heart when we bring our offering of praise.

SCRIPTURE READING: LEVITICUS 5:5-13

April 20
CARRYING US IN HIS HEART
(WEEK 16: DAY 5)

Christ the Priest

Westminster Catechism Question #25:

How does Christ fulfill the office of a priest? *Answer:* Christ fulfills the office of a priest by offering himself once as a sacrifice to satisfy the Father's righteous anger against sin, thereby reconciling us to God, and interceding for us now.

Theme verse: 'Such a high priest meets our need — one who is holy, blameless, pure, set apart from sinners, exalted above the heavens' (Heb. 7:26).

During Old Testament times no one was allowed to enter the sanctuary except the high priest who offered the sacrifice. The people were required to remain at a distance, waiting for the high priest to come out to see if the Lord had accepted the sacrifice offered on behalf of the people. As he entered the sanctuary the Old Testament high priest bore the names of Israel on his shoulders and had twelve precious stones fastened on his breastplate. These gems represented the names of the sons of Israel. 'Whenever Aaron enters the Holy Place, he will bear the names of the sons of Israel over his heart on the breastpiece of decision as a continuing memorial before the Lord' (Exod. 28:29). It was a reminder that Aaron served as the people's mediator before God and his solemn task was to bring the needs of a sinful people to the throne of grace. There was a sense of unworthiness among the people, knowing that should the offering be received by the Lord it was pure mercy. In the same way, Jesus bore our sins on the cross. He now bears us, as it were, in his heart. This is the bedrock of our faith, our hope that we have favour with God. We sense our own unworthiness and cast all our hope and confidence on our great Mediator, our great High Priest, in expectation of his blessing.

SCRIPTURE READING: EXODUS 28:15-21; EXODUS 29-30

April 21

Christ the Priest

Westminster Catechism Question #25:

How does Christ fulfill the office of a priest? *Answer*: Christ fulfills the office of a priest by offering himself once as a sacrifice to satisfy the Father's righteous anger against sin, thereby reconciling us to God, and interceding for us now.

Theme verse: 'Such a high priest meets our need — one who is holy, blameless, pure, set apart from sinners, exalted above the heavens' (Heb. 7:26).

When Jesus made his public appearance in Jerusalem, most of the religious leaders rejected the idea that Jesus could be the Messiah. They didn't believe his words or the claims he made about himself and therefore dismissed him as a prophet. They also scoffed at the idea that Jesus could be any kind of a king. Besides a few misguided fishermen from Galilee, where was his following or his kingdom? But what settled the matter completely for them was that Jesus could not be a priest. He could not trace his lineage to the tribe of Levi, a requirement to hold the office of priest. Jesus was from the tribe of Judah. Therefore, in their mind, Jesus held none of the three offices of prophet, priest, or king. Of course, to disregard the words of Christ the religious leaders also had to overlook his mighty miracles (John 10:24-25). Because their minds were sealed shut to spiritual truth they could not understand the nature of his spiritual kingdom. But with regards to his role as a High Priest, they completely missed King David's prophecy in Psalm 110. 'You are a priest forever, in the order of Melchizedek' (Ps. 110:4). The author to the Hebrews amplified on this reality, recognizing that Jesus 'has become a priest not on the basis of a regulation as to his ancestry but on the basis of the power of an indestructible life' (Heb. 7:16). Such a priest meets our every need.

SCRIPTURE READING: HEBREWS 7:11-22

April 22
THE GREAT TRANSACTION
(WEEK 16: DAY 7)

Christ the Priest

Westminster Catechism Question #25:

How does Christ fulfill the office of a priest? *Answer:* Christ fulfills the office of a priest by offering himself once as a sacrifice to satisfy the Father's righteous anger against sin, thereby reconciling us to God, and interceding for us now.

Theme verse: 'Such a high priest meets our need — one who is holy, blameless, pure, set apart from sinners, exalted above the heavens' (Heb. 7:26).

When Jesus shed his blood on the cross he experienced the agony of separation from his Father. The Apostle Paul described the transaction that took place at Calvary this way: 'God made him who had no sin to be sin for us, so that in him we might become the righteousness of God' (2 Cor. 5:21). There are three amazing truths in that verse. First, Jesus had no sin. When you think of it, that is an incredible statement. Jesus is the only person who ever lived who had no blemishes on his record. He was pure perfection and was untainted by the world or by his own heart. The second marvel is this: the sinless Jesus actually took on sin (even stronger, *became* sin) for us. Who would do such a thing? We cannot enter into the physical agony of the cross nor can we begin to understand how loathsome it was for the Redeemer to have the filth of sin placed on him; none the less, Jesus willingly accepted his Father's purpose for him in doing so. The third shocker is this: our Heavenly Father decreed that this transaction should occur in order that you and I, so sick with sin and polluted from head to toe, might become righteous like Jesus by receiving his righteousness. This is the gospel in a nutshell. Jesus, as our High Priest, took the punishment we deserved in order to make it possible for us to be reconciled to God.

SCRIPTURE READING: 2 CORINTHIANS 5:16-21

April 23
The great King
(WEEK 17: DAY 1)

Christ the King

Westminster Catechism Question #26:

How does Christ fulfill the office of a king? *Answer*: Christ fulfills the office of a king by subduing us to himself, in ruling and defending us, and in restraining and conquering all his and our enemies.

Theme verse: 'For he must reign until he has put all his enemies under his feet. The last enemy to be destroyed is death' (1 Cor. 15:25-26).

Along with the offices of Prophet and Priest, Jesus also holds the office of King. As the great King, Jesus ushered in a spiritual kingdom while here on earth. His followers are the subjects of a gracious and benevolent King who conquered them for himself, rules over them as Lord and defends them. While on earth he conquered our worst enemies: sin, the devil, death and hell. His strength was unparalleled. Earthly kings are often weak and impotent, but Jesus is the Lord of the universe. When he returns to this earth at the end of history we will see him in all the fulness and glory of his kingly office as he judges the nations, establishes a new heaven and new earth, and brings all things to their ordained conclusion. In this new order Christ will be exalted as the eternal King and his people will joyfully serve him for ever. Our theme verse speaks of his power and authority. Before the end of human history Jesus will destroy all rivals, both human and demonic. Only those who belong to him will be saved. 'Therefore, you kings, be wise; be warned you rulers of the earth. Serve the Lord with fear and rejoice with trembling. Kiss the Son, let he be angry and you be destroyed in your way, for his wrath can flare up in a moment. Blessed are all who take refuge in him' (Ps. 2:11-13).

SCRIPTURE READING: PSALM 2

April 24

NEW SUBJECTS FOR THE KING

(WEEK 17: DAY 2)

Christ the King

Westminster Catechism Question #26:

How does Christ fulfill the office of a king? *Answer*: Christ fulfills the office of a king by subduing us to himself, in ruling and defending us, and in restraining and conquering all his and our enemies.

Theme verse: 'For he must reign until he has put all his enemies under his feet. The last enemy to be destroyed is death' (1 Cor. 15:25-26).

As with many earthly kings, our King, the Lord Jesus, wants to expand his kingdom in our world. The Great Commission (Matt. 28:16-20), tells us how we fit into Christ's plan for expanding his kingdom. We are told to be proactive. 'Go,' Jesus says, moving forward in making new followers for him, discipling them and baptizing new converts to his cause. These new subjects are to be taught and trained to obey what Jesus has commanded in his holy Word. The result the King is seeking is none other than his Church, an ever-expanding kingdom of faithful followers, committed to his cause and obedient to his commands. We engage in recruiting for the King with confidence, knowing that our efforts will be successful since the Lord promises to go with us: 'surely I am with you always, to the very end of the age' (Matt. 28:20). King Jesus declares that the Church will always prevail against its enemies; in fact, 'the gates of Hades will not overcome it' (Matt. 16:18). All forces opposed to Christ and his kingdom will be overthrown. While there is time, we are to warn persons everywhere to no longer be indifferent or rebellious towards our conquering King. Instead, we are to call sinners from every land to join us in giving glad worship and service to King Jesus before he comes again.

SCRIPTURE READING: MATTHEW 28:16-20

April 25
THE KING'S UNIVERSAL REIGN
(WEEK 17: DAY 3)

Christ the King

Westminster Catechism Question #26:

How does Christ fulfill the office of a king? *Answer*: Christ
fulfills the office of a king by subduing us to himself, in ruling
and defending us, and in restraining and conquering all his and
our enemies.

Theme verse: 'For he must reign until he has put all his enemies
under his feet. The last enemy to be destroyed is death'
(1 Cor. 15:25-26).

Human kingdoms are limited in time and space. No one king has
ever ruled the entire earth and no king has ever ruled for more
than a few decades. But the Bible declares that Jesus reigns in
heaven and will do so for ever: 'For he must reign until he has put
all his enemies under his feet' (1 Cor. 15:25). All the holy angels
delight to obey his commands. The various orders of cherubim
and seraphim attend to the King. All the principalities and powers
in heavenly places do homage to the Lord for ever. Believers who
have died and entered heaven all worship the Lord Jesus there,
proclaiming him as their King and High Priest who has purchased
them by his own blood. Some of God's chosen people are near the
throne, falling down before him and laying their crowns at his feet,
saying: 'You are worthy, our Lord and God, to receive glory and
honor and power' (Rev. 4:11). Yet, while the Lord reigns in sovereign majesty today in heaven, there are still rebels in the world he
has made. But at the end of human history Jesus will make quick
work of them. 'Then the end will come, when he hands over the
kingdom to God the Father after he has destroyed all dominion,
authority and power' (1 Cor. 15:24). While there is time we are
wise to lay down arms and seek peace with this great King.

SCRIPTURE READING: 1 CORINTHIANS 15:20-28

April 26
The great Warrior-King
(WEEK 17: DAY 4)

Christ the King

Westminster Catechism Question #26:

How does Christ fulfill the office of a king? *Answer*: Christ fulfills the office of a king by subduing us to himself, in ruling and defending us, and in restraining and conquering all his and our enemies.

Theme verse: 'For he must reign until he has put all his enemies under his feet. The last enemy to be destroyed is death' (1 Cor. 15:25-26).

Revelation 19:11-21 is a description of the Lord returning to the earth as the great Warrior-King. It is beyond our powers of imagination to understand the image of Christ that is revealed in this passage. Jesus is riding a white horse to emphasize his holiness. He is 'faithful and true' to inform us that he can be fully trusted since there is no fakery about him; he is who he claims to be. He is just, a Judge who judges righteously and correctly. 'His eyes are like flaming fire' (Rev. 19:12). They are all-penetrating, burning and they shrivel up the unrighteous. His crowns represent his kingship. His robe speaks of his mighty work at Calvary. He is the Word of God in the flesh who will destroy his enemies by the word of his mouth. Words are written on his robe and thigh: 'King of kings, and Lord of lords'. He comes with his army from heaven to wage war against Satan who is the source and head of all anti-Christian activity. 'Then I saw the beast and the kings of the earth and their armies gathered together to make war against the rider on the horse and his army' (Rev. 19:19). When the King comes to wrap up human history and wage war against his enemies he will capture his foes and cast them into the lake of fire. The question for each of us will be, 'Whose side am I on?'

SCRIPTURE READING: REVELATION 19:11-21

April 27
LAVISH REWARDS
(WEEK 17: DAY 5)

Christ the King

Westminster Catechism Question #26:

How does Christ fulfill the office of a king? *Answer*: Christ fulfills the office of a king by subduing us to himself, in ruling and defending us, and in restraining and conquering all his and our enemies.

Theme verse: 'For he must reign until he has put all his enemies under his feet. The last enemy to be destroyed is death' (1 Cor. 15:25-26).

If there is one thing that the Bible teaches emphatically it is that we are saved by grace, not by works. There is nothing we can do to 'earn' our salvation; there is nothing we can do to impress God or to work our way to heaven. But alongside that truth, the Bible also teaches that true followers of Jesus will be rewarded or 'judged' according to how we have lived our lives. Have we lived to honour the Lord? Have we served the King with hearts of love? Notice the generosity of Jesus towards followers who serve him well: 'To him who overcomes and does my will to the end, I will give authority *over the nations*' (Rev. 2:26). Jesus is stating that those followers who remain faithful to him will share in his rule over the nations as a reward for their faithfulness. In both the Parable of the Talents (Matt. 25) and the Parable of the Ten Minas (Luke 19), Jesus teaches that faithful service will be lavishly rewarded. 'Well done, my good servant!' his master replied. 'Because you have been trustworthy in a very small matter, take charge of ten cities' (Luke 19:17). When Christ comes as conquering King he will reward his followers extravagantly according to their love and service to the King. Although the Bible warns us against building up treasures on earth, it does teach that we should pursue heavenly rewards.

SCRIPTURE READING: LUKE 19:11-27

April 28

Christ the King

Westminster Catechism Question #26:

How does Christ fulfill the office of a king? *Answer*: Christ fulfills the office of a king by subduing us to himself, in ruling and defending us, and in restraining and conquering all his and our enemies.

Theme verse: 'For he must reign until he has put all his enemies under his feet. The last enemy to be destroyed is death' (1 Cor. 15:25-26).

There had been previous attempts on the life of Jesus. Angry mobs had tried to throw him over a hill. Stones had been picked up in order to stone him to death. Plans had been made to secretly assassinate the Messiah. But when it was God's time to allow his Son to die for sinners it was necessary for the Sanhedrin to present to Pilate actual charges against Jesus. 'We have found this man subverting our nation. He opposes payment of taxes to Caesar and claims to be Christ, a king' (Luke 23:2). So Pilate asked Jesus, 'Are you the king of the Jews?' 'Yes, it is as you say,' Jesus replied (Luke 23:3). The charges against Jesus were that he claimed to be both the Messiah and 'King of the Jews'. While Pilate asked Jesus about the main charge of his claiming to be a king, the Lord posed no threat to Pilate. Jesus was accompanied by no army or adherents. He was poorly dressed. There were no pretensions to earthly power. Yet when asked, the Lord Jesus shocked Pilate by saying that he was indeed a king: 'in fact, for this reason I was born, and for this I came into the world' (John 18:37). Jesus was born to usher in a spiritual kingdom that was not understood or appreciated by Pilate. But now, if you understand why Jesus came, 'Repent, for the kingdom of heaven is near' (Matt. 3:2).

SCRIPTURE READING: LUKE 23:1-25

April 29

Christ the King

Westminster Catechism Question #26:

How does Christ fulfill the office of a king? *Answer*: Christ
fulfills the office of a king by subduing us to himself, in ruling
and defending us, and in restraining and conquering all his and
our enemies.

Theme verse: 'For he must reign until he has put all his enemies
under his feet. The last enemy to be destroyed is death'
(1 Cor. 15:25-26).

God reveals a fantastic vision of the future to the Apostle John
in Revelation 21:1-8. 'A new heaven and earth' has replaced this
polluted, decaying and dying one. The old separation of heaven
and earth has ended. Satan and his anti-Christian forces, which
have committed such terrible horrors on this earth, have been destroyed and God's heaven and the new heaven and earth are joined
together and made one. 'I saw the Holy City, the new Jerusalem,
coming down out of heaven from God, prepared as a bride beautifully dressed for her husband' (Rev. 21:2). A voice from the throne
then says: 'Now the dwelling of God is with men, and he will live
with them' (Rev. 21:3). This is the ultimate fulfilment of what it
means for Jesus to be called 'Immanuel', God with us. This is the
enthroned King coming down out of heaven to join his people in
eternal celebration of his triumph over his and our enemies, particularly through his victory at the cross. 'And having disarmed
the powers and authorities, he made a public spectacle of them,
triumphing over them by the cross' (Col. 2:15). Here is our challenge from the lips of King Jesus: 'He who overcomes will inherit
all this, and I will be his God and he will be my son' (Revelation
21:7). Is this your inheritance?

SCRIPTURE READING: COLOSSIANS 2:6-15

April 30
GLORY IN HUMILIATION
(WEEK 18: DAY 1)

Christ's humiliation

Westminster Catechism Question #27:

What did Christ's humiliation consist of? *Answer*: Christ's humiliation consisted of his being born, and that under humble circumstances, under the Old Testament law; his experiencing the miseries of this life, the wrath of God, the curse of death on the cross, burial and the power of death for a time.

Theme verse: 'And being found in appearance as a man, he humbled himself and became obedient to death — even death on a cross!' (Phil. 2:8).

This week we consider the humble, servant role our Lord Jesus assumed while here on earth. Theologians call Christ's time on earth his 'humiliation'. The biblical scholars who drew up the *Westminster Confession of Faith* believed it was important to understand this doctrine in order to appreciate better Christ's exaltation to the Father's right hand. The incarnation of Christ (his coming into the world) is as great and significant a miracle as his death and resurrection. The catechism question emphasizes that Christ lived under the Old Testament law and that he fulfilled the law perfectly by never sinning. The great God of the universe lived under the constraints of the law and became the only person ever to follow every detail of that law. At the crucifixion Jesus bore the wrath of his Father against sin, being forsaken by his Father when he became sin for us. His death and burial were final acts of voluntary humiliation. An ancient hymn of the church is recorded by the Apostle Paul for us in Philippians 2:6-11. The passage deals both with Christ's humiliation and exaltation. Our theme verse is taken from verse 8 of that hymn. Paul states his amazement that Christ would be willing to die for us at all, but then the final humiliation — death on a cross! And yet, we glory in nothing else.

SCRIPTURE READING: PHILIPPIANS 2:1-8

May 1
FULFILLED PROPHECY
(WEEK 18: DAY 2)

Christ's humiliation

Westminster Catechism Question #27:

What did Christ's humiliation consist of? *Answer*: Christ's humiliation consisted of his being born, and that under humble circumstances, under the Old Testament law; his experiencing the miseries of this life, the wrath of God, the curse of death on the cross, burial and the power of death for a time.

Theme verse: 'And being found in appearance as a man, he humbled himself and became obedient to death — even death on a cross!' (Phil. 2:8).

Luke 2:1 informs us that Caesar Augustus was emperor at the time of Christ's birth. The name 'Augustus' means 'exalted' and it was a title given him by the Roman senate. A decree went out from Caesar Augustus that a census should be taken of all citizens of the Roman Empire. This was done for the purpose of collecting taxes and registering men for military service. But God had his own purposes for Augustus issuing such a decree. In the back-waters of the Roman Empire, in an insignificant portion of Palestine, a poor man and his fiancée were thus forced to leave their little village of Nazareth in Galilee and head south to Bethlehem, the town of David, in Judea, in order to register. This seemingly insignificant event fulfilled Old Testament prophecy: 'But you, Bethlehem Ephrathah, though you are small among the clans of Judah, out of you will come for me one who will be ruler over Israel, whose origins are from of old, from ancient times' (Micah 5:2). The 'exalted' Caesar made his decree but the ancient prophecy was about the humble Jesus. 'He will stand and shepherd his people in the strength of the Lord, in the majesty of the name of the Lord his God. And they will live securely, for then his greatness will reach to the ends of the earth. And he will be their peace' (Micah 5:4-5).

SCRIPTURE READING: MICAH 5:1-5

May 2
LEARNING FROM CHRIST'S HUMILITY
(WEEK 18: DAY 3)

Christ's humiliation

Westminster Catechism Question #27:

What did Christ's humiliation consist of? *Answer*: Christ's humiliation consisted of his being born, and that under humble circumstances, under the Old Testament law; his experiencing the miseries of this life, the wrath of God, the curse of death on the cross, burial and the power of death for a time.

Theme verse: 'And being found in appearance as a man, he humbled himself and became obedient to death — even death on a cross!' (Phil. 2:8).

When Jesus gave us the Beatitudes in his Sermon on the Mount, he gave us a description of his own life. 'Blessed are the poor in spirit' (Matt. 5:3), Jesus said, and he was that. Blessed are the meek, those who hunger and thirst for righteousness, the merciful. Jesus lived out his sermon in his own life. Peter preached that Jesus 'went around doing good and healing all who were under the power of the devil' (Acts 10:38). The Apostle Paul described Jesus this way: He 'did not consider equality with God something to be grasped, but made himself nothing, taking the very nature of a servant' (Phil. 2:6-7). If we study this aspect of the life of Jesus we are astounded by his self-giving. Jesus is so unlike us. We are, by nature, proud people. We tend to want our own way and our feelings are easily hurt. But here is the Apostle Paul's admonition to us that our attitude should be the same as that of Christ: 'Do nothing out of selfish ambition or vain conceit, but in humility consider others better than yourselves' (Phil. 2:3). Jesus told us that we can break the enslaving 'me-first' attitude and consider others as better than ourselves by following his example: 'Take my yoke upon you and learn from me, for I am gentle and humble in heart, and you will find rest for your souls' (Matt. 11:29).

SCRIPTURE READING: MATTHEW 11:25-30

Christ's humiliation

Westminster Catechism Question #27:

What did Christ's humiliation consist of? *Answer*: Christ's humiliation consisted of his being born, and that under humble circumstances, under the Old Testament law; his experiencing the miseries of this life, the wrath of God, the curse of death on the cross, burial and the power of death for a time.

Theme verse: 'And being found in appearance as a man, he humbled himself and became obedient to death — even death on a cross!' (Phil. 2:8).

As they were walking along the road, a man said to him, 'I will follow you wherever you go.' Jesus replied, 'Foxes have holes and birds of the air have nests, but the Son of Man has no place to lay his head' (Luke 9:57-58). Jesus was warning all potential followers that there is cost to following him. It can mean choosing Christ over the wishes of family members or accepting hardships that come with cross-bearing. Jesus had less in the way of creature comforts than the wild animals. At least the foxes had dens and birds had nests. But Jesus had no fixed address where he could lay his head to rest. His life was consumed with doing his Father's will and spiritual priorities superseded earthly comforts. Still, Jesus enjoyed visiting with Mary, Martha and Lazarus. Here was a place where Jesus could kick off his sandals and recover from his labour. The amazing condescension of the Son of God is hard to grasp. He flung the stars in space and made every living thing, yet he toiled and sweated under the sun and slept in an uncomfortable boat when the waves were high and the winds were howling. It is stranger still that our hope for eternal life rests on the shoulders of this self-denying, homeless man. Be warned that to follow Jesus means taking up your cross every day and following him regardless of the cost.

SCRIPTURE READING: LUKE 9:51-62

May 4

Christ's humiliation

Westminster Catechism Question #27:

What did Christ's humiliation consist of? *Answer*: Christ's humiliation consisted of his being born, and that under humble circumstances, under the Old Testament law; his experiencing the miseries of this life, the wrath of God, the curse of death on the cross, burial and the power of death for a time.

Theme verse: 'And being found in appearance as a man, he humbled himself and became obedient to death — even death on a cross!' (Phil. 2:8).

During his time of ministry Jesus was constantly monitored by those who wanted to kill him. When Jesus healed on the Sabbath day the Pharisees and teachers of the law 'were furious and began to discuss with one another what they might do to Jesus' (Luke 6:11). It is impossible for us to imagine the animosity and intense hatred from evil people that Christ endured as part of his daily life. When the catechism answer informs us that Jesus 'experienced the miseries of this life' we should not assume that the depth of his humiliation was purely physical. After Jesus preached in the synagogue of his hometown of Nazareth the people were furious with him. They 'took him to the brow of the hill on which the town was built, in order to throw him down the cliff' (Luke 4:29). When Jesus claimed he was God in the flesh 'they picked up stones to stone him' (John 8:59). He bore the mental and psychological challenge of speaking and living the truth in the face of angry and powerful mobs and among those who made it their intent to torture him. Jesus understands better than we know what it means to have evil spoken of us. It was because he lived a godly life. Cruel words should not discourage us. 'In fact, everyone who wants to live a godly life in Christ Jesus will be persecuted' (2 Tim. 4:12).

SCRIPTURE READING: LUKE 2:23 – 3:6

May 5

The Garden of Gethsemane
(week 18: day 6)

Christ's humiliation

Westminster Catechism Question #27:

What did Christ's humiliation consist of? *Answer*: Christ's humiliation consisted of his being born, and that under humble circumstances, under the Old Testament law; his experiencing the miseries of this life, the wrath of God, the curse of death on the cross, burial and the power of death for a time.

Theme verse: 'And being found in appearance as a man, he humbled himself and became obedient to death — even death on a cross!' (Phil. 2:8).

The mental anguish of the Saviour's suffering is most clearly seen in the Garden of Gethsemane. 'And being in anguish, he prayed more earnestly, and his sweat was like drops of blood falling to the ground' (Luke 22:44). In the garden the Lord was facing the greatest of temptations. He who knew no sin was now being asked by his Father to become sin, to become filth, to be crushed by the weight of our sin and to die bearing it on the cross. God's wrath was to be poured out on his only Son. It tells us something about the unalterable nature of God's justice. Jesus had to fully bear the wrath of God against sin. Nothing was to be withheld. If he was to be our substitute he had to enter our world as a servant and accept the humiliation of the cross. When people are in anguish blood naturally flows to the internal organs to protect what is vital for life. The heart is filled with blood while the cheeks and hands and feet go pale. But in the Garden of Gethsemane the blood flowed out of Jesus. Nails were unnecessary as the Saviour's blood flowed freely without assistance; such was his love for sinners. This was a voluntary offering up of himself so that we might live. With grateful hearts we gaze at the agony of Jesus in the garden and marvel at the fullness of the offering he made for us.

Scripture reading: Luke 22:39-53

May 6

Christ's humiliation

Westminster Catechism Question #27:

What did Christ's humiliation consist of? *Answer*: Christ's humiliation consisted of his being born, and that under humble circumstances, under the Old Testament law; his experiencing the miseries of this life, the wrath of God, the curse of death on the cross, burial and the power of death for a time.

Theme verse: 'And being found in appearance as a man, he humbled himself and became obedient to death — even death on a cross!' (Phil. 2:8).

When Pilate delivered Jesus to be scourged they most likely tied his hands around a column and used a whip made of the sinews of oxen. They inter-twisted sharp bones in the whip in order that every lash would inflict lacerations to the body of the victim. Jesus endured thirty-nine lashes, a beating so severe that many died from the blows. Roman soldiers then took him to another place of torture where a crown of thorns was pushed onto his head. They drove large nails into his hands and feet and hung him, naked, on a cross. Isaiah prophesied about all this: 'he was pierced for our transgressions; he was crushed for our iniquities' (Isa. 53:5). Isaiah tells us that it was the Father's will 'to crush him and cause him to suffer ... and to make his life a guilt offering' (Isa. 53:10). Of course, the Redeemer's great humiliation had a wonderful purpose: 'the punishment that brought us peace was upon him, and by his wounds we are healed' (Isa. 53:5). The good news is that the grave could not hold him. 'After the suffering of his soul he will see the light of life and be satisfied; by his knowledge my righteous servant will justify many, and he will bear their iniquities' (Isa. 53:11). Has your sin been transferred to the dying Saviour? Then rejoice in your deliverance and adore the one on whom your sins were laid.

SCRIPTURE READING: ISAIAH 53:1-12

May 7

Christ's exaltation

Westminster Catechism Question #28:

What does Christ's exaltation consist of? *Answer*: Christ's exaltation consists of his rising again from the dead on the third day, his ascension up into heaven, his sitting at the right hand of God the Father and his coming to judge the world at the last day.

Theme verse: 'Therefore God exalted him to the highest placed and gave him the name that is above every name' (Phil. 2:9).

It was God's plan from the beginning to send his Son into the world to die and redeem his people from their sins. This was essential to fulfil the desire of both the Father and the Son for Christ's exaltation and glorification. Before Jesus went to the cross he prayed, 'Father, I want those you have given me to be with me where I am, and to see my glory, the glory you have given me because you loved me before the creation of the world' (John 17:24). The great goal of Christ's agony at the cross was to bring his children home to be with him. There we shall see his glory as the exalted King. We will agree with the Father that it is right that Jesus receive the highest place of honour and a 'name that is above every name' (Phil. 2:9). The catechism answer also states that Jesus is coming back at the end of human history to judge the nations. This is a privilege and responsibility which his Father has given him. When Christ comes to judge the world on the last day he will separate the sheep from the goats (Matt. 25:31-46) — that is, he will separate those who love him from those who do not. Some will be waiting for his return but others will be completely taken by surprise and shocked that the Judge of all the earth has come not to save but to punish. In which camp will you find yourself?

SCRIPTURE READING: MATTHEW 25:31-46

May 8

Christ's exaltation

Westminster Catechism Question #28:

What does Christ's exaltation consist of? *Answer*: Christ's exaltation consists of his rising again from the dead on the third day, his ascension up into heaven, his sitting at the right hand of God the Father and his coming to judge the world at the last day.

Theme verse: 'Therefore God exalted him to the highest placed and gave him the name that is above every name' (Phil. 2:9).

God the Father demonstrated 'mighty strength, which he exerted in Christ when he raised him from the dead and seated him at his right hand in the heavenly realms' (Eph. 1:20). After Jesus had completed his work on earth, Jesus was laid in a rich man's tomb. The Father supernaturally cared for Christ's body, ensuring that it suffered no decay so that the perfect body of Jesus would not be ceremonially defiled (Acts 2:27). On the third day, the Father powerfully raised Jesus from the grave. Days later Jesus ascended, in full view of his followers, back to heaven. At Pentecost the Apostle Peter testified that the patriarch King David 'spoke of the resurrection of the Christ, that he was not abandoned to the grave, nor did his body see decay. God has raised this Jesus to life, and we are all witnesses of the fact. [He is] exalted to the right hand of God' (Acts 2:31-33). Peter, at a later time, applies this good news of the resurrection to God's people: 'In his great mercy he has given us new birth into a living hope through the resurrection of Jesus Christ from the dead, and into an inheritance that can never perish, spoil or fade' (1 Peter 1:3). Christ's resurrection provides us with a firm conviction that we too will one day rise to join him in heaven, an inheritance of joy in Christ's presence that will last for ever.

SCRIPTURE READING: ACTS 2:22-36

May 9

Christ's exaltation

Westminster Catechism Question #28:

What does Christ's exaltation consist of? *Answer*: Christ's exaltation consists of his rising again from the dead on the third day, his ascension up into heaven, his sitting at the right hand of God the Father and his coming to judge the world at the last day.

Theme verse: 'Therefore God exalted him to the highest placed and gave him the name that is above every name' (Phil. 2:9).

Late in Christ's earthly ministry his disciples were greatly discouraged. 'From that time on Jesus began to explain to his disciples that he must go to Jerusalem and suffer many things at the hands of the elders, chief priests and teachers of the law, and that he must be killed and on the third day be raised to life' (Matt. 16:21). Peter even rebuked Jesus for his negativity. But Jesus was only warning his disciples of the inevitable suffering of his pre-determined path. It is interesting, then, to see how Jesus encouraged them. Several days later Jesus took Peter, James and John up a high mountain. Before their eyes Jesus was transfigured. 'His face shone like the sun, and his clothes became as white as the light' (Matt. 17:2). Here was a revelation of the glory that Christ possesses when he is in heaven. The disciples even heard the voice of God thunder, 'This is my Son, whom I love; with him I am well pleased. Listen to him!' (Matt. 17:5). This manifestation of his glory was a preview of what they would behold one day in heaven. What an encouragement for the disciples! What a powerful way to fortify their courage! If you are experiencing discouragement today be strengthened by a vision of the glory of Christ and remember that one day you, too, will see the exalted one.

SCRIPTURE READING: MATTHEW 17:1-9

May 10

Christ's exaltation

Westminster Catechism Question #28:

What does Christ's exaltation consist of? *Answer*: Christ's exaltation consists of his rising again from the dead on the third day, his ascension up into heaven, his sitting at the right hand of God the Father and his coming to judge the world at the last day.

Theme verse: 'Therefore God exalted him to the highest placed and gave him the name that is above every name' (Phil. 2:9).

In Philippians 2:6-11 we probably have not one hymn, but two. The first of these hymns (vv. 6-8) underscores the depth of Christ's humiliation. It eloquently portrays the self-emptying of God the Son in his servant role and torturous death. The second hymn (vv. 9-11) highlights the Father's enthusiasm in Christ's exaltation. The second hymn pictures the delight of the Father in his Son and his excitement to raise Jesus to the very pinnacle of honour in the universe. It is as if the proud Father was saying 'Look at my boy! Isn't he amazing?' The first hymn concentrates our attention on the self-denial of Christ. The second hymn has us see the glory and happiness of the Heavenly Father. The first hymn focuses on the cross. The second hymn focuses on the results of Christ's perfect sacrifice: Jesus exalted to the highest place and given a name above every name. Downward went Christ to the lowest depths, then upward to the highest heights. He died voluntarily as one cursed, hanging on wood. This is the noblest act the world has ever seen. It merits being raised above every other act in the universe. All people in all ages will one day bow before this exalted King and confess that Jesus Christ is Lord to the glory of God the Father. The only question will be whether we confess him as Lord voluntarily or involuntarily.

SCRIPTURE READING: PHILIPPIANS 2:1-11

May 11

Christ's exaltation

Westminster Catechism Question #28:

What does Christ's exaltation consist of? *Answer*: Christ's exaltation consists of his rising again from the dead on the third day, his ascension up into heaven, his sitting at the right hand of God the Father and his coming to judge the world at the last day.

Theme verse: 'Therefore God exalted him to the highest placed and gave him the name that is above every name' (Phil. 2:9).

The Apostle John uses striking imagery in Revelation 5 to describe the exalted Christ seated on his throne. The passage sees Christ as full of power (represented by seven horns) and omniscient (the seven eyes represent his ability to know and see all things). He alone is able to open the scroll and bring human history to a conclusion by judging the world in his righteousness. A new song is sung to celebrate a new demonstration of Christ's total sovereignty as he brings all of human history to a close. Those around the throne worship Christ in awe and adoration and exclaim why it is right that he alone should bring the world as we know it to an end. 'You are worthy to take the scroll and to open its seals, because you were slain, and with your blood you purchased men for God from every tribe and language and people and nation' (Rev. 5:9). Jesus is worthy and it is right for him to possess such an exalted position because of his sacrificial death that rescued us from sin and turned us into lovers of God. The picture in heaven is one of countless thousands of angels encircling the throne and the redeemed people of God. Everyone, in a spine-tingling act of other-worldly praise and worship, are seeking, if it were possible, to exalt and raise Jesus even higher. Let us join them here below.

SCRIPTURE READING: REVELATION 5:1-14

May 12

Christ's exaltation

Westminster Catechism Question #28:

What does Christ's exaltation consist of? *Answer*: Christ's exaltation consists of his rising again from the dead on the third day, his ascension up into heaven, his sitting at the right hand of God the Father and his coming to judge the world at the last day.

Theme verse: 'Therefore God exalted him to the highest placed and gave him the name that is above every name' (Phil. 2:9).

When the Apostle Paul wanted to encourage the believers at Thessalonica he wrote to them about the imminent return of the Lord Jesus and that they would be with the Lord for ever. 'After that, we who are still alive and are left will be caught up together with them in the clouds to meet the Lord in the air. And so we will be with the Lord forever. Therefore encourage each other with these words' (1 Thess. 4:17-18). When the Apostle Peter wanted to exhort the early Church to persevere in the midst of suffering he wrote that their trials 'have come so that your faith ... may be proved genuine ... when Jesus Christ is revealed' (1 Peter 1:7). The author to the Hebrews, in order to encourage regular attendance at worship services, urged the believers to 'not give up meeting together ... but let us encourage one another — and all the more as you see the Day approaching' (Heb. 10:25). However, for unbelievers, the return of Christ has the opposite effect. 'Look, he is coming with the clouds, and every eye will see him, even those who pierced him; and all the peoples of the earth will mourn because of him' (Rev. 1:7). While the world will be sad that King Jesus is coming to bring the affairs of this world to an end, believers are challenged to make his return their source of daily consolation and encouragement.

SCRIPTURE READING: REVELATION 1:1-8

May 13

Christ's exaltation

Westminster Catechism Question #28:

What does Christ's exaltation consist of? *Answer*: Christ's exaltation consists of his rising again from the dead on the third day, his ascension up into heaven, his sitting at the right hand of God the Father and his coming to judge the world at the last day.

Theme verse: 'Therefore God exalted him to the highest placed and gave him the name that is above every name' (Phil. 2:9).

There are three parables in Matthew 25 dealing with Christ's sudden and unexpected return at the end of time. In the first parable Jesus describes five wise and five foolish virgins. The five wise virgins have plenty of oil to keep their torches lit. When the bridegroom arrives they are ready and waiting for him. The five foolish virgins, without oil for their torches, are left out in the cold. In the second parable Jesus explains the coming kingdom through the example of an employer who goes on a long journey. He entrusts his property to his workers. When he returns he discovers that two of his servants were productive and serving their employer during his absence. They were richly rewarded. But one worker was wicked and lazy. He was fired and eternally judged. In the third parable the Son of Man returns to earth in splendour and glory. He gathers the nations before him and separates believers and unbelievers. Those who are blessed have served their Lord joyously. They receive rich rewards. The 'goats' are surprised that Jesus is not including them in his eternal kingdom. They had never seen Jesus thirsty or hungry. They had, in fact, been completely indifferent to the mission of Christ's kingdom. When the King returns will you be gladly serving him, watching and prayerfully waiting?

SCRIPTURE READING: MATTHEW 25:1-13

May 14

Redemption

Westminster Catechism Question #29:

How are we able to partake in the redemption purchased by Christ? *Answer*: We are able to partake in the redemption purchased by Christ, by the Holy Spirit who effectually applies it to us.

Theme verse: 'Repent and be baptized, every one of you, in the name of Jesus Christ for the forgiveness of your sins. And you will receive the gift of the Holy Spirit' (Acts 2:38).

How does Christ's work at Calvary, two thousand years ago, become real and meaningful for us today? It is through his Holy Spirit. Our Saviour's mighty work at the cross only becomes life-changing and personal when the Holy Spirit enters our lives and applies the atoning sacrifice to our souls. The theme verse (Acts 2:38) is a clear gospel presentation from the lips of the Apostle Peter to a crowd of intent listeners: 'Repent.' Show that you are serious about your repentance by willingly making a public confession of your desire to follow Christ through baptism. Seek the Lord's forgiveness for sinning against him. God promises the incredible gift of the Holy Spirit and his indwelling presence to repentant sinners. Through the Holy Spirit 'he who began a good work in you will carry it onto completion until the day of Christ Jesus' (Phil. 1:6). The Holy Spirit will continue to convict us of sin and cause us to rest upon Christ alone for our redemption. The Spirit of God will not only bring redemption to us at our conversion, but will also continue throughout our Christian lives to apply Christ's atoning sacrifice to us. It is the third Person of the Trinity who fills us 'with the fruit of righteousness that comes through Jesus Christ — to the glory and praise of God' (Phil. 1:11).

SCRIPTURE READING: PHILIPPIANS 1:3-11

May 15

Redemption

Westminster Catechism Question #29:

How are we able to partake in the redemption purchased by Christ? *Answer*: We are able to partake in the redemption purchased by Christ, by the Holy Spirit who effectually applies it to us.

Theme verse: 'Repent and be baptized, every one of you, in the name of Jesus Christ for the forgiveness of your sins. And you will receive the gift of the Holy Spirit' (Acts 2:38).

The Bible tells us that it was the Holy Spirit who raised Jesus from the dead on the third day. We are also told that the same Holy Spirit who raised Jesus will also give us life when Christ returns on Judgement Day. 'If the Spirit of him who raised Jesus from the dead is living in you, he who raised Christ from the dead will also give life to your mortal bodies through his Spirit, who lives in you' (Rom. 8:11). In this verse the Apostle Paul is not assuming that all his readers are true Christians and Paul is not interested in judging us. We are to judge ourselves and here is how we can determine if we are true believers or not: Does the Holy Spirit live in us? 'If anyone does not have the Spirit of Christ, he does not belong to Christ. But if Christ is in you, your body is dead because of sin, yet your spirit is alive because of righteousness' (Rom. 8:9-10). This is not an impossible criterion. The heart that possesses God's Spirit hears and feels the Spirit's promptings and is moved to follow that prompting by the power that the Spirit supplies. The Spirit is present with us when we hear the Word of God and God's Word is to motivate us, compelling us to obey, and controlling our thoughts and actions. We are not to create imaginary voices; rather, this is the Christian listening to God through his Word.

SCRIPTURE READING: ROMANS 8:5-14

May 16

Redemption

Westminster Catechism Question #29:

How are we able to partake in the redemption purchased by Christ? *Answer*: We are able to partake in the redemption purchased by Christ, by the Holy Spirit who effectually applies it to us.

Theme verse: 'Repent and be baptized, every one of you, in the name of Jesus Christ for the forgiveness of your sins. And you will receive the gift of the Holy Spirit' (Acts 2:38).

Salvation has an order to it. First, God chooses us to be his own as trophies of his grace. 'In him we were also chosen, having been predestined according to the plan of him who works out everything in conformity with the purpose of his will' (Eph. 1:11). Secondly, this choosing becomes effective when we hear the Word of God and respond in repentance and faith: 'you also were included in Christ when you heard the word of truth, the gospel of your salvation' (Eph. 1:13). Thirdly, at conversion God sends his Spirit into our hearts to guide us and take possession of us for Christ. 'Having believed, you were marked in him with a seal, the promised Holy Spirit, who is a deposit guaranteeing our inheritance until the redemption of those who are God's possession' (Eph. 1:13-14). The Holy Spirit is the guarantee that we belong to Jesus, and the one who prompts us to praise and glorify our new Master. The phrase 'marked in him with a seal' is a statement of accomplished fact. The Holy Spirit in us is the guarantee and pledge that we will receive a gracious inheritance in the future. That inheritance is nothing less than living in the presence of King Jesus for all eternity. Such a guarantee causes us to join the Apostle Paul in declaring — 'to the praise of his glory' (Eph. 1:14).

SCRIPTURE READING: EPHESIANS 1:11-14

May 17

Redemption

Westminster Catechism Question #29:

How are we able to partake in the redemption purchased by Christ? *Answer*: We are able to partake in the redemption purchased by Christ, by the Holy Spirit who effectually applies it to us.

Theme verse: 'Repent and be baptized, every one of you, in the name of Jesus Christ for the forgiveness of your sins. And you will receive the gift of the Holy Spirit' (Acts 2:38).

To explain how the Holy Spirit actually applies the redemption purchased for us by Christ the Bible informs us that God 'saved us through the washing of rebirth and renewal by the Holy Spirit, whom he poured out on us generously through Jesus Christ our Savior' (Titus 3:5-6). This means that God the Father gives us new life by washing and renewing us by the Holy Spirit. God makes us spiritually alive by accepting what Christ did on our behalf when he died at Calvary. The Father then proceeds further by applying to our lives what Jesus did for us. He accomplishes this by cleansing us from sin through the Holy Spirit. This mighty work begins our spiritual life. It affects every part of us, body and soul, making us children of God that are 'born of the Spirit'. By this washing and rebirth we become inheritors of heaven. This new life that is applied to us by the Holy Spirit makes us wholly different. We take on new characteristics that are God-honouring. The Bible describes us as having put off the 'old self with its practices and have put on the new self which is being renewed in knowledge in the image of its Creator' (Col. 3:10). Astonishingly, the Bible tells us that when we put on this new self we are 'created to be like God in true righteousness and holiness' (Eph. 4:24).

SCRIPTURE READING: TITUS 3:3-8

May 18

Redemption

Westminster Catechism Question #29:

How are we able to partake in the redemption purchased by Christ? *Answer*: We are able to partake in the redemption purchased by Christ, by the Holy Spirit who effectually applies it to us.

Theme verse: 'Repent and be baptized, every one of you, in the name of Jesus Christ for the forgiveness of your sins. And you will receive the gift of the Holy Spirit' (Acts 2:38).

In Old Testament times God's plan for redemption was spelled out by the covenant made with Moses and the children of Israel. God promised that he would bless the chosen people. In return, the people were required to demonstrate obedience and singular devotion to God. At this the people of Israel failed miserably. Therefore, God told the people through Jeremiah the prophet: 'The time is coming when I will make a new covenant with the house of Israel ... I will put my law in their minds and write it on their hearts' (Jer. 31:31,33). This new covenant is far superior to the old covenant because God's laws become inner principles that make us want to do God's will. The Old Testament prophet Ezekiel explained what the new covenant means: 'I will give you a new heart and put a new spirit in you ... And I will put my Spirit in you and move you to follow my decrees and be careful to follow my laws' (Ezek. 36:26-27). Now instead of a holy God distancing himself from us there can be intimate fellowship. The Holy Spirit places God's laws and truths into our minds and hearts, making us to understand our God and his purposes for us. Best of all, forgiveness of sins will be a permanent reality as the Holy Spirit cleanses us, renews us, and secures us for eternity.

SCRIPTURE READING: JEREMIAH 31:31-40

May 19

Redemption

Westminster Catechism Question #29:

How are we able to partake in the redemption purchased by Christ? *Answer*: We are able to partake in the redemption purchased by Christ, by the Holy Spirit who effectually applies it to us.

Theme verse: 'Repent and be baptized, every one of you, in the name of Jesus Christ for the forgiveness of your sins. And you will receive the gift of the Holy Spirit' (Acts 2:38).

The Apostle Paul was very thankful to God for the church at Thessalonica. His work among them had been productive and when he preached the Gospel the people responded positively. Paul knew it wasn't his dazzling personality or his persuasive rhetoric that had won them over. Instead, he recognized that God had simply used him to demonstrate his love for each of the believers there. 'But we ought always to thank God for you, brothers loved by the Lord, because from the beginning God chose you to be saved through the sanctifying work of the Spirit and through belief in the truth' (2 Thess. 2:13). Paul had seen the two things necessary for redemption very much in evidence in their lives. First, he had witnessed the life-changing work of the Holy Spirit who had purified them; and secondly, they had embraced the Word of God. Paul had taught them what they needed to know about Christ's ministry and his work of redemption at the cross, but the Holy Spirit had worked in their hearts to make them open to the message. He praised God that the Holy Spirit had applied Christ's redemption to them and challenged them to 'stand firm and hold to the teachings we passed on to you' (2 Thess. 2:14). By the power of the Spirit within us, we are called to do the same.

SCRIPTURE READING: 2 THESSALONIANS 2:13-17

May 20

Redemption

Westminster Catechism Question #29:

How are we able to partake in the redemption purchased by Christ? *Answer*: We are able to partake in the redemption purchased by Christ, by the Holy Spirit who effectually applies it to us.

Theme verse: 'Repent and be baptized, every one of you, in the name of Jesus Christ for the forgiveness of your sins. And you will receive the gift of the Holy Spirit' (Acts 2:38).

The Scriptures teach that when the Holy Spirit effectively applies Christ's redemption to us it is just the beginning of a life of ever-deepening growth and trust in the Lord Jesus. The Apostle Paul wrote to the church at Ephesus, 'I pray that out of his glorious riches he may strengthen you with power through his Spirit in your inner being, so that Christ may dwell in your hearts through faith' (Eph. 3:16-17). This strengthening is to come to us by 'his Spirit' and always the Holy Spirit works in conjunction with the Word of God. At Pentecost the Spirit was poured out on the church. Since then the ministry of the Holy Spirit has been to supply believers everywhere with ever-new power. The Spirit's work is to regenerate and fill the 'inner being'; our hearts, minds, souls, and strength in order for us to be 'filled to the measure of all the fullness of God' (Eph. 3:19). Paul's longing was that the believers at Ephesus would not be satisfied with a weak and impotent faith, with little knowledge of Christ and the Spirit's power. No, he prayed that God might grant them power 'to grasp how wide and long and high and deep is the love of Christ' (Eph. 3:18). It is the kind of earnest prayer we should pray for our own lives, for our families, for fellow believers, and for our churches.

SCRIPTURE READING: EPHESIANS 3:14-21

May 21

Justification

Westminster Catechism Question #33:

What is justification? *Answer*: Justification is an act of God's free grace received by faith alone, by which he pardons all our sins and accepts us as righteous in his sight.

Theme verse: 'For all have sinned and fall short of the glory of God, and are justified freely by his grace through the redemption that came by Christ Jesus' (Rom. 3:23-24).

Justification is when God freely, of his own accord, approves of us. Of course, as we all know, there is plenty about us that is disappointing and meets with God's disapproval. A holy God can only approve of us when we are free from the guilt of sin and the punishment that our sin deserves. What do we need to receive God's approval? We need the righteousness of Christ applied to our lives by the Holy Spirit. Therefore, we are moved to pray and ask God to apply this righteousness of Christ to our lives. When we long for Christ's righteousness we do so with faith that God will cleanse us and make us righteous in his sight. When this transaction takes place and we are set free from our sin, the Bible tells us that we are now 'justified freely by his grace through the redemption that came by Christ Jesus' (Rom. 3:23-24). God can only justify saving us from our sin if there is someone who will be our substitute and bear the punishment for our sin. That person is the Lord Jesus Christ who was the sacrifice to atone for our transgressions. This makes God righteous in saving sinners, and 'the one who justifies those who have faith in Jesus' (Rom. 3:26). How can God 'justify' himself in saving sinners like us? He can only be just if someone who is perfectly holy stands in our place.

SCRIPTURE READING: ROMANS 3:21-26

May 22
JUSTIFIED BY GRACE
(WEEK 21: DAY 2)

Justification

Westminster Catechism Question #33:

What is justification? *Answer*: Justification is an act of God's free grace received by faith alone, by which he pardons all our sins and accepts us as righteous in his sight.

Theme verse: 'For all have sinned and fall short of the glory of God, and are justified freely by his grace through the redemption that came by Christ Jesus' (Rom. 3:23-24).

Justification is the doctrine in the Bible that really lets you know you will never receive God's approval by 'doing the best you can'. Doing our best just is not good enough. Our theme verse explains our hopeless condition: 'for all have sinned and fall short of the glory of God' (Rom. 3:23). Our best efforts are never going to impress God. He knows our sinful hearts. The Apostle Paul put it this way: 'Where, then, is boasting? It is excluded ... For we maintain that a man is justified by faith apart from observing the law' (Rom. 3:27-28). Even godly Abraham could not please God except by faith in the future Saviour. 'If, in fact, Abraham was justified by works, he had something to boast about — but not before God. What does the Scripture say? "Abraham believed God, and it was credited to him as righteousness"' (Rom. 4:2-3). The rabbis cited Abraham as an example of receiving God's approval by 'works', that is, by human effort. But the Apostle Paul used Abraham as an example of one saved from his sin by faith in the future Messiah. When it comes to our salvation the only proper attitude is one of reverent humility since 'it is by grace you have been saved, through faith — and this not from yourselves, it is the gift of God — not by works, so that no one can boast' (Eph. 2:8-9).

SCRIPTURE READING: ROMANS 4:1-8

May 23

Justification

Westminster Catechism Question #33:

What is justification? *Answer*: Justification is an act of God's
free grace received by faith alone, by which he pardons all our
sins and accepts us as righteous in his sight.

Theme verse: 'For all have sinned and fall short of the glory of
God, and are justified freely by his grace through the redemption
that came by Christ Jesus' (Rom. 3:23-24).

One day Jesus told a parable about a Pharisee and a tax collector
who both went up to the temple to pray. The Pharisee stood up
and prayed about himself: 'God, I thank you that I am not like
other men — robbers, evildoers, adulterers — or even like this tax
collector' (Luke 18:11). But the tax collector, in grief and contrition, prayed, 'God, have mercy on me, a sinner' (Luke 18:13). The
contrast could not be more obvious. The Pharisee was proud of
his religious zeal. He believed that he did not need to be justified in God's sight because he was convinced God approved of his
lifestyle and personal efforts. He felt that he needed no Saviour to
rescue him since he was already righteous, and that he could take
care of himself. But the tax collector knew he was a sinner and
that he could never win God's approval by his own efforts. He believed that if he was to be justified in God's sight, he would need
a Saviour to rescue him. This is where the Saviour and his work at
the cross is the centrepiece of our faith. Without his substitution
for us, taking our sin upon himself, there simply can be no salvation. Jesus tells us that the tax collector rather than the Pharisee
'went home justified before God. For everyone who exalts himself
will be humbled, and he who humbles himself will be exalted'
(Luke 18:14).

SCRIPTURE READING: LUKE 18:9-14

Justification

Westminster Catechism Question #33:

What is justification? *Answer*: Justification is an act of God's free grace received by faith alone, by which he pardons all our sins and accepts us as righteous in his sight.

Theme verse: 'For all have sinned and fall short of the glory of God, and are justified freely by his grace through the redemption that came by Christ Jesus' (Rom. 3:23-24).

When the Apostle Paul went about preaching the gospel of Jesus he did not leave these 'lofty' doctrines such as justification for a later time when the people were spiritually mature. In fact, justification by grace was the central point of his evangelistic message. In Acts 13, Paul was allowed to preach in the synagogue of Pisidian Antioch. He began by giving an overview of God's dealings among the Jewish people in the Old Testament. Paul then introduced Jesus as the Son of David, the promised Saviour. He spoke about Christ's death and resurrection and then reached the climax of his preaching by declaring, 'Therefore, my brothers, I want you to know that through Jesus the forgiveness of sins is proclaimed to you. Through him everyone who believes is justified from everything you could not be justified from by the law of Moses' (Acts 13:38-39). Everything turns on whether we understand and embrace this doctrine. It defines the saving significance of Christ's life. Justification makes clear that true faith is belief in Christ's atoning death for the forgiveness of sins and that we trust alone in Jesus for righteousness. Justification displays God's justice in condemning and punishing sin and his mercy in pardoning and accepting sinners. God's punishment for sin fell on Jesus that you might be justified in his sight.

SCRIPTURE READING: ACTS 13:13-41

Justification

Westminster Catechism Question #33:

What is justification? *Answer*: Justification is an act of God's free grace received by faith alone, by which he pardons all our sins and accepts us as righteous in his sight.

Theme verse: 'For all have sinned and fall short of the glory of God, and are justified freely by his grace through the redemption that came by Christ Jesus' (Rom. 3:23-24).

Understanding justification makes it easier to understand many other Christian beliefs and practices. For instance, all Christians believe it is essential to obey the law, whether we are talking about the Ten Commandments or about laws that our government establishes. But what is our motivation for law-keeping? Are we afraid that we will go to hell if we don't keep the law? If that is the case, all of us are doomed. Our theme verse has already informed us that we 'all have sinned and fall short of the glory of God'. No, Christians keep the law out of gratitude to the Saviour whose gift of righteousness makes law-keeping needless as a requirement for acceptance with God. Does that mean we can break the law and God does not mind? The Apostle Paul addressed this issue when he wrote: 'Shall we sin because we are not under law but under grace?' (Rom. 6:15). His answer was an emphatic 'No!' Christ's work at the cross, when applied to our lives, frees us from sin and makes us 'slaves of righteousness' (Rom. 6:18). We now keep the Ten Commandments and obey the laws of the land because we love the Saviour who justifies us 'freely by his grace through the redemption that came by Christ Jesus'. If you are thankful that Christ died for your sins then he has made you a willing law-keeper.

SCRIPTURE READING: ROMANS 6:11-23

May 26

Justification

Westminster Catechism Question #33:

What is justification? *Answer*: Justification is an act of God's free grace received by faith alone, by which he pardons all our sins and accepts us as righteous in his sight.

Theme verse: 'For all have sinned and fall short of the glory of God, and are justified freely by his grace through the redemption that came by Christ Jesus' (Rom. 3:23-24).

Some Jewish converts to the Christian faith in the days of the Apostle Paul believed that all Christians, even if they were not ethnic Jews, should still practise some of the Jewish ceremonial customs. They insisted that Gentile (non-Jewish) Christians should still abide by certain Old Testament rites, particularly circumcision. They would travel to places, such as Galatia where Paul had already preached, and seek to impose many of the legal requirements set down in the Old Testament on new believers who had been converted under Paul's preaching. Paul responded to this by warning that such teaching was perverting the true gospel of justification by faith alone in Christ's work at the cross. 'We who are Jews by birth ... know that a man is not justified by observing the law, but by faith in Jesus Christ' (Gal. 2:15-16). He believed that if anyone taught any other gospel than 'justification by faith alone' it really was not the true Gospel at all. 'I am astonished that you are so quickly deserting the one who called you by the grace of Christ and are turning to a different gospel — which is really no gospel at all' (Gal. 1:6-7). Paul sought to protect his new converts to Christ from the bondage of legalism. Make sure you do not add rules and regulations on top of the pure gospel of Christ alone for salvation.

SCRIPTURE READING: GALATIANS 2:11-21

May 27
Imputed righteousness
(week 21: day 7)

Justification

Westminster Catechism Question #33:

What is justification? *Answer*: Justification is an act of God's free grace received by faith alone, by which he pardons all our sins and accepts us as righteous in his sight.

Theme verse: 'For all have sinned and fall short of the glory of God, and are justified freely by his grace through the redemption that came by Christ Jesus' (Rom. 3:23-24).

'Imputation' is another theological term that will help us understand the doctrine of justification. The dictionary defines imputation as meaning 'to ascribe' or 'to reckon'. For God to justify us he imputed Christ's righteousness on us by ascribing his work to our lives. In doing that God declares the sinful man or woman to be righteous in his sight. The doctrine of justification means that before the eyes of God the sinful man or woman is now 'in Christ' and has perfectly kept the Law of God. We can even say that 'in Christ' we have loved the Lord our God with all our heart, soul, mind, and strength and our neighbour as ourselves. This means that we look to Christ and his dying for us as 'our righteousness'. No other righteousness will do. Our human efforts to keep the law or to please God fall hopelessly short. We cannot have faith in our Christian service, our worship services, or even our religious experiences. It is pointless to trust in our religious background or what others think of us. The righteousness we need comes from outside of us and must be imputed to us. So we look to Christ who has power to pardon all our sins and accept us as righteous in his sight. The greater our understanding of this central truth of the Christian faith, the more intense will be our love for Christ and his free grace.

SCRIPTURE READING: ROMANS 5:1-11

May 28

Adoption

Westminster Catechism Question #34:

What is adoption? *Answer*: Adoption is an act of God's free grace, by which we are received into the family of God, and have a right to all the privileges which belong to the children of God.

Theme verse: 'How great is the love the Father has lavished on us, that we should be called children of God! And that is what we are!' (1 John 3:1).

Adoption is perhaps the most appealing of all biblical doctrines. The idea that God — out of sheer kindness and mercy — embraces us, takes us out of slavery to sin and makes us part of his family is a thought almost too wonderful to express in words. As an added blessing, all the rights and privileges that are associated with being part of such a happy and joyous family are ours. Unlike Jesus, who is his Father's only begotten Son, we were foreigners and aliens before being adopted into the family. But now, 'you are no longer foreigners and aliens, but fellow citizens with God's people and members of God's household' (Eph. 2:19). Sometimes we hear people say, 'Well, we are all children of God here,' assuming that all people everywhere are part of the family of God. But the Scriptures reserve true inclusion in the family of God to those who have been justified by grace through faith. Adoption is an act of God's free grace to those who have received the righteousness of Christ by faith, whose sins have been covered by the work of Christ at the cross. Only justified sinners can enthusiastically proclaim our theme verse: 'How great is the love the Father has lavished on us, that we should be called children of God!' And amazingly, because of the lavish love of the Father, that is what we really are!

SCRIPTURE READING: EPHESIANS 2:11-22

May 29
THE SPIRIT OF ADOPTION
(WEEK 22: DAY 2)

Adoption

Westminster Catechism Question #34:

What is adoption? *Answer*: Adoption is an act of God's free grace, by which we are received into the family of God, and have a right to all the privileges which belong to the children of God.

Theme verse: 'How great is the love the Father has lavished on us, that we should be called children of God! And that is what we are!' (1 John 3:1).

Adoption is a term that the Apostle Paul borrowed from the Roman legal system. Under the Roman system the adopted son received all the rights and privileges of a biological son, including rights of inheritance. The Apostle Paul, in writing to the Romans, described Christians as those who were once slaves to sin but who have now 'received the Spirit of adoption' (Rom. 8:15). We were once strangers to God's grace and lived as orphans, far removed from the fellowship or love of God. But now, as true children of God, we are marked by the Holy Spirit living within us who urges us to approach God in childlike love, crying, 'Abba, Father' (Rom. 8:15). Such expressions of love speak of an especially close relationship to God, similar to a warm and joyful relationship between a child and parent. Children know who their parents are. And sons and daughters of the Heavenly Father are conscious that they are children of God as well. The Holy Spirit provides them with an inner testimony based on passage after passage from the Word of God, establishing this clear sense that they are adopted into the family of God. Nor is this all we receive. We are promised the inheritance of heaven and eternal fellowship with the Lord Jesus who died for us. He made entrance possible for family members.

SCRIPTURE READING: ROMANS 8:12-17

May 30
Living a delusion
(week 22: day 3)

Adoption

Westminster Catechism Question #34:

What is adoption? *Answer*: Adoption is an act of God's free grace, by which we are received into the family of God, and have a right to all the privileges which belong to the children of God.

Theme verse: 'How great is the love the Father has lavished on us, that we should be called children of God! And that is what we are!' (1 John 3:1).

Most of us are confident that we really are the children of God, adopted into his family. But how can we be so certain? When Jesus addressed the Jews of his day they were sure that Abraham was their father and that God was their Heavenly Father. Yet Jesus shocked them by telling them that just the opposite was the case. 'You belong to your father, the devil, and you want to carry out your father's desire' (John 8:44). Jesus gave reasons why they were children of the devil rather than children of God. 'You are ready to kill me, because you have no room for my word' (John 8:37), and, 'If God were your Father, you would love me, for I came from God and now am here' (John 8:42). One of the clear proofs that persons do not belong to God is when they refuse to listen to and obey the commands of Christ. There is no love expressed to Christ in disobedient or indifferent lives. We may say we love God, attend church services, and perhaps even be involved in Christian ministries. But is there loving obedience to Christ and his words? It is easy to delude ourselves. Even persons mixed up in false religions have a sense of security that all is well with their souls. But the wise man or woman listens attentively and responds to Christ's admonitions. 'He who belongs to God hears what God says' (John 8:47).

SCRIPTURE READING: JOHN 8:31-47

May 31
PRIVILEGED PEOPLE
(WEEK 22: DAY 4)

Adoption

Westminster Catechism Question #34:

What is adoption? *Answer*: Adoption is an act of God's free grace, by which we are received into the family of God, and have a right to all the privileges which belong to the children of God.

Theme verse: 'How great is the love the Father has lavished on us, that we should be called children of God! And that is what we are!' (1 John 3:1).

Because Christians are the adopted children of God they are the most privileged people in the world. Think of it, we were once objects of God's wrath but are now objects of his mercy. We were once aliens to God's grace; we now are sons and daughters of the God of the universe. We were strangers. God has made us his family. We were once enemies. God has made us his friends. We once had no rights. Now we have all the rights and privileges which belong to the children of God. We once were poor. God has made us rich by giving us an 'inheritance that can never perish, spoil, or fade — kept in heaven for you' (1 Peter 1:4). What a dramatic and radical change. The Scriptures teach that we will one day share in the glory of our Great Brother, our Lord Jesus Christ. It is staggering to think that we can be elevated to such a place of dignity and honour. When we understand and embrace all that we have been given in our adoption, our complaints must disappear. How can we mutter or groan about trifling matters now that 'you are a chosen people, a royal priesthood, a holy nation, a people belonging to God, that you may declare the praises of him who called you out of darkness into his wonderful light' (1 Peter 2:9). We offer our heartfelt praise today that we are part of the family of God.

SCRIPTURE READING: 1 PETER 1:3-12

June 1

Adoption

Westminster Catechism Question #34:

What is adoption? *Answer*: Adoption is an act of God's free grace, by which we are received into the family of God, and have a right to all the privileges which belong to the children of God.

Theme verse: 'How great is the love the Father has lavished on us, that we should be called children of God! And that is what we are!' (1 John 3:1).

Our theme verse above is an exclamation of astonishment. It is shouting: 'Just take a look at this love!' To see it clearly is to shake our heads in wonder. It is beyond all comprehension. 1 John 3:1 is a statement that expresses not a hope but a fact: 'We are children of God!' The verse tells us that the Father is infinite in his love. He accepts us as his children, and all his love and the gifts that he is happy to bestow on us are ours. In some relationships there is equality in the giving and sharing. We receive gifts from others at special events knowing that we will likely have an opportunity to reciprocate. We ask a favour of a friend knowing we can return the kindness. But in this relationship it is all one-sided: God gives, and we only receive in gratitude. 'To all who received him, to those who believed in his name, he gave the right to become children of God — children born not of natural descent, nor of human decision or a husband's will, but born of God' (John 1:12-13). Here is the Father's divine initiative to establish fellowship with us: 'this is how God showed his love among us: He sent his one and only Son into the world that we might live through him. This is love, not that we loved God, but that he loved us and sent his Son as an atoning sacrifice for our sins' (1 John 4:9-10).

SCRIPTURE READING: JOHN 1:1-13

June 2

Adoption

Westminster Catechism Question #34:

What is adoption? *Answer*: Adoption is an act of God's free grace, by which we are received into the family of God, and have a right to all the privileges which belong to the children of God.

Theme verse: 'How great is the love the Father has lavished on us, that we should be called children of God! And that is what we are!' (1 John 3:1).

If we want to consider ourselves children of God, adopted into his family, then we need to get along with all the members of the family. The Apostle John states emphatically that you are not a child of God if you do not love your brother. 'This is how we know who the children of God are and who the children of the devil are: Anyone who does not do what is right is not a child of God; nor is anyone who does not love his brother' (1 John 3:10). So the apostle draws a circle around the children of God and separates them from children of the devil by their fathers and by their conduct within the family. The evidence to prove which family a person belongs to is the love or absence of love towards family members. Because of God's lavish love for us and his forgiving us all our sin we express our love both to God and to all persons as we have opportunity by expressing love to them. We especially demonstrate love to our spiritual family members. 'As we have opportunity, let us do good to all people, especially to those who belong to the family of believers' (Gal. 6:10). Here is another indicator as to whether you are a child of God: 'We know that we have passed from death to life, because we love our brothers' (1 John 3:14). Jesus said the same: 'You are my disciples if you love one another' (John 13:35).

SCRIPTURE READING: 1 JOHN 3:1-15

June 3
THE PURPOSE OF DISCIPLINE
(WEEK 22: DAY 7)

Adoption

Westminster Catechism Question #34:

What is adoption? *Answer*: Adoption is an act of God's free grace, by which we are received into the family of God, and have a right to all the privileges which belong to the children of God.

Theme verse: 'How great is the love the Father has lavished on us, that we should be called children of God! And that is what we are!' (1 John 3:1).

Like any loving parent, God disciplines his children. In fact, God's discipline of us is evidence that we are his children. Rather than discouraging us, discipline is a solid reason for real encouragement since it informs us that God cares about us. When discipline comes our way it is designed to make us more like Jesus. 'Endure hardship as discipline; God is treating you as sons. For what son is not disciplined by his father?' (Heb. 12:7). When we suffer as Christians we should see it as corrective and instructive training for our spiritual development. It is the way God makes us more like Christ. 'My son, do not make light of the Lord's discipline, and do not lose heart when he rebukes you, because the Lord disciplines those he loves, and he punishes everyone he accepts as a son' (Heb. 12:5-6). All chastisement that God lets us bear in this life is to correct us and to drive out the sin that is still in us, but only in order that we may be more truly the sons and daughters that God would have us be. God always disciplines us for our good 'that we may share in his holiness' (Heb. 12:10). Do not seek it, but be prepared as a child in the family of God to receive his discipline. 'It produces a harvest of righteousness and peace for those who have been trained by it' (Heb. 12:11).

SCRIPTURE READING: HEBREWS 12:4-11

June 4

Sanctification

Westminster Catechism Question #35:

What is sanctification? *Answer*: Sanctification is the work of
God's free grace, by which he renews every part of us in his
image, enabling us increasingly to die to sin and to live
for righteousness.

Theme verse: 'For if you live according to the sinful nature, you
will die; but if by the Spirit you put to death the misdeeds of the
body, you will live' (Rom. 8:13).

Sanctification is a process that involves a moral and spiritual
change in us once we receive salvation. Spiritually, we are given
a new heart and a new spirit is created in us by God. God's work
of conversion means that we are now sanctified, set apart as holy,
and loved by God. Our catechism answer states that sanctification extends to every part of our being, yet it remains incomplete
in this life. In Romans 7:7-25 the Apostle Paul describes the warfare between the old, corrupt nature and the new nature, which is
given to us and controlled by the Holy Spirit. This battle lasts our
entire Christian lives, but the continual supply of strength from
the Spirit of Christ enables us, as believers, to gain fresh victo-
ries and increase in our love for and obedience to the Lord Jesus.
With the Holy Spirit and God's Word dwelling within us, we begin to manifest increasingly holy lives. Sin's power over our lives is
broken, sin has less hold on us and we increasingly demonstrate
the fruits of the Spirit (love, joy, peace, patience, kindness, goodness, faithfulness, gentleness and self-control). All this is possible
by the power of Christ's sacrificial death and glorious resurrection applied to our lives. Here is our confidence: 'He who began
a good work in you will carry it on to completion until the day of
Christ Jesus' (Phil. 1:6).

SCRIPTURE READING: ROMANS 7:7-25

SANCTIFIED BY GOD
(WEEK 23: DAY 2)

Sanctification

Westminster Catechism Question #35:

What is sanctification? *Answer*: Sanctification is the work of God's free grace, by which he renews every part of us in his image, enabling us increasingly to die to sin and to live for righteousness.

Theme verse: 'For if you live according to the sinful nature, you will die; but if by the Spirit you put to death the misdeeds of the body, you will live' (Rom. 8:13).

Sanctification is a beautiful thing. It makes God and the angels fall in love with us. To advance and grow in sanctification requires the involvement of all three Persons of the Trinity. First, it is the Father who adopts us into his family. We respond to the Father personally and daily examine our lives as we relate to him. We seek to eradicate everything that is displeasing and at the same time do everything that is pleasing to him. 'Just as he who called you is holy, so be holy in all you do' (1 Peter 1:15). Secondly, we are related to Jesus through our union with him. He is not only our Redeemer, but he is also our Brother and our pattern to follow. We seek to walk as he walked. 'Whoever claims to live in him must walk as Jesus did' (1 John 2:6). He is unrivalled for love, compassion, gentleness, meekness and humility. He hated sin and gave himself as an offering to conquer sin in us. In justifying us he now calls us to be like him. Thirdly, the Holy Spirit monitors all our thought patterns. He represents us and only by his power are we able to pray. 'The Spirit himself intercedes for us with groans that words cannot express' (Rom. 8:26). He motivates us, directs us, interprets the Word of God to us, and empowers us for worship and service. In all of this, God's intention is to re-fashion us into his image.

SCRIPTURE READING: ROMANS 8:18-27

June 6

Sanctification

Westminster Catechism Question #35:

What is sanctification? *Answer*: Sanctification is the work of God's free grace, by which he renews every part of us in his image, enabling us increasingly to die to sin and to live for righteousness.

Theme verse: 'For if you live according to the sinful nature, you will die; but if by the Spirit you put to death the misdeeds of the body, you will live' (Rom. 8:13).

Putting sin to death in us is not optional. It is essential. Our theme verse is direct: 'For if you live according to the sinful nature, you will die' (Rom. 8:13). Putting sin to death involves all the power of the will. This is not something that is done for us. It is up to each of us to 'put to death the misdeeds of the body'. Without doubt, this is accomplished through the empowering of the Holy Spirit, but putting sin to death is still our responsibility. 'Put to death, therefore, whatever belongs to your earthly nature; sexual immorality, impurity, lust, evil desires and greed, which is idolatry' (Col. 3:5). The 'therefore' refers to the radical break with the world of sin, which has come about through our union with Christ. In Christ's death we have died to the old sinful patterns of living. While we live in this world there will be remaining corruption in us, but we have the promise that the Holy Spirit will help us, waging war against our old nature. Killing off sin in us is like clearing away the rubble on a building site to make room for the new structure. It is impossible for the old rubble to form part of the new building. 'You also, like living stones, are being built into a spiritual house to be a holy priesthood, offering spiritual sacrifices acceptable to God through Jesus Christ' (1 Peter 2:5).

SCRIPTURE READING: ROMANS 8:5-17

June 7

Sanctification

Westminster Catechism Question #35:

What is sanctification? *Answer*: Sanctification is the work of God's free grace, by which he renews every part of us in his image, enabling us increasingly to die to sin and to live for righteousness.

Theme verse: 'For if you live according to the sinful nature, you will die; but if by the Spirit you put to death the misdeeds of the body, you will live' (Rom. 8:13).

Throughout church history God has dealt with his people not only individually, but also corporately: Noah and his family, Abraham and his family, Israel as a nation, and now with his Church. Every local church is a microcosm of the whole Church and every believer needs to be aligned to a body of believers. This is essential for our sanctification because we derive so much spiritual benefit from participation in the body of Christ. The interdependence of members in a local church is vividly expressed in the text, 'From him the whole body, joined and held together by every supporting ligament, grows and builds itself up in love, as each part does its work' (Eph. 4:16). We are taught together through the preaching. We benefit together from the Lord's Supper and baptism. We learn from one another in fellowship. We serve together. We rejoice together and we suffer together. We gain inspiration from leaders and the example of godly members in the church. We are encouraged and corrected by fellow believers. 'Therefore encourage one another and build each other up, just as in fact you are doing' (1 Thess. 5:11). For our sanctification we need the blessing of fellowship and interaction with God's people. 'As iron sharpens iron, so one man sharpens another' (Prov. 27:17).

SCRIPTURE READING: EPHESIANS 4:1-16

June 8

Sanctification

Westminster Catechism Question #35:

What is sanctification? *Answer*: Sanctification is the work of God's free grace, by which he renews every part of us in his image, enabling us increasingly to die to sin and to live for righteousness.

Theme verse: 'For if you live according to the sinful nature, you will die; but if by the Spirit you put to death the misdeeds of the body, you will live' (Rom. 8:13).

God has called us to be conformed to the image of Christ. In sanctification the Holy Spirit gradually and progressively transforms us to the likeness of Christ, for we 'are being transformed into his likeness with ever-increasing glory, which comes from the Lord, who is the Spirit' (2 Cor. 3:18). The Lord accomplishes this change in us by renewing our minds. 'Do not conform any longer to the pattern of this world, but be transformed by the renewing of your mind' (Rom. 12:2). The word 'transformation' is the equivalent of 'metamorphosis' in English, denoting a change which is inward, permeating and thorough, in the same way a caterpillar is transformed into a butterfly. How are we made to be like Christ? The answer is that we are conformed to him in the attributes of love, meekness, humility, patience, gentleness, love for righteousness and hatred for evil. Practically, Christ-likeness can only take place as we study our actions in detail and compare them with the life and example of our Lord Jesus and the requirements of God's Word. To advance in holiness requires critical self-examination. But we must never grow tired of pursuing such an excellent ideal: 'Therefore we do not lose heart. Though outwardly we are wasting away, yet inwardly we are being renewed day by day' (2 Cor. 4:16).

SCRIPTURE READING: 2 CORINTHIANS 3:7-18

June 9

A LIFE OF SANCTIFICATION

(WEEK 23: DAY 6)

Sanctification

Westminster Catechism Question #35:

What is sanctification? *Answer*: Sanctification is the work of God's free grace, by which he renews every part of us in his image, enabling us increasingly to die to sin and to live for righteousness.

Theme verse: 'For if you live according to the sinful nature, you will die; but if by the Spirit you put to death the misdeeds of the body, you will live' (Rom. 8:13).

In our spiritual lives there is never a time when we can be caught off guard. This has been likened to the professional soldier who is always in training and always on the alert (2 Tim. 2:3), and the athlete who has a disciplined conditioning schedule (1 Cor. 9:24). The Apostle Paul exhorts Timothy to train himself to be godly. Just like weight-lifting, cardiovascular training, stretching, and other exercises to keep our body strong, there are spiritual disciplines and habits which keep us from being weak and flabby Christians. 'If anyone competes as an athlete, he does not receive the victor's crown unless he competes according to the rules' (2 Tim. 2:5). A disciplined Christian lifestyle includes daily private prayer and regular times of praying with others, and regular time devoted to the study and meditation on the Word of God, allowing us opportunity for self-examination in light of God's Word. The Apostle Paul was an example of this kind of lifestyle and commended it to us: 'You know all about my way of life' (2 Tim. 3:10). We too can benefit from the example set by Paul of a life of patience, love and endurance. 'Everyone who competes in the games goes into strict training. They do it to get a crown that will not last; but we do it to get a crown that will last forever' (1 Cor. 9:25).

SCRIPTURE READING: 1 CORINTHIANS 9:19-27

June 10
SANCTIFICATION THROUGH TRIALS
(WEEK 23: DAY 7)

Sanctification

Westminster Catechism Question #35:

What is sanctification? *Answer*: Sanctification is the work of God's free grace, by which he renews every part of us in his image, enabling us increasingly to die to sin and to live for righteousness.

Theme verse: 'For if you live according to the sinful nature, you will die; but if by the Spirit you put to death the misdeeds of the body, you will live' (Rom. 8:13).

God sends us trials to drive us closer in dependence on him. 'Consider it pure joy, my brothers, whenever you face trials of many kinds, because you know that the testing of your faith develops perseverance ... so that you may be mature and complete' (James 1:2-4). The cardinal book in the Bible on this theme is Job. Job suffered extremely and in his trials made great progress in his life of sanctification. His friends were sure that Job was being punished for some sin he had committed. They attempted to compel some confession of specific sin from him. However, we are informed at the beginning of the book that Job was a blameless and upright man who feared God. He was not being punished. His trials were not permitted in order to correct him in the sense that he needed a radical change in his lifestyle. Instead, he was being tested in order that his sufferings would develop a sanctified life of deepening dependence on God. On the other hand, there are times when the Lord does punish us for our sin. King David was acutely conscious of the fact that his later trials were sent to chasten him. 'Create in me a pure heart, O God, and renew a steadfast spirit within me' (Ps. 51:10). Whether the Lord tests or chastens us, his intention is to humble us, make us like Jesus, and grow us in sanctification.

SCRIPTURE READING: JAMES 1:1-8

June 11

Death Benefits

Westminster Catechism Question #37:

What benefits do believers receive from Christ at death?
Answer: At their death the souls of believers are made perfect in holiness and immediately pass into glory; and their bodies, being still united to Christ, rest in their graves until the resurrection.

Theme verse: 'We ... would prefer to be away from the body and at home with the Lord' (2 Cor. 5:8).

We would all like to know what will happen to us when we die. Unfortunately, most people have no assurance of their future state. Even believers in Christ can be confused about the Bible's teaching concerning the soul at the time of death, and the future of the body. The catechism answer above clearly explains the Bible's comforting truths to these questions. The souls of believers immediately enter into the glorious presence of the Lord. Their earthly bodies are left behind to decay. The souls of believers remain in heaven with the Lord until his return to earth. When Jesus comes to judge the world he will resurrect their mortal, earthly bodies and clothe them with an immortal, spiritual body. It does not matter whether a Christian's lifeless body has been buried, cremated or lost at sea. When Christ returns we will be given a new, immortal body which cannot be subjected to any form of decay. With this new body, believers will be equipped to honour the Lord in the new heavens and new earth for ever. In our theme verse, the Apostle Paul states that even though he will have to leave his earthly body behind at the time of his death, he would prefer to be in heaven with the Lord, waiting for the day the Lord returns to give believers their immortal, incorruptible bodies.

SCRIPTURE READING: 2 CORINTHIANS 5:1-10

June 12

Death Benefits

Westminster Catechism Question #37:

What benefits do believers receive from Christ at death?
Answer: At their death the souls of believers are made perfect in holiness and immediately pass into glory; and their bodies, being still united to Christ, rest in their graves until the resurrection.

Theme verse: 'We ... would prefer to be away from the body and at home with the Lord' (2 Cor. 5:8).

The Lord knows how weak we are. We should be able to believe his words without all sorts of proofs to comfort us along the way. But God stoops to our weakness and gives us bread and wine as visible reminders of his death for us. He provided the rainbow to assure us that he will never again flood the earth and destroy us. He answered Gideon's request for a fleece. He gave the people of Israel a pillar of cloud by day and of fire by night to assure them of his constant presence. When we need assurance that there is life after this life — that is, life after death, God has given us the best possible visible proof. He raised Jesus from the dead. Christ's resurrection is the guarantee of our resurrection. Jesus is the first to be resurrected from the dead never to die again. 'But Christ has indeed been raised from the dead, the firstfruits of those who have fallen asleep' (1 Cor. 15:20). This means that Jesus is the first to be resurrected in the harvest of Christian people. If Christ has been raised, we will be raised as well. It was also kind of the Lord not to rush off to heaven after he was raised. He was seen by Peter and the twelve apostles, then by more than 500 believers at the same time (1 Cor. 15:5-6). 'For as in Adam all die, so in Christ all will be made alive' (1 Cor. 15:22).

SCRIPTURE READING: 1 CORINTHIANS 15:1-19

June 13

Death Benefits

Westminster Catechism Question #37:

What benefits do believers receive from Christ at death?
Answer: At their death the souls of believers are made perfect in holiness and immediately pass into glory; and their bodies, being still united to Christ, rest in their graves until the resurrection.

Theme verse: 'We ... would prefer to be away from the body and at home with the Lord' (2 Cor. 5:8).

The Bible teaches that at the moment of death the souls of believers immediately enter into the presence of God. It may be difficult to picture how a person can be in heaven without a body. Even the Apostle Paul seemed to share our uneasiness about the idea of not having a physical body in heaven: 'Meanwhile we groan, longing to be clothed with our heavenly dwelling, because when we are clothed, we will not be found naked ... because we do not wish to be unclothed but to be clothed with our heavenly dwelling' (2 Cor. 5:2-4). Paul had this on his mind when he wrote to the church at Philippi: 'I am torn between the two: I desire to depart and be with Christ, which is better by far: but it is more necessary for you that I remain in the body' (Phil. 1:23-24). Paul was happy with either option. He would love to be with Christ, even temporarily without a physical body, but he was also happy to carry on working for the Lord as long as he was useful. That should also be our attitude. While we are still alive on planet earth, let us serve and exercise our bodies for useful service to the King. But let us always be ready to leave these temporary bodies behind and join the angels and departed saints in heaven, who live in a world which is better by far.

SCRIPTURE READING: PHILIPPIANS 1:19-30

June 14
THE RESURRECTION BODY
(WEEK 24: DAY 4)

Death Benefits

Westminster Catechism Question #37:

What benefits do believers receive from Christ at death?
Answer: At their death the souls of believers are made perfect in holiness and immediately pass into glory; and their bodies, being still united to Christ, rest in their graves until the resurrection.

Theme verse: 'We ... would prefer to be away from the body and at home with the Lord' (2 Cor. 5:8).

The Bible tells us that when a Christian dies the body is like a seed of wheat. Although our bodies decay and are destroyed, the Lord will take seeds (perhaps molecules) from our earthly bodies and infuse them with new, eternal life. Just as a seed which is dropped into the ground dies in order to produce a new plant, so our mortal bodies will flower into powerful, resurrected bodies at the Lord's command. 'So will it be with the resurrection of the dead. The body that is sown is perishable, it is raised imperishable. It is sown in dishonor, it is raised in glory; it is sown in weakness, it is raised in power, it is sown a natural body; it is raised a spiritual body' (1 Cor. 15:42-44). Adam was formed from the dust of the ground, and as with Adam, our earthly bodies return to the dust. Jesus, 'the last Adam', came to us from heaven. 'And just as we have borne the likeness of the earthly man, so shall we bear the likeness of the man from heaven' (1 Cor. 15:49). Although when we die we shall be absent from our physical body, Jesus will one day return. On that great day we will receive new bodies that will be united to our spirit. The spiritual bodies we receive will be incorruptible, powerful, heavenly and full of glory and honour. They will serve us well in giving praise to him who is seated on the throne.

SCRIPTURE READING: 1 CORINTHIANS 15:35-49

June 15

Death Benefits

Westminster Catechism Question #37:

What benefits do believers receive from Christ at death?
Answer: At their death the souls of believers are made perfect in
holiness and immediately pass into glory; and their bodies, being
still united to Christ, rest in their graves until the resurrection.

Theme verse: 'We ... would prefer to be away from the body and
at home with the Lord' (2 Cor. 5:8).

It is understandable how people can be confused about the resurrection body. We all know that bodies of deceased persons are still
buried in the local cemetery. The confusion becomes even greater
when we read two seemingly opposing doctrines in the Bible. Our
theme verse informs us that when we are 'away from the body' we
will be 'at home with the Lord' (2 Cor. 5:8). We read that at the return of Christ believers will accompany Jesus to earth: 'we believe
that God will bring with Jesus those who have fallen asleep in
him' (1 Thess. 4:14). But then we are told, 'The Lord himself will
come down from heaven, with a loud command ... and the dead
in Christ will rise first' (1 Thess. 4:16). How is it that believers
return with Christ and yet are raised by him from the dead? The
answer is that at death the souls of believers in Christ are taken to
be with the Lord in heaven. The Scriptures teach that Christians
already in heaven will return to earth with the Saviour when he
comes to judge the world. At that time the Lord will raise their
mortal, earthly bodies and give them immortal, spiritual bodies.
When they descend from heaven to earth, their bodies will ascend
from the earth to join the Saviour in the air! 'Therefore, encourage each other with these words' (1 Thess. 4:18).

SCRIPTURE READING: 1 THESSALONIANS 4:13-18

June 16
RAISED FROM THE DEAD
(WEEK 24: DAY 6)

Death Benefits

Westminster Catechism Question #37:

What benefits do believers receive from Christ at death?
Answer: At their death the souls of believers are made perfect in holiness and immediately pass into glory; and their bodies, being still united to Christ, rest in their graves until the resurrection.

Theme verse: 'We ... would prefer to be away from the body and at home with the Lord' (2 Cor. 5:8).

Our faith and hope as Christians rest on whether the resurrection of Christ is true. 'If Christ has not been raised, our preaching is useless and so is your faith' (1 Cor. 15:14). The proof that Jesus is the true God is that he 'was declared with power to be the Son of God by his resurrection from the dead: Jesus Christ our Lord' (Rom. 1:4). Christ's authority to rule over all things is because 'Christ died and returned to life so that he might be the Lord of both the dead and the living' (Rom. 14:9). If he is to be our Saviour, cleansing us from our sin and declaring us righteous in his sight, then his resurrection is essential: 'He was delivered over to death for our sins and was raised to life for our justification' (Rom. 4:25). For certain, our ultimate resurrection is tied up with Christ's resurrection: 'If the Spirit of him who raised Jesus from the dead is living in you, he who raised Christ from the dead will also give life to your mortal bodies through his Spirit, who lives in you' (Rom. 8:11). All of the blessings of the Christian life depend on the reality of Christ's resurrection. If there is to be life after this life, then we rest on this central theme: 'Christ has indeed been raised from the dead' (1 Cor. 15:20).

SCRIPTURE READING: ROMANS 4:16-25

June 17

Death Benefits

Westminster Catechism Question #37:

What benefits do believers receive from Christ at death?
Answer: At their death the souls of believers are made perfect in
holiness and immediately pass into glory; and their bodies, being
still united to Christ, rest in their graves until the resurrection.

Theme verse: 'We ... would prefer to be away from the body and
at home with the Lord' (2 Cor. 5:8).

God made a beautiful world: its seas and rivers, its sunrises and
sunsets, and its mountains and valleys. But as beautiful as the
world is, there are many things in it to remind us that it is not
home. A home should be a place of comfort and consistency. The
world is constantly changing, moving, altering and passing away.
A home should be a place of joy. The world is full of people with
difficulties with their marriages, children and siblings, with money concerns, health issues and many other trials. A home should
be full of life. The world is full of people who have lost loved ones
on the battlefield, in car accidents, or to disease. A world so full
of trials and disappointments is no place to call home. God has
an answer to the disappointment of this world. He has a home
prepared for those who love him (John 14:2), a place where the
changeless Jesus waits for us. Jesus said: 'Come to me, all you who
are weary and burdened, and I will give you rest' (Matt. 11:28).
He invites us to a permanent home filled with kindness, joy and
eternal communion with the Lord. 'There will be no more death
or mourning or crying or pain, for the old order of things has
passed away' (Rev. 21:4). Jesus informed us that his Father's house
has many rooms. Is one reserved for you?

SCRIPTURE READING: JOHN 14:1-14

June 18

Obedience

Westminster Catechism Question #39:

What is the duty which God requires of man? *Answer*: The duty which God requires of man is obedience to his revealed will.

Theme verse: 'He has showed you, O man, what is good. And what does the Lord require of you? To act justly and to love mercy and to walk humbly with your God' (Micah 6:8).

There was once a man who asked the Lord Jesus a very sombre question. 'Lord, are only a few people going to be saved?' Jesus could tell that such a question had prompted keen interest in all those assembled to hear him. So Jesus took the opportunity to direct everyone's thinking to their clear responsibility. He urged them forcefully, 'Make every effort to enter through the narrow door, because many, I tell you, will try to enter and will not be able to' (Luke 13:24). Whether few or many are saved is God's prerogative and should not be the issue that primarily concerns us. What is important is that we seek to enter the kingdom of God through what Jesus describes as 'the narrow door' or 'the narrow gate'. 'I am the gate; whoever enters through me will be saved' (John 10:9). Now is the accepted time; now is the day of salvation. When Jesus died he paid our debt to God and bore our punishment at the cross. The Lord has also told us to strive to enter that gate. There is a direction we must choose to go, even though it is filled with testing and trial. While our own efforts can never save us, through the power of the Holy Spirit, the Lord requires that we 'make every effort to be found spotless, blameless, and at peace with him' (2 Peter 3:14). People who love Christ are not lazy; they strive to obey God's revealed will.

SCRIPTURE READING: LUKE 13:22-30

June 19

Obedience

Westminster Catechism Question #39:

What is the duty which God requires of man? *Answer*: The duty which God requires of man is obedience to his revealed will.

Theme verse: 'He has showed you, O man, what is good. And what does the Lord require of you? To act justly and to love mercy and to walk humbly with your God' (Micah 6:8).

We have all heard about spiritual leaders who are caught committing the very sins they preach against. The Pharisees at the time of Christ fit into this category. Jesus noted it: 'On the outside you appear to people as righteous but on the inside you are full of hypocrisy and wickedness' (Matt. 23:28). They tended to make a great show of their acts of worship, but Jesus could tell they were often more interested in how the world saw them than true devotion. Jesus denounced them with harsh words: 'You snakes! You brood of vipers! How will you escape being condemned to hell?' (Matt. 23:33). Why was our gracious Lord so severe in his words since the Pharisees were a seemingly moral and decent group? He was offended that that they were more concerned about appearing religious than with a true relationship with the Lord. This is a call for self-examination. Do we attend worship, and if we do, what is our motive? Do we attend simply out of habit? Do we pray? If we do, what is the energy level of our prayers? Do we pray earnestly, as Elijah did? (James 5:17). Do we study God's Word? If we do, what is our level of interest in discovering God's will within its pages? If the Lord loves authentic faith, we are wise to take inventory to see if our faith passes the test.

SCRIPTURE READING: MATTHEW 23:1-12

June 20

Obedience

Westminster Catechism Question #39:

What is the duty which God requires of man? *Answer*: The duty which God requires of man is obedience to his revealed will.

Theme verse: 'He has showed you, O man, what is good. And what does the Lord require of you? To act justly and to love mercy and to walk humbly with your God' (Micah 6:8).

In 1 Samuel 15, King Saul was commanded by God to enter into battle against the Amalekites. Saul was ordered to take no prisoners as a divine demonstration of God's judgement against wickedness. But Saul did not listen to the Lord. Instead, he kept the Amalekite king and also spared the best of the sheep and cattle. Saul was proud of his skill in battle and anticipated the acclaim he would receive from his own people for his stunning victory. When Samuel the prophet arrived on the scene Saul deliberately lied to him, telling him that the animals had been spared to sacrifice to the Lord. It was pure hypocrisy. Saul was not interested in offering acceptable worship in an attitude of submission, obedience and true devotion; he was interested in personal acclaim. He blamed his soldiers, rather than himself, for coveting the animals which had been taken as booty. So Samuel prophesied against him: 'Does the Lord delight in burnt offerings and sacrifices as much as in obeying the voice of the Lord? To obey is better than sacrifice, and to heed is better than the fat of rams' (1 Sam. 15:22). Saul's rebellion was serious and his disobedience to God's revealed will stripped him of his kingdom. What God requires of us, more than anything else, is humble obedience to his revealed will.

SCRIPTURE READING: 1 SAMUEL 15

June 21

Obedience

Westminster Catechism Question #39:

What is the duty which God requires of man? *Answer*: The duty which God requires of man is obedience to his revealed will.

Theme verse: 'He has showed you, O man, what is good. And what does the Lord require of you? To act justly and to love mercy and to walk humbly with your God' (Micah 6:8).

The well-known story of Abraham offering his son Isaac as a sacrifice is a story of the beauty of obedience. When God commanded Abraham to offer his only son in sacrifice Abraham promptly obeyed, for 'early the next morning, Abraham got up and saddled his donkey' (Gen. 22:3). Abraham, we are told in the book of Hebrews, 'reasoned that God could raise the dead' (Heb. 11:19), and therefore, obeyed unflinchingly. When he was about to slay Isaac the angel of the Lord called out to him. 'Do not lay a hand on the boy,' he said, 'Do not do anything to him. Now I know that you fear God' (Gen. 22:12). A ram was offered in place of Isaac as a substitute for sin, pre-figuring the substitution of Christ for sinners. Tremendous blessing flowed from Abraham's obedience. God said to him: 'I will surely bless you and make your descendants as numerous as the stars in the sky and as the sand on the seashore' (Gen. 22:17). Abraham became the father of many nations, all because of obedience. In the same way, Jesus was greatly blessed because of his perfect obedience to his Father's will. The Father 'exalted him to the highest place and gave him the name that is above every name' (Phil. 2:9). God's promise is to bless all those who are obedient to his will.

SCRIPTURE READING: GENESIS 22:1-19

June 22
HYPOCRISY FROM WITHIN
(WEEK 25: DAY 5)

Obedience

Westminster Catechism Question #39:

What is the duty which God requires of man? *Answer*: The duty which God requires of man is obedience to his revealed will.

Theme verse: 'He has showed you, O man, what is good. And what does the Lord require of you? To act justly and to love mercy and to walk humbly with your God' (Micah 6:8).

There are times when God does not wait for Judgement Day to execute his judgement. Ananias and Sapphira were members of the early church. We are told that they sold a piece of property and pretended to give all the proceeds of the sale to the apostles for the benefit of the believers. In reality, however, they lied about this, for they kept back part of the money for themselves. The couple tried to make their sin appear as an act of Spirit-filled love. But then Peter said, 'Ananias, how is it that Satan has so filled your heart that you lied to the Holy Spirit and have kept back some of the money you received for the land?' (Acts 5:3). Consequently, both Ananias and Sapphira died that very day by the hand of God. The deceit of Ananias and Sapphira, which happened when the Christian church was just beginning in Jerusalem, and the severe penalty they received, are recorded as a warning for the entire New Testament church. We read, 'Great fear seized the whole church and all who heard about these events' (Acts 5:11). There are dangers that can come upon us from the outside. But many attacks by Satan on the church come from within the congregation itself. If left uncorrected, hypocrisy destroys the church's witness and vitality. It deadens the Spirit's freedom to bless. Above all, God hates it.

SCRIPTURE READING: ACTS 5:1-11

June 23
THE ALL-SUFFICIENT SCRIPTURES
(WEEK 25: DAY 6)

Obedience

Westminster Catechism Question #39:

What is the duty which God requires of man? *Answer*: The duty which God requires of man is obedience to his revealed will.

Theme verse: 'He has showed you, O man, what is good. And what does the Lord require of you? To act justly and to love mercy and to walk humbly with your God' (Micah 6:8).

It is important to remind ourselves that we can only learn obedience to God's revealed will from the Word of God itself. Listening to good preaching, receiving counsel from others and our own common sense can be valuable helps, but only to the degree that they line up with Scripture. The Scriptures carry divine authority. When the prophets spoke they would often introduce their proclamations by stating that 'the word of the Lord' had come to them. Jesus would declare, 'A new command I give to you'. The Scriptures are sufficient to thoroughly equip us for every good work (2 Tim. 3:17), so that we are able 'to act justly and to love mercy and to walk humbly' with God. When we wonder which way to turn in order to know God's will, we should always turn back to the study and meditation of Scripture. 'The law of the Lord is perfect, reviving the soul. The statutes of the Lord are trustworthy, making wise the simple. The precepts of the Lord are right, giving joy to the heart' (Ps. 19:7-8). The nineteenth psalm carries this theme further by speaking of the preciousness and sweetness of the Word of God and its ability to warn us when we are straying from the Lord's appointed path. We do well when we hold fast to the words of God: 'in keeping them there is great reward' (Ps. 19:11).

SCRIPTURE READING: PSALM 19

June 24
DOING GOOD
(WEEK 25: DAY 7)

Obedience

Westminster Catechism Question #39:

What is the duty which God requires of man? *Answer*: The duty which God requires of man is obedience to his revealed will.

Theme verse: 'He has showed you, O man, what is good. And what does the Lord require of you? To act justly and to love mercy and to walk humbly with your God' (Micah 6:8).

Most villages in Israel seem to have been visited by the Saviour during his earthly ministry. His life was one of constant, yet un-hurried, movement and activity. We are told that 'he went around doing good and healing all who were under the power of the devil, because God was with him' (Acts 10:38). Christ's life is described as one of constant giving. He was a preacher and his message pointed people to eternal life through belief in his name. He healed personally, touching the leper with his own finger and vis-iting the sick bed to touch and cure. Despite many obstacles and dangers the Lord Jesus carried on serving others, anointed by the Holy Spirit and motivated to do his Father's will. Only Jesus can say unreservedly, 'I have set you an example that you should do as I have done for you' (John 13:15). God has called his children to 'act justly and to love mercy'. This is clearly his will for our lives. Life is too short to consume our energies on ourselves when the world is longing for the witness of Christ's love through us. It is true that to live as Christ did is costly. He denied himself and his followers are called to a life of servant hood. But it is worth it. 'To this you were called, because Christ suffered for you, leaving you an example, that you should follow in his steps' (1 Peter 2:21).

SCRIPTURE READING: ACTS 10:34-48

PART 3:

THE MORAL LAW

June 25
The greatest commandment
(week 26: day 1)

The Ten Commandments

Westminster Catechism Question #42:

What is the sum of the Ten Commandments? *Answer*: The sum of the Ten Commandments is: To love the Lord our God with all our heart, with all our soul, with all our strength and with all our mind; and our neighbor as ourselves.

Theme verse: 'Jesus replied: "Love the Lord your God with all your heart and with all your soul and with all your mind." This is the first and greatest commandment. And the second is like it: "Love your neighbor as yourself." All the Law and Prophets hang on these two commandments' (Matt. 22:37-40).

Jesus was asked on several occasions which commandment was the most important. His answer, which is our theme verse, was a call to the total surrender of our entire beings to the Lord: heart, soul, strength and mind. First, to manifest a deep love for God requires a dramatic change of our hearts. Jesus calls us to practise our love for God not just by loving those who are easy to love, such as family or friends, but to love all our neighbours, even the unlovely ones. Secondly, the soul is the centre of our passions and the source of our energy and focus. Jesus told us that our passions must be redirected so that our focus is on God. Thirdly, Jesus called us to use our physical and spiritual strength in this all-important pursuit of God (Mark 12:30), who is supremely worth loving. Finally, Jesus told us to love God with our minds so that our thought patterns will be 'renewed in knowledge in the image of its Creator' (Col. 3:10). Loving God so completely, with heart, soul, strength and mind is a high standard. Only those who are born from above can fulfil these commandments to any degree. In our own strength we lack the love necessary to keep the requirements of the greatest commandment. But in the power of the Holy Spirit we can, and in so doing, keep all Ten Commandments as well.

Scripture reading: Matthew 22:23-40

June 26
NOT FAR FROM THE KINGDOM
(WEEK 26: DAY 2)

The Ten Commandments

Westminster Catechism Question #42:

What is the sum of the Ten Commandments? *Answer*: The sum of the Ten Commandments is: To love the Lord our God with all our heart, with all our soul, with all our strength and with all our mind; and our neighbor as ourselves.

Theme verse: 'Jesus replied: "Love the Lord your God with all your heart and with all your soul and with all your mind." This is the first and greatest commandment. And the second is like it: "Love your neighbor as yourself." All the Law and Prophets hang on these two commandments' (Matt. 22:37-40).

Our theme verse was prompted by a question from one of the Jewish teachers of the law. He asked Jesus, 'Of all the commandments, which is the most important?' (Mark 12:28). Then Jesus responded by telling him the greatest commandment. At this, the teacher of the law heartily agreed, and mentioned that loving God and neighbour is 'more important than all burnt offerings and sacrifices' (Mark 12:33). This discussion probably took place in the temple court where burnt offerings were sacrificed. Offerings and sacrifices at the temple were a major part of Jewish religious practice at that time. For many of the religious leaders and people the offerings and sacrifices were of greater importance than a right attitude of heart towards God. Ceremony was everything. Reverence and devotion towards God were less important. When the teacher of the law agreed with Jesus, the Lord said to him, 'You are not far from the kingdom of God' (Mark 12:34). Jesus could see that the man intelligently embraced the truth of the gospel. Jesus was now urging him to take the next step and enter this kingdom where one leaves behind ceremony and human effort as a way to appease God, in order to live in the power and joy of God's grace. This man realized that God required his full devotion. What does God require of you?
SCRIPTURE READING: MARK 12:28-34

June 27
OUR MORAL COMPASS
(WEEK 26: DAY 3)

The Ten Commandments

Westminster Catechism Question #42:

What is the sum of the Ten Commandments? *Answer*: The sum of the Ten Commandments is: To love the Lord our God with all our heart, with all our soul, with all our strength and with all our mind; and our neighbor as ourselves.

Theme verse: 'Jesus replied: "Love the Lord your God with all your heart and with all your soul and with all your mind." This is the first and greatest commandment. And the second is like it: "Love your neighbor as yourself." All the Law and Prophets hang on these two commandments' (Matt. 22:37-40).

The Ten Commandments have a profound influence on all believers. Not only are the commandments used to bring about a conviction of sin before conversion, but they are also essential if we are to progress in holiness and Christ-likeness after conversion. The Ten Commandments serve as a powerful daily guide by which to live. The Apostle Paul tells us that the Ten Commandments taught him that he was a sinner: 'I would not have known what sin was except through the law … if the law had not said, "Do not covet"' (Rom. 7:7). Believers in Christ are now under greater obligation to live according to these moral laws because we have been united to Christ and sanctified by the Holy Spirit. God has used his laws to convict us of sin and now he provides them to us as our moral compass. If we are married to Christ we want to please him by observing carefully what he loves and hates, and by avoiding everything that offends the majesty and holiness of his character. Our adoption into the family of God carries with it the obligation to honour the Lord by living as a true child of God. Above all, the privilege we enjoy of possessing the gift of the Holy Spirit as he guides and teaches us, means that we have an ability now to love God's law from the heart and the power to keep it.

SCRIPTURE READING: DEUTERONOMY 5:6-21

June 28

The Ten Commandments

Westminster Catechism Question #42:

What is the sum of the Ten Commandments? *Answer*: The sum of the Ten Commandments is: To love the Lord our God with all our heart, with all our soul, with all our strength and with all our mind; and our neighbor as ourselves.

Theme verse: 'Jesus replied: "Love the Lord your God with all your heart and with all your soul and with all your mind." This is the first and greatest commandment. And the second is like it: "Love your neighbor as yourself." All the Law and Prophets hang on these two commandments' (Matt. 22:37-40).

When God is emphasizing what is important to him he knows how to get our attention. That is certainly the case when he gave us the Ten Commandments. The Lord made Mount Sinai his throne and surrounded it with thunder, lightning, a thick cloud and an impenetrable darkness. All this was accompanied by very loud trumpet blasts (Exod. 19:16). The whole mountain trembled violently and smoke billowed from it as from a furnace. The people of Israel were seized with fear. Then the Lord spoke face to face to the people out of the fire from the mountain (Deut. 5:4). God's speech to the people was not in a whisper but with a very loud voice to the whole assembly. Nothing like it has ever been known before or since. 'Has any other people heard the voice of God speaking out of fire, as you have, and lived?' (Deut. 4:33). The point God was making was that the giving of the Ten Commandments was special and unique. To make it even more special, God wrote these ten laws on two stone tablets himself. One tablet he gave to the people and one was for the Lord to keep. Here was a binding agreement between two parties. Why are the Ten Commandments so special? It is because they reflect the holy character of our God. And God wants us to reflect his character.

SCRIPTURE READING: EXODUS 19:16-25

June 29
LOVING OUR NEIGHBOUR
(WEEK 26: DAY 5)

The Ten Commandments

Westminster Catechism Question #42:

What is the sum of the Ten Commandments? *Answer*: The sum of the Ten Commandments is: To love the Lord our God with all our heart, with all our soul, with all our strength and with all our mind; and our neighbor as ourselves.

Theme verse: 'Jesus replied: "Love the Lord your God with all your heart and with all your soul and with all your mind." This is the first and greatest commandment. And the second is like it: "Love your neighbor as yourself." All the Law and Prophets hang on these two commandments' (Matt. 22:37-40).

We cannot improve on the command to 'love the Lord your God with all your heart and with all your soul and with all your mind.' If we love God with our entire being it follows that we will not break his rules. Notice that the first four commandments focus on our relationship to God and the other six commandments on our relationship to people. If we honour God by living according to the first four vertical commands, it logically follows that we will have a righteous concern and love for our fellow humans and live out the six horizontal commands. Some have reasoned that they do love God but admit that they have less love for their obstinate, difficult neighbour. But the Ten Commandments are a unit and if you break one command you break them all. 'For whoever keeps the whole law and yet stumbles at just one point is guilty of breaking all of it' (James 2:10). It is the law of our King. If you put a crack into one of his stone tablets that crack runs through the whole tablet so that it falls apart. None of us break just one part of the law. We are only fooling ourselves if we think we can love God and not our neighbour. In fact, our theme verse makes clear that Jesus added the command 'love your neighbor as yourself' as the indicator whether your love for God is real.

SCRIPTURE READING: JAMES 2:1-13

194

June 30
THE GOOD SAMARITAN
(WEEK 26: DAY 6)

The Ten Commandments

Westminster Catechism Question #42:

What is the sum of the Ten Commandments? *Answer*: The sum of the Ten Commandments is: To love the Lord our God with all our heart, with all our soul, with all our strength and with all our mind; and our neighbor as ourselves.

Theme verse: 'Jesus replied: "Love the Lord your God with all your heart and with all your soul and with all your mind." This is the first and greatest commandment. And the second is like it: "Love your neighbor as yourself." All the Law and Prophets hang on these two commandments' (Matt. 22:37-40).

In the Parable of the Good Samaritan a Jewish man is badly beaten by robbers, leaving him half dead. Both a priest and a Levite, two respected Jewish leaders, returning home from religious duties in Jerusalem, passed by but refused to help. Both had their excuses: robbers were near, and they might be assaulted themselves. To be found near the man might cast suspicion on them. But then a Samaritan, a despised 'half-breed', comes to the rescue of the poor Jewish victim. It is difficult for us to appreciate the force of Christ's illustration, since we cannot enter into the feeling of hostility that existed between the Jews and their northern neighbours, the Samaritans. Both cultures were separated by race, culture and religion. The Samaritans were cursed publicly in the synagogue with the prayer that they might have no part in the resurrection. The Samaritans hated the Jews in return. Yet here, in Christ's parable, the Samaritan shows unusual compassion which demanded both his money and time. Christ's application is that we all are like the selfish priest and Levite until the beauty of his transforming grace comes to us, giving us an ability to love others that knows no national boundaries or prejudice. Only then can we say that we love God and our neighbours as ourselves.

SCRIPTURE READING: LUKE 10:25-37

July 1

The Ten Commandments

Westminster Catechism Question #42:

What is the sum of the Ten Commandments? *Answer*: The sum of the Ten Commandments is: To love the Lord our God with all our heart, with all our soul, with all our strength and with all our mind; and our neighbor as ourselves.

Theme verse: 'Jesus replied: "Love the Lord your God with all your heart and with all your soul and with all your mind." This is the first and greatest commandment. And the second is like it: "Love your neighbor as yourself." All the Law and Prophets hang on these two commandments' (Matt. 22:37-40).

True love finds its direction in the Law of God. Love is not a warm and undefined feeling; it shows itself by the way we express our love to God and our neighbour. That expression of love is through the keeping of the Ten Commandments. The commands will never be abolished. They are the norm for Christian conduct. 'Let no debt remain outstanding, except the continuing debt to love one another, for he who loves his fellowman has fulfilled the law' (Rom. 13:8). Jesus said to his disciples: 'If you love me, you will obey what I command' (John 14:15). And the Apostle John declared: 'We know that we have come to know him if we keep his commandments' (1 John 2:3). Of course, now that Christ has entered our world, we look to him as the one who, 'born under the law', perfectly fulfils the law of love. Jesus kept all of the commandments perfectly; in fact, he fulfilled them through his sinless life and sacrificial death. By his grace and power we can live a life of love. 'The commandments, "Do not commit adultery," "Do not murder," "Do not steal," "Do not covet," and whatever other commandment there may be, are summed up in this one rule: "Love your neighbor as yourself." Love does no harm to its neighbor. Therefore love is the fulfillment of the law' (Rom. 13:9-10).

SCRIPTURE READING: ROMANS 13:8-14

July 2

GOD AS OUR GOD

(WEEK 27: DAY 1)

The only true God

Westminster Catechism Question #46:

What is required in the First Commandment? *Answer*: The First Commandment requires us to know and acknowledge God to be the only true God, and our God, and to worship and glorify him accordingly.

Theme verse: 'You shall have no other gods before me' (Exod. 20:3).

Every Christian is required to know and acknowledge God to be the only true God. The first command speaks to each of us on an individual level. You shall have no other gods before me. This commandment is not, first of all, to the Israelites as a nation or to the church. It is to be applied to every single life. This commandment is first because it is the foundation of our faith. We must give the triune God pre-eminence in our lives and he must be foremost over all other created things. The Bible teaches that there is only one God, the true God of the Bible, who is unique, personal, plural (meaning there are three distinguishable persons within the Godhead), that God is a Spirit, eternal, over and above all things, unchangeable, holy in his being and all his actions, loving, and that he is our Creator, Ruler, and Judge. A recent survey taken in Western Europe found seventy-five per cent of adults acknowledged the existence of God. But when those same people were asked if they believed in the God as defined in the Bible the percentages dropped to thirty-two per cent. For Christians, however, the God of the Bible is our God and we adore him. Hezekiah's prayer is the believer's prayer: 'O Lord, God of Israel, enthroned between the cherubim, you alone are God over all the kingdoms of the earth. You have made heaven and earth' (2 Kings 19:15).

SCRIPTURE READING: 2 KINGS 19:14-19

July 3

The only true God

Westminster Catechism Question #46:

What is required in the First Commandment? *Answer*: The First Commandment requires us to know and acknowledge God to be the only true God, and our God, and to worship and glorify him accordingly.

Theme verse: 'You shall have no other gods before me' (Exod. 20:3).

We do not choose a marriage partner without first getting to know the person. Only after discovering a person's qualities will we begin to love on an emotional level. It is the same with God. The Bible is where we look to learn about him, where God is described as perfect in his attributes, glorious in his character, majestic in his holiness, rich in mercy and faithful in his promises. To know God is to love him and to love him is to increasingly desire him. Just before his death, Joshua gathered the tribes of Israel together in order to exhort them to renew their covenant with the true God of Israel. He recounted Israel's history and God's faithfulness to them. He described carefully what God is like. Sadly, the people really were unsure who to follow, the gods of the Egyptians and other neighbouring tribes, or the true God of Israel. Finally, Joshua proclaimed, 'As for me and my household, we will serve the Lord' (Josh. 24:15). Joshua was not asking the people whether they approved of God, or even if they believed he existed. He challenged them to turn away from the false gods of their neighbours, and instead to love the true God of Israel with heart, soul, strength and mind. We are called to do the same. There is no other way to worship and glorify God acceptably.

SCRIPTURE READING: JOSHUA 24:1-27

July 4
THE FEAR OF THE LORD
(WEEK 27: DAY 3)

The only true God

Westminster Catechism Question #46:

What is required in the First Commandment? *Answer*: The First Commandment requires us to know and acknowledge God to be the only true God, and our God, and to worship and glorify him accordingly.

Theme verse: 'You shall have no other gods before me' (Exod. 20:3).

Shadrach, Meshach and Abednego feared the Lord more than they feared King Nebuchadnezzar. They refused to worship the false gods of Babylon or the image of gold the king had erected. Nebuchadnezzar was furious at their rebuff and ordered that they be thrown into a blazing furnace. The response of the three men was fearless. 'If we are thrown into the blazing furnace, the God we serve is able to save us from it, and he will rescue us from your hand, O king' (Dan. 3:17). So Nebuchadnezzar had the furnace heated seven times hotter than usual and had the three men hurled into it. Not only did God intervene, protecting his three servants, but the Lord also joined them in the fiery furnace. Miraculously, they emerged from their ordeal unharmed. What gave Shadrach, Meshach and Abednego such amazing courage? Their knowledge of the true God, their steadfast faith in him, and their fear of dishonouring him outweighed their fear of the king. Greater noises drown out lesser noises, thunder drowns out the noise of a raging river, and the voice of the true and living God is more powerful and awe-inspiring than the voice of any earthly king. Love for the Lord and the fear of offending him will cause a person to make choices that honour the Saviour, and that boldly testify of Christ's supremacy in all matters.

SCRIPTURE READING: DANIEL 3:1-30

July 5
TRUSTING GOD
(WEEK 27: DAY 4)

The only true God

Westminster Catechism Question #46:

What is required in the First Commandment? *Answer*: The First Commandment requires us to know and acknowledge God to be the only true God, and our God, and to worship and glorify him accordingly.

Theme verse: 'You shall have no other gods before me' (Exod. 20:3).

As believers, we are called to trust God in all circumstances, whether life is progressing smoothly or we are experiencing days of trial. But what does trusting God look like when we lose our job, or cannot pay the mortgage, or a family member dies, or divorce is threatened? The prophet Habakkuk witnessed the horrifying results of the Babylonian invasion on his own land. Yet he was able to say, 'Though the fig tree does not bud and there are no grapes on the vines ... no sheep in the pen and no cattle in the stalls, yet I will rejoice in the Lord, I will be joyful in God my Savior' (Hab. 3:17-18). Habakkuk had learned the lesson of trusting God's providence regardless of the circumstances. Even if God sent suffering and devastation he would still rejoice in the Lord. Reaching the point where we can join Habakkuk in resting confidently in the Lord's purposes is rarely achieved overnight. It occurs when we are 'growing in the knowledge of God ... so that you may have great endurance and patience' (Col. 1:11). Faith that rests on the promise of God, 'never will I leave you; never will I forsake you' (Heb. 13:5) is the cure during the fearful times. We can say with confidence, 'The Lord is my helper; I will not be afraid' (Heb. 13:6). If God has promised you heaven, trust him for your daily needs.

SCRIPTURE READING: HABAKKUK 3:8-19

HEAR, O ISRAEL

(WEEK 27: DAY 5)

The only true God

Westminster Catechism Question #46:

What is required in the First Commandment? *Answer*: The First Commandment requires us to know and acknowledge God to be the only true God, and our God, and to worship and glorify him accordingly.

Theme verse: 'You shall have no other gods before me' (Exod. 20:3).

'Hear, O Israel: The Lord our God, the Lord is one' (Deut. 6:4) is known in Hebrew as the *Shema*, which means 'Hear'. It has become the Jewish confession of faith, recited daily by pious Jews and every Sabbath day in synagogues around the world. This really is the starting point for a clear understanding of our faith. God made himself known as the one true God. He is the Creator of all things; he sustains and governs all things. No one can rival his authority. Israel's neighbours attempted to appease scores of gods, each god vying for the people's affection and competing with one another. These gods were as immoral as the people who invented them. What a contrast and comfort as the people of Israel heard God say: 'I am the Lord your God. Do not turn to idols or make gods of cast metal for yourselves. I am the Lord your God' (Lev. 19:4). Only much later, when we understood unswervingly that God is one, did the Lord fully reveal that he exists in three persons: Father, Son and Holy Spirit. And this knowledge brings even further comfort since we know that the Father has promised to protect and bless his children, the Son has died to save us from sin and judgement, and the Holy Spirit has applied the gift of salvation to us and promises to be with us for ever.

SCRIPTURE READING: DEUTERONOMY 6:1-25

July 7
SECRET GODS
(WEEK 27: DAY 6)

The only true God

Westminster Catechism Question #46:

What is required in the First Commandment? *Answer*: The First
Commandment requires us to know and acknowledge God to be
the only true God, and our God, and to worship and glorify
him accordingly.

Theme verse: 'You shall have no other gods before me'
(Exod. 20:3).

What are your idols? Some people are very open about their idols.
They are proud to be seen with the newest electronic gadgets
and fanciest cars. Some are consumed with their jobs and stock
portfolios. Other people try to hide their idols. Alcoholics stash
liquor in the basement and men obsessed with internet pornogra-
phy keep their online identities secret. Still others make idols of
their relationships. Young lovers fawn over each other and parents
can become consumed with their children's lives. Whether carved
in stone or merely etched in our brains, idols take our focus off
of the Lord. When the first commandment states, 'You shall have
no other gods before me', God is literally saying that he does not
want false gods flaunted in front of his face. We all know what it
is like to feel cheated, when someone steals our idea and claims
it for himself or when we work hard and someone else is praised
for the work we accomplished. God feels the same way when we
worship idols in his presence. 'Cursed is the man who carves an
image or casts an idol, a thing detestable to the Lord … and sets
it up in secret' (Deut. 27:15). We need to examine whether there
are any secret idols still lurking within us, and ask God to free us
from them in order for us to live wholly consecrated lives.

SCRIPTURE READING: EXODUS 34:1-17

July 8

The only true God

Westminster Catechism Question #46:

What is required in the First Commandment? *Answer*: The First Commandment requires us to know and acknowledge God to be the only true God, and our God, and to worship and glorify him accordingly.

Theme verse: 'You shall have no other gods before me' (Exod. 20:3).

The rich young man was earnest. He really wanted to know the way to heaven. 'Good teacher,' he asked, 'what must I do to inherit eternal life?' (Mark 10:17). Jesus looked at him and loved him. His intentions were good. But the Lord knew that if this young man was to experience the joy of intimacy with Christ he would have to be rid of his money-god. When confronted with the clear choice, the young man went away sad, unable to give up his false god for the true God. The Bible describes any covetous man as an idolater: 'No immoral, impure or greedy person — such a man is an idolater — has any inheritance in the kingdom of Christ and of God' (Eph. 5:5). Jesus described riches as deceitful (Matt. 13:22). Money and possessions promise happiness but they do not deliver. They leave us unsatisfied and our souls empty. The first commandment offers us much better. 'The Almighty will be your gold, the choicest silver for you. Surely then you will find delight in the Almighty and will lift up your face to God' (Job 22:25-26). To live for and serve the true God is in our best interest. He says to us: 'I am your shield, your very great reward' (Gen. 15:1). No one ever needed to repent for having made the only true God their highest interest in this life. It was their comfort and their crown on their deathbed.

SCRIPTURE READING: JOB 22:19-30

July 9

CORRECT WORSHIP
(WEEK 28: DAY 1)

Idolatry forbidden

Westminster Catechism Question #50:

What is required in the Second Commandment? *Answer*: The Second Commandment requires that we observe and keep pure all religious worship that God has commanded in his Word.

Theme verse: 'You shall not make for yourselves an idol … You shall not bow down to them or worship them; for I, the Lord your God, am a jealous God' (Exod. 20:4-6).

In the second commandment we are told that God hates idolatry because it robs him of the glory due to his name. He is the Creator of all things, the Lord of the universe and the hope of the world. Therefore, he rightfully refuses to share his glory with another. The catechism answer reminds us that if we obey God by keeping his commands, especially in this area of proper religious worship, we will be protected from the sin of idolatry. In the book of Acts we are told that the early church 'devoted itself to the apostles' teaching and to the fellowship, to the breaking of bread and to prayer' (Acts 2:42). They were careful to observe the biblical teaching in order to worship, fellowship and pray correctly. Such care and concern for purity in worship glorifies God, who detests ignorant worship which leads to idolatry. People fall into superstitious practices due to an ignorance of what the Word of God teaches. Proper worship must be 'in spirit and truth', empowered by the Holy Spirit and sanctified by the truth of God's Word. God has a right to prescribe how he will be worshiped, and therefore, he has given us directives in his Word on how to worship him correctly. The first commandment prohibited worshiping a false god. In this second commandment God forbids us to worship him in any way we choose.

SCRIPTURE READING: ACTS 2:40-47

July 10

The golden calf

(week 28: day 2)

Idolatry forbidden

Westminster Catechism Question #50:

What is required in the Second Commandment? *Answer*: The Second Commandment requires that we observe and keep pure all religious worship that God has commanded in his Word.

Theme verse: 'You shall not make for yourselves an idol … You shall not bow down to them or worship them; for I, the Lord your God, am a jealous God' (Exod. 20:4-6).

Perhaps the most flagrant violation of the second commandment recorded in the Bible is the manufacture and worship of the golden calf by the people of Israel. Moses had gone up Mount Sinai to meet with God. The people grew impatient waiting for Moses and asked Aaron to fashion a gold replica of one of the gods of Egypt. This idol was formed into the shape of a calf. Soon the people were bowing down to their idol, holding a festival in its honour, and indulging in immoral behaviour. Then the Lord said to Moses, 'Leave me alone so that my anger may burn against them and that I may destroy them' (Exod. 32:10). But Moses pleaded with God, reminding him of the covenants he had made with the patriarchs. What is shocking about this episode was how quickly the people forgot the true God and turned away to idols. In anger, Moses threw the tablets containing the Law of God out of his hands, breaking them to pieces. His action testified against Israel that they had broken the covenant agreement. About three thousand of the people were killed because of their wickedness. It is a reminder that one day God will judge idolaters. 'Blessed are those who wash their robes, that they may have the right to the tree of life … Outside are … the idolaters and everyone who loves and practices falsehood' (Rev. 22:14-15). Lord, save us.

SCRIPTURE READING: EXODUS 32

July 11

Idolatry forbidden

Westminster Catechism Question #50:

What is required in the Second Commandment? *Answer*: The Second Commandment requires that we observe and keep pure all religious worship that God has commanded in his Word.

Theme verse: 'You shall not make for yourselves an idol … You shall not bow down to them or worship them; for I, the Lord your God, am a jealous God' (Exod. 20:4-6).

It was not only important to God that the people of Israel received the Ten Commandments at Mount Sinai, but also *how* they received them. The mountain was ablaze. Deep darkness covered it. Then God's booming voice was heard, but the people saw no form. 'You saw no form of any kind the day the Lord spoke to you at Horeb out of the fire. Therefore, watch yourselves very carefully, so that you do not become corrupt and make for yourselves an idol, an image of any shape' (Deut. 4:15). God is a Spirit and must be worshiped in spirit and truth. Any attempt to make an image of God would result in a false, inadequate representation. The invisible God cannot be reduced to a level comprehensible to human beings. He is great, mighty and beyond description. And since false gods are not to be worshiped, making forms of them is equally sinful. So how should we conceive of God? Think of God as he has revealed himself in Jesus Christ: 'Do not believe me unless I do what my Father does' (John 10:37). The Apostle John tells us that 'no one has ever seen God, but God the One and Only, who is at the Father's side, has made him known' (John 1:18). Jesus humbled himself, taking on the form of a servant, laying aside his glory, in order to make the invisible glory visible.

SCRIPTURE READING: DEUTERONOMY 4:9-31

July 12

Idolatry forbidden

Westminster Catechism Question #50:

What is required in the Second Commandment? *Answer*: The Second Commandment requires that we observe and keep pure all religious worship that God has commanded in his Word.

Theme verse: 'You shall not make for yourselves an idol … You shall not bow down to them or worship them; for I, the Lord your God, am a jealous God' (Exod. 20:4-6).

Intellectually, we have no difficulty seeing the utter silliness of carving a god out of wood, then bowing down and worshiping what our hands have made. There is no contest between the true God and a god of our own making. Yet, in the face of the obvious, and having received protection and blessings beyond counting, the people of Israel chose to forsake the God of Israel and run after foreign gods. More than any other prophet, Isaiah showed the foolishness of worshiping idols. 'To whom, then, will you compare God? What image will you compare him to?' (Isa. 40:18). God 'sits enthroned above the circle of the earth, and its people are like grasshoppers' (Isa. 40:22). The rulers of the world are nothing to him (Isa. 40:23). God never grows tired or weary and his understanding no one can fathom (Isa. 40:28). With biting sarcasm, Isaiah contrasts the omnipotent God of the universe with the impotence of the carved idol: 'The craftsman encourages the goldsmith, and he who smooths with the hammer spurs on him who strikes the anvil. He says of the welding, "It is good." He nails down the idol so it will not topple' (Isa. 41:7). Their foolishness warns us to remain vigilant, and to be watchful and prayerful in a world of enticements, temptations and idols that vie for our affection.

SCRIPTURE READING: ISAIAH 40:15-31

July 13

Idolatry forbidden

Westminster Catechism Question #50:

What is required in the Second Commandment? *Answer*: The Second Commandment requires that we observe and keep pure all religious worship that God has commanded in his Word.

Theme verse: 'You shall not make for yourselves an idol … You shall not bow down to them or worship them; for I, the Lord your God, am a jealous God' (Exod. 20:4-6).

Isaiah's satire and denunciation of false gods reaches its climax in Isaiah 44. Here are idols made by human hands, products of the human imagination. They resemble us (Isa. 44:13), even in our sinfulness. 'Half of the wood he burns in the fire; over it he prepares his meal … from the rest he makes a god, his idol; he bows down to it and worships. He prays to it and says, "Save me; you are my god"' (Isa. 44:16-17). Amazingly, Isaiah declares, 'No one stops to think, no one has the knowledge or understanding to say, "Half of it I used for fuel"' (Isa. 44:19). This is the great distinction between Christianity and false religion. Our faith is not something we could have invented. Who would have thought that the God of the universe would enter our world as a servant, live a perfect and sinless life, die for sinners, and then return to the highest place of honour to intercede for those he purchased with his own blood? False religions have their followers making long treks, carving images, repeating rote prayers, and reciting the 'wisdom' sayings of their leaders. It is all made and invented by human thought and relies on human effort to attain acceptance with God. But 'this is what the Lord says — Israel's King and Redeemer, the Lord almighty: I am the first and I am the last; apart from me there is no God' (Isa. 44:6).

SCRIPTURE READING: ISAIAH 44:6-23

July 14

Idolatry forbidden

Westminster Catechism Question #50:

What is required in the Second Commandment? *Answer*: The Second Commandment requires that we observe and keep pure all religious worship that God has commanded in his Word.

Theme verse: 'You shall not make for yourselves an idol ... You shall not bow down to them or worship them; for I, the Lord your God, am a jealous God' (Exod. 20:4-6).

The believers in Corinth were divided about whether to eat meat that had been offered to idols. The Apostle Paul informed them that there is no real power in an idol. At the same time, however, Paul warned that demons are the real objects of idol worship and therefore participation in pagan festivals and worship was expressly forbidden. 'You cannot drink the cup of the Lord and the cup of demons too; you cannot have a part in both the Lord's table and the table of demons. Are we trying to arouse the Lord's jealousy? Are we stronger than he?' (1 Cor. 10:21-22). Here is a clear word of exhortation for us. If we claim to be followers of Christ we cannot be participants in idolatry. That is not a warning for other people, but for us, since our loyalties can be divided by sinful addictions. 'Put to death, therefore, whatever belongs to your earthly nature: sexual immorality, impurity, lust, evil desires and greed, which is idolatry' (Col. 3:5). Another example of divided loyalty is the challenge for some believers to balance faith and family. Family members cannot understand the believer's new faith in Christ and pressure is exerted to participate with the family in their false religious practices. Idolatry is infectious and is an equal-opportunity destroyer. We must put it to death.

SCRIPTURE READING: 1 CORINTHIANS 10:1-22

July 15

Idolatry forbidden

Westminster Catechism Question #50:

What is required in the Second Commandment? *Answer*: The Second Commandment requires that we observe and keep pure all religious worship that God has commanded in his Word.

Theme verse: 'You shall not make for yourselves an idol … You shall not bow down to them or worship them; for I, the Lord your God, am a jealous God' (Exod. 20:4-6).

When God established his covenant with the Israelites it was like a marriage agreement between God and Israel. 'I will take you as my own people and I will be your God' (Exod. 6:7). Mutual fidelity defined the union. When the people of Israel deserted the Lord and ran after other gods the Bible pictures the Lord as a betrayed lover. 'How can I give you up, Ephraim? How can I hand you over, Israel' (Hosea 11:8). Similarly, Scripture portrays our union with Christ as a sacred bonding of God's people with their God. At the end of time we will be united to Christ for ever, never to stray. It is the marriage of the Lamb; the Lord Jesus with his bride. 'Let us rejoice and be glad and give him glory! For the wedding of the Lamb has come, and his bride has made herself ready' (Rev. 19:7). We are 'married' to Christ just as God was 'married' to Israel through the covenant. God strongly forbids Israel from making idols since Israel belongs to him, and the Lord sees our relationship to him in the same way. In the second commandment the Lord is very open about his feelings towards idolatry. The worship of idols makes him jealous. What does the Father ask of his people? 'Obey God's commands and remain faithful to Jesus' (Rev. 14:12) and 'Dear children, keep yourselves from idols' (1 John 5:21).

SCRIPTURE READING: HOSEA 11:1-11

July 16
Taming the tongue
(week 29: day 1)

Reverence for God's name

Westminster Catechism Question #54:

What is required in the Third Commandment? *Answer*: The Third Commandment requires the holy and reverent use of God's names, titles, attributes, ordinances, Word, and works.

Theme verse: 'You shall not misuse the name of the Lord your God, for the Lord will not hold anyone guiltless who misuses his name' (Exod. 20:7).

The third commandment prohibits the misuse (or profaning) of God's name. This commandment has a much broader application than most people realize. It not only forbids the misuse of God's name in our language, but also any irreverence when worshiping God, praying to him, speaking about him, or reading the Scriptures. When the commandment is understood in this broader sense it has a direct bearing on all worship of the Lord: our worship services, preparation and approach to the Lord's Table and devotional life. There are two sides to this third commandment. The 'you shall not' side requires us to never dishonour the name of Christ in word or deed. The 'you shall' side requires us to uphold and revere the Lord's name at all times. This commandment, then, has implications for our communication about God and other people. The Apostle James describes the tongue as 'a restless evil, full of deadly poison' (James 3:8). If we attack a person's character and impugn their name there is the potential of being sued for libel. More severe punishment, the Lord tells us, awaits the person who misuses his name, 'for the Lord will not hold anyone guiltless who misuses his name'. 'Out of the same mouth come praise and cursing. My brothers, this should not be' (James 3:10).

SCRIPTURE READING: JAMES 3:1-12

July 17

Reverence for God's name

Westminster Catechism Question #54:

What is required in the Third Commandment? *Answer*: The Third Commandment requires the holy and reverent use of God's names, titles, attributes, ordinances, Word and works.

Theme verse: 'You shall not misuse the name of the Lord your God, for the Lord will not hold anyone guiltless who misuses his name' (Exod. 20:7).

As a young man, Absalom plotted the overthrow of his father, David, in order to make himself king. He would stand by the city gate, and like a good politician, do a lot of kissing and hand-shaking in an attempt to win the hearts of the people. After four years of this the Scriptures tell us 'he stole the hearts of the men of Israel' (2 Sam. 15:6). Absalom now felt the time was right. He requested of his father that he might go to Hebron, the former capital city, in order to fulfil a religious vow. In reality, he believed Hebron was the perfect place to stage his coup, since there was resentment among the citizens of Hebron that the capital had been moved to Jerusalem. 'Then Absalom sent secret messengers throughout the tribes of Israel to say, "As soon as you hear the sound of the trumpets, then say, 'Absalom is king in Hebron'."' (2 Sam. 15:10). The action Absalom took was wicked from its conception, but he intensified his treachery by pretending to fulfil a vow he had made to the Lord. When any wicked action is baptized in the name of God it is a gross misuse of the Lord's name. Jesus told us to forget about making pious oaths that hide false motives and learn to speak the truth. 'Simply let your "Yes" be "Yes" and your "No", "No"; anything beyond this comes from the evil one' (Matt. 5:37).

SCRIPTURE READING: 2 SAMUEL 15:1-12

July 18

Reverence for God's name

Westminster Catechism Question #54:

What is required in the Third Commandment? *Answer*: The Third Commandment requires the holy and reverent use of God's names, titles, attributes, ordinances, Word and works.

Theme verse: 'You shall not misuse the name of the Lord your God, for the Lord will not hold anyone guiltless who misuses his name' (Exod. 20:7).

Throughout the Psalms we are directed to praise the Lord. It is the very finest way to avoid profaning the Lord's holy name. 'Sing to God, sing praise to his name, extol him who rides on the clouds — his name is the Lord — and rejoice before him' (Ps. 68:4). This one verse mentions three different ways for us to revere God's name. First, we honour God's name when we sing hymns and choruses that praise the name of Jesus. Secondly, when we extol God for his character and attributes, we are joining the angels who shower praise on the Lord who is 'high and lifted up'. Thirdly, we honour the name of Christ when we rejoice in his presence, when our hearts overflow in joy at the sheer goodness of Christ in saving us and being our God. God's name is the manifestation of his character. All the perfect and holy attributes of God are bound up in the name of the Lord. His name is an extension of all he is in his grace towards us, protection of us, and salvation of us. The psalmist tells us that we are the great beneficiaries if we use our voices, not to curse God, but to become experts at praising God: 'Blessed are those who have learned to acclaim you, who walk in the light of your presence, O Lord. They rejoice in your name all day long; they exult in your righteousness' (Ps. 89:15).

SCRIPTURE READING: PSALM 89:9-18

July 19
USELESS WORSHIP
(WEEK 29: DAY 4)

Reverence for God's name

Westminster Catechism Question #54:

What is required in the Third Commandment? *Answer*: The Third Commandment requires the holy and reverent use of God's names, titles, attributes, ordinances, Word and works.

Theme verse: 'You shall not misuse the name of the Lord your God, for the Lord will not hold anyone guiltless who misuses his name' (Exod. 20:7).

After an initial burst of spiritual enthusiasm, the Jews that returned from exile and rebuilt the temple fell into a religious malaise. Much of the land had not been recovered and the city of Jerusalem was not fully restored. In the face of these and other discouragements the people's worship degenerated into mere ritual and they no longer took God's Word and commands seriously. Through the prophet Malachi, the Lord rebuked the priests for their indifference. '"If I am a father, where is the honor due me? If I am a master, where is the respect due me?" says the Lord. "It is you, O priests, who show contempt for my name"' (Mal. 1:6). The priests were astounded. 'How have we shown contempt for your name?' Then the Lord pointed to their irreverence in worship. They were bringing diseased and crippled animals to the altar of sacrifice, offering them to God instead of unblemished animals. The Lord was so irate that he wanted the temple doors closed so that useless fires would no longer be offered on his altar. The priests were simply going through the motions. The Lord vowed that one day his name would be revered, when the nations would bring pure offerings of earnest prayer and praise (Mal. 1:11). What kind of offering will you bring to the Lord of heaven today?

SCRIPTURE READING: MALACHI 1:6-14

July 20
Reverence at the Lord's Supper
(WEEK 29: DAY 5)

Reverence for God's name

Westminster Catechism Question #54:

What is required in the Third Commandment? *Answer*: The Third Commandment requires the holy and reverent use of God's names, titles, attributes, ordinances, Word and works.

Theme verse: 'You shall not misuse the name of the Lord your God, for the Lord will not hold anyone guiltless who misuses his name' (Exod. 20:7).

The third commandment requires that our worship be reverent and holy. This includes our approach to the ordinances of baptism and the Lord's Supper. In this regard, the Apostle Paul had no praise for the Corinthian church: 'Your meetings do more harm than good' (1 Cor. 11:17). The congregation had formed cliques, and when they came together to eat the Lord's Supper 'each of you goes ahead without waiting for anybody else' (1 Cor. 11:21). The Lord's Supper was being profaned by their gluttony and divisiveness. People brought food to share, but because of their discriminatory behaviour, some gorged themselves while the poor went home hungry. Others were actually getting drunk. Paul explained a more excellent way. He had the Corinthians note how reverently the Lord Jesus instituted the Lord's Supper on the night he was betrayed (Luke 22:14-22). Then Paul gave the Corinthians a harsh warning: 'Whoever eats this bread and drinks the cup of the Lord in an unworthy manner will be guilty of sinning against the body and blood of the Lord' (1 Cor. 11:27). The unruly nature of their 'love' feasts had to come to an end. This is such a good reminder to us that when we approach the Lord's Supper or baptism we are to reflect on the cross, confess sin, allow for self-examination, and praise God's name from a reverent heart.

SCRIPTURE READING: LUKE 14:7-22

July 21

Reverence for God's name

Westminster Catechism Question #54:

What is required in the Third Commandment? *Answer*: The
Third Commandment requires the holy and reverent use of
God's names, titles, attributes, ordinances, Word and works.

Theme verse: 'You shall not misuse the name of the Lord your
God, for the Lord will not hold anyone guiltless who misuses
his name' (Exod. 20:7).

No more terrible profaning of God's name was ever uttered than
those hours leading up to Christ's death at the cross. 'The men
who were guarding Jesus began mocking and beating him. They
blindfolded him and demanded, "Prophesy! Who hit you?" And
they said many other insulting things to him' (Luke 22:63-65).
The blasphemy intensified as Jesus was dying. The rulers sneered
at him, 'He saved others; let him save himself if he is the Christ
of God, the Chosen One' (Luke 23:35). Even in public, the religious leaders threw away their dignity and gave way to their hatred. Since they could no longer spit on Jesus, they stabbed him as
deeply as possible with their language. They accused the Lord of
never having saved anybody since he was unable to save himself.
They said that if he was the Messiah of God, he should come
down from the cross. The fact that Jesus was dying on the cross
was evidence to these blasphemers that God had not elected Jesus
to his high office. So how will the Father rectify this horrible profaning of Christ? 'Therefore God exalted him to the highest place
and gave him the name that is above every name, that at the name
of Jesus every knee should bow, in heaven and on earth and under
the earth, and every tongue confess that Jesus Christ is Lord, to
the glory of God the Father' (Phil. 2:9-11). Hallelujah!

SCRIPTURE READING: LUKE 23:32-43

July 22

Reverence for God's name

Westminster Catechism Question #54:

What is required in the Third Commandment? *Answer*: The Third Commandment requires the holy and reverent use of God's names, titles, attributes, ordinances, Word and works.

Theme verse: 'You shall not misuse the name of the Lord your God, for the Lord will not hold anyone guiltless who misuses his name' (Exod. 20:7).

If you want an example of how to properly use God's name, consider the angels. 'Great and marvelous are your deeds, Lord God Almighty. Just and true are your ways, King of the ages. Who will not fear you, O Lord, and bring glory to your name?' (Rev. 15:3-4). Believers who now reside in heaven have a new song to sing: 'You are worthy to take the scroll and to open its seals, because you were slain, and with your blood you purchased men for God from every tribe and language and people and nation' (Rev. 5:9). Suddenly, a chorus of praise erupts throughout the universe: 'To him who sits on the throne and to the Lamb be praise and honor and glory and power for ever and ever!' (Rev. 5:13). In heaven there will be perfect control of our speech, we will speak only the truth, and with sinless hearts and minds, praise will be on our lips. We will direct our praise and adoration to the Lord Jesus and the work he has done. It is interesting to note the request the saints in heaven make to the Lord: 'The time has come for judging the dead, and for rewarding your servants the prophets and your saints and those who reverence your name' (Rev. 11:18). At the end of time, rewards will be given to those who have reverenced Christ's name, for those who have kept the third commandment.

SCRIPTURE READING: REVELATION 11:15-19

July 23

The Sabbath

Westminster Catechism Question #58:

What is required in the Fourth Commandment? *Answer*: The Fourth Commandment requires that we keep holy to God one whole day in seven, to be a holy Sabbath to him.

Theme verse: 'Remember the Sabbath day by keeping it holy. Six days you shall labor and do all your work, but the seventh day is a Sabbath to the Lord your God' (Exod. 20:8-11).

God created an order of six days that were followed by one of rest and contemplation. God himself rested on the seventh day, not because he was tired, but because his work of creation was complete. This mighty work was perfect and did not need to be repeated or changed in any way. So the Lord rested in order to commemorate his work; he blessed the day and set it apart as holy. God wanted his work at creation to be remembered, so he established the fourth commandment. 'For in six days the Lord made the heavens and the earth, the sea, and all that is in them, but he rested on the seventh day. Therefore the Lord blessed the Sabbath day and made it holy' (Exod. 20:11). The Ten Commandments reflect God's character and express his will. We demonstrate our love for God when we keep his commands. That is why the people of Israel were commanded to keep the Sabbath. 'Remember that you were slaves in Egypt and that the Lord your God brought you out of there with a mighty hand and an outstretched arm. Therefore the Lord your God has commanded you to observe the Sabbath day' (Deut. 5:15). Observing the Sabbath demonstrated the people's gratitude, even as our love and enjoyment of Christ on this day sets us apart as God's chosen and grateful people.

SCRIPTURE READING: DEUTERONOMY 5:12-15; EXODUS 20:8-11

July 24

The Sabbath

Westminster Catechism Question #58:

What is required in the Fourth Commandment? *Answer*: The Fourth Commandment requires that we keep holy to God one whole day in seven, to be a holy Sabbath to him.

Theme verse: 'Remember the Sabbath day by keeping it holy. Six days you shall labor and do all your work, but the seventh day is a Sabbath to the Lord your God' (Exod. 20:8-11).

The fourth commandment is the last in the Ten Commandments which deals with our vertical relationship to God. It is probably the one which is most flagrantly violated. Much of the Christian community has lost the blessing of making the Christian Sabbath a special day of worship, praise and rest. Christians ought to make the Lord's Day special through private and public worship, and by breaking with regular Monday-to-Saturday routines. There are, of course, works of necessity and mercy which must be performed on the Lord's Day, such as the need for doctors and nurses and a number of other professions. Yet if possible, according to the light of God's Word and our own consciences, the Lord wants us to rest from our regular activities in order to concentrate on our souls, maximizing the potential for spiritual good on the Lord's Day. Jesus said that he was Lord of the Sabbath but that the Sabbath was made for our benefit (Mark 2:27-28). On the Lord's Day the spiritual instruction and enjoyment, the refreshment of worship and the advantages of fellowship with other believers, all contribute towards the Christian's sanctification and growth in Christ-likeness.

SCRIPTURE READING: MARK 2:23 – 3:6

July 25
TWICE AS MUCH
(WEEK 30: DAY 3)

The Sabbath

Westminster Catechism Question #58:

What is required in the Fourth Commandment? *Answer*: The Fourth Commandment requires that we keep holy to God one whole day in seven, to be a holy Sabbath to him.

Theme verse: 'Remember the Sabbath day by keeping it holy. Six days you shall labor and do all your work, but the seventh day is a Sabbath to the Lord your God' (Exod. 20:8-11).

When the people of Israel grumbled against Moses and Aaron about a lack of food, God intervened and sent them quail in the evening and strange bread, manna, that fell from heaven. Each person was to gather as much manna as needed but 'on the sixth day, they gathered twice as much — two omers for each person' (Exod. 16:22). The reason for gathering twice as much on the sixth day was because, as Moses declared: 'This is what the Lord commanded: "Tomorrow is to be a day of rest, a holy Sabbath to the Lord"' (Exod. 16:23). None the less, some people went out on the seventh day to gather manna, but they found none. God was angry with their rebellion and reiterated that the seventh day was to be a day of rest. From the very outset the people of God found it difficult to obey this command, which is dear to God and reflects his holy character. Through Isaiah the prophet, God promises to bless and prosper those who make praising and worshiping him their priority on the Lord's Day. 'If you keep your feet from breaking the Sabbath and from doing as you please on my holy day, if you call the Sabbath a delight and the Lord's holy day honorable … then you will find your joy in the Lord, and I will cause you to ride on the heights of the land and to feast on the inheritance of your father Jacob' (Isa. 58:13-14).

SCRIPTURE READING: EXODUS 16:19-31

July 26

The Sabbath

Westminster Catechism Question #58:

What is required in the Fourth Commandment? *Answer*: The Fourth Commandment requires that we keep holy to God one whole day in seven, to be a holy Sabbath to him.

Theme verse: 'Remember the Sabbath day by keeping it holy. Six days you shall labor and do all your work, but the seventh day is a Sabbath to the Lord your God' (Exod. 20:8-11).

Nehemiah was a man of amazing energy and vision. Upon hearing the dismal conditions in Jerusalem after the exile, he prayed hard, received the king's permission, and set about rebuilding the walls. He also wisely governed and helped to settle the newly returned exiles. During Ezra and Nehemiah's leadership of Jerusalem, God sent a true religious revival. However, while Nehemiah was away for a period of time, sinful practices returned. One of the most glaring was in the area of Sabbath-keeping. 'In those days I saw men in Judah treading winepresses on the Sabbath and bringing in grain and loading it on donkeys' (Neh. 13:15). Nehemiah warned them to stop, rebuking the nobles and merchants of the city. On the Sabbath, Nehemiah stationed men to guard the entrances to the city so that no commerce could be conducted. 'Then I commanded the Levites to purify themselves and go and guard the gates in order to keep the Sabbath day holy' (Neh. 13:22). Nehemiah knew that God would send his blessing if he succeeded in changing the people's priorities on the Sabbath. It was an act of faith. His motive was the honour of God's name and the blessing that comes from obedience to his commandments. Nehemiah wanted the people to find their delight not in their groceries, but in the Lord.

SCRIPTURE READING: NEHEMIAH 13:15-22

July 27

The Sabbath

Westminster Catechism Question #58:

What is required in the Fourth Commandment? *Answer*: The Fourth Commandment requires that we keep holy to God one whole day in seven, to be a holy Sabbath to him.

Theme verse: 'Remember the Sabbath day by keeping it holy. Six days you shall labor and do all your work, but the seventh day is a Sabbath to the Lord your God' (Exod. 20:8-11).

When the psalmist declared 'This is the day the Lord has made; let us rejoice and be glad in it' (Ps. 118:24) he was referring to Christ's victory day, the day of resurrection, the first day of the week. On that day our victorious Saviour rose from the dead and in so doing, he perfectly fulfilled his declaration that he was Lord of the Sabbath. Only the Lord of the Sabbath has the right to change the Sabbath from Saturday to Sunday, from the last to the first day of the week. By doing so, the Lord retains the rest and contemplation of the creation, but also adds the service of joy and worship that the fourth commandment requires, a Sabbath *to the Lord your God* (Exod. 20:10). It is the day Christians have set aside to specially remember the Lord Jesus ever since. On the first day of creation God created light. That day of light corresponds with the Lord's Day. We must pray for and look for maximum spiritual light on this day. The Holy Spirit was poured out on Pentecost, the first day of the week, and we should particularly look to the Lord's Day as a day of receiving empowerment through the Holy Spirit's work in our lives. The conditions of modern-day living devour our time and emotional resources. We live in a world of exhausted, stressed and hurting people. Perhaps God has given us a remedy that we have been neglecting.

SCRIPTURE READING: PSALM 118

July 28

A GOOD HABIT

(WEEK 30: DAY 6)

The Sabbath

Westminster Catechism Question #58:

What is required in the Fourth Commandment? *Answer*: The Fourth Commandment requires that we keep holy to God one whole day in seven, to be a holy Sabbath to him.

Theme verse: 'Remember the Sabbath day by keeping it holy. Six days you shall labor and do all your work, but the seventh day is a Sabbath to the Lord your God' (Exod. 20:8-11).

Jesus made a habit of worship on the Sabbath. 'He went to Nazareth, where he had been brought up, and on the Sabbath day he went into the synagogue, as was his custom' (Luke 4:16). That would have been a bad day to be absent from worship! We are told that 'he taught in their synagogues, and everyone praised him' (Luke 4:15). Tremendous spiritual growth occurs when there is sound preaching, and the Lord's teaching was the very best. When the Sabbath was changed from Saturday to Sunday believers in Jesus followed his example and formed a habit of public worship. They honoured the resurrection of Jesus and declared Sunday to be the Lord's Day. On the very day Jesus rose from the dead, a Sunday evening, the disciples were assembled when 'Jesus himself stood among them and said to them, "Peace be with you"' (Luke 24:36). One Sunday later the disciples were assembled in the same room when Jesus appeared to them again. This time, Thomas was in worship with them! Paul preached and the believers celebrated the Lord's Supper on Sunday (Acts 20:7). The people worshiped and took up an offering on Sunday (1 Cor. 16:1-2). Pentecost took place on a Sunday (Acts 2:1). Much of our spiritual growth and the Spirit's work will take place on the Lord's Day. Make it your day of days for all the right reasons.

SCRIPTURE READING: ACTS 20:7-12

July 29
Our use of the Lord's Day
(week 30: day 7)

The Sabbath

Westminster Catechism Question #58:

What is required in the Fourth Commandment? *Answer*: The Fourth Commandment requires that we keep holy to God one whole day in seven, to be a holy Sabbath to him.

Theme verse: 'Remember the Sabbath day by keeping it holy. Six days you shall labor and do all your work, but the seventh day is a Sabbath to the Lord your God' (Exod. 20:8-11).

Jesus did not spend the whole Sabbath day in the synagogue. He taught and healed people both inside and outside the synagogue, and spent time with his disciples as they walked through fields of grain (Matt. 12:1-14). The Pharisees, who had turned observance of the Sabbath into a form of legalistic bondage, could not appreciate the freedom that Christ enjoyed, or the way his Father was honoured by his conduct. He set a pattern for us to follow. The art of making it the day of the Lord, the day of days, consists of laying aside all work except works of necessity, or to show mercy to others. If progress is to be made in our own sanctification then a correct use of the Lord's Day is of great importance. For so many of us with hectic schedules, Sunday may be the only opportunity available to make the welfare of our souls our top priority. If you have been born into a Christian home and live beyond seventy years of age, it is possible that ten years of your life can be set aside and devoted to the worship of God and to spiritual growth on this one day alone. How much grace, knowledge, self-control, perseverance, good works, love for God and man, and overall godliness will have been added to your life through a Sabbath decade of time? Pursue it, before you enter your eternal Sabbath rest (Heb. 4:6).

SCRIPTURE READING: MATTHEW 12:1-14

July 30
RELATIONSHIPS
(WEEK 31: DAY 1)

Honouring our parents

Westminster Catechism Question #64:

What is required in the Fifth Commandment? *Answer*: The Fifth Commandment requires that we preserve the honor of others and fulfill our responsibility to them whether they are superior, inferior, or equal in their relationship to us.

Theme verse: 'Honor your father and your mother, so that you may live long in the land the Lord your God is giving you' (Exod. 20:12).

The fifth commandment requires that children honour their parents. This is, of course, a responsibility which lasts a lifetime. But the command also gives us God's perspective on other relationships. How do we relate to employers and others in positions of authority? How do we relate to our spouses and to fellow believers? How do we relate to employees or small children? The Apostle Paul gave us a list of biblical precepts regarding relationships when he wrote, 'Love must be sincere ... Be devoted to one another in brotherly love. Honor one another above yourselves ... Share with God's people who are in need. Practice hospitality. Bless those who persecute you ... Rejoice with those who rejoice; mourn with those who mourn. Live in harmony with one another. Do not be proud, but be willing to associate with people of low position. Do not be conceited' (Rom. 12:9-16). Love is the essential ingredient in all our relationships and is the supreme fruit of real, justifying faith. 'Love must be sincere' is another way of stating that hypocrisy in our relationships is not allowed. Counterfeit love tries to hide itself behind the mask of words that have the sound of love. But the fifth commandment tells us to love from the heart and to be sincere in honouring others in all our relationships.

SCRIPTURE READING: ROMANS 12:9-21

July 31
HARSH PUNISHMENT
(WEEK 31: DAY 2)

Honouring our parents

Westminster Catechism Question #64:

What is required in the Fifth Commandment? *Answer*: The Fifth Commandment requires that we preserve the honor of others and fulfill our responsibility to them whether they are superior, inferior, or equal in their relationship to us.

Theme verse: 'Honor your father and your mother, so that you may live long in the land the Lord your God is giving you' (Exod. 20:12).

At one point when the Lord spoke to Moses on various laws he placed this command at the top of the list, 'Be holy because I, the Lord your God, am holy. Each of you must respect his mother and father' (Lev. 19:1-2). In Jewish culture during the time of Moses, a child defying a father or mother's discipline was unthinkable. The Jews believed that a child who would not listen to his parents would not listen to any authority, even to God. In that context we can better understand the Lord imposing such a harsh sentence on a rebellious son. 'If a man has a stubborn and rebellious son who does not obey his father and mother and will not listen to them when they discipline him, his father and mother shall take hold of him and bring him to the elders at the gate of his town' (Deut. 21:18-19). If the parents testified against their son and the elders agreed with their testimony the son would be stoned to death. One of the purposes of such a harsh sentence was to spread fear throughout Israel that rebellion would not be tolerated. When Eli's sons arrogantly went about their religious duties, since no one else would remove them, God took care of the matter and put them to death (1 Sam. 2:12-25). They serve as a strong warning that the fifth commandment will be obeyed. If it is not, the Lord will judge.

SCRIPTURE READING: 1 SAMUEL 2:12-25

August 1

Honouring our parents

Westminster Catechism Question #64:

What is required in the Fifth Commandment? *Answer*: The Fifth
Commandment requires that we preserve the honor of others
and fulfill our responsibility to them whether they are superior,
inferior, or equal in their relationship to us.

Theme verse: 'Honor your father and your mother, so that you
may live long in the land the Lord your God is giving you'
(Exod. 20:12).

A strange tradition was practised during the time of Jesus. It was
known as 'corban', meaning 'offering'. By using this word in a
religious vow an irresponsible Jewish son could dedicate money
to God (or the temple) which should have gone to his parents.
This money might not actually be given to the temple, but was
often kept by the young man. However, his vow would keep him
from honouring his parents because he would not be able to support them in their old age. The teachers of the law taught that a
Corban vow was binding and could not be broken, even if it was
uttered rashly. Jesus condemned the teachers of the law for their
approval of such outrageous behavior: 'You have a fine way of
setting aside the commands of God in order to observe your own
traditions!' (Mark 7:9). Then the Lord quoted Moses, 'Honor
your father and your mother' and 'Anyone who curses his father
or mother must be put to death' (Exod. 21:17). Jesus emphatically
reinforced the importance of demonstrating real honour and love
towards parents. It is clear that Jesus believes our relationship with
our parents is critical. If this relationship is right, characterized
by obedience and respect, then it will produce right relationships
within society, respect for God, and blessing to God's people.

SCRIPTURE READING: MARK 7:1-22

August 2

Honouring our parents

Westminster Catechism Question #64:

What is required in the Fifth Commandment? *Answer*: The Fifth Commandment requires that we preserve the honor of others and fulfill our responsibility to them whether they are superior, inferior, or equal in their relationship to us.

Theme verse: 'Honor your father and your mother, so that you may live long in the land the Lord your God is giving you' (Exod. 20:12).

So much of our approach to human relationships is based on what we learned in childhood. If a child learns reverence, respect and obedience at a young age then the basis for having proper relationships will be present throughout life. To achieve proper respect and obedience a child must be taught, since a child does not come into the world with these disciplines. As we know, children do not need to learn how to disobey or to be selfish. They already possess an active sin nature. So if the fifth commandment is to be adhered to, parents need to instruct their children properly, so that their children can obey. We are told that from a youth 'Jesus grew in wisdom and stature and in favor with God and men' (Luke 2:52). That informs us that children are inferior to their parents in four areas: wisdom (intelligence), stature (physical growth), favour with God (spiritual growth) and favour with men (social maturity). Who will provide the instruction to meet these needs if not parents? Parents, as their children's superiors, are not infallible, but it is necessary for children to learn authority and submission. At the same time, parents are not to exasperate their children (Eph. 6:4) but 'should train a child in the way he should go, and when he is old he will not turn from it' (Prov. 22:6).

SCRIPTURE READING: EPHESIANS 6:1-4

August 3
EQUALITY IN MARRIAGE
(WEEK 31: DAY 5)

Honouring our parents

Westminster Catechism Question #64:

What is required in the Fifth Commandment? *Answer*: The Fifth Commandment requires that we preserve the honor of others and fulfill our responsibility to them whether they are superior, inferior, or equal in their relationship to us.

Theme verse: 'Honor your father and your mother, so that you may live long in the land the Lord your God is giving you' (Exod. 20:12).

Our catechism answer covers all kinds of relationships. We are to preserve the honour of kings and bosses as our 'superiors', children and employees as our 'inferiors' and honour those relationships where there is equality, such as with fellow believers in our church family. The importance of equality is especially emphasized in Scripture when addressing the marriage relationship. In the Apostle Paul's handling of this subject he commands that each partner 'submit to one another out of reverence for Christ' (Eph. 5:21). To fulfil the fifth commandment within marriage there must be an attitude of conciliation. Spirit-filled spouses honour each other out of reverence for Christ. The wife is called to submit to her husband as an act of submission to the Lord (Eph. 5:24). The husband is to devote himself to his wife and actively demonstrate his submission by giving himself to her in the same way that Jesus gave up his life for his bride, the church. From both spouses, the emphasis is on a caring, cherishing and self-giving expression of love. This is to be especially seen in Christian marriages so that non-believers witness love that is expressed out of love for Christ. The Bible ascribes authority in the home to the husband, but the Christian marriage should be so bathed in love, that mutual submission occurs naturally and joyfully.

SCRIPTURE READING: EPHESIANS 5:21-33

August 4
HONOURING AUTHORITY FIGURES
(WEEK 31: DAY 6)

Honouring our parents

Westminster Catechism Question #64:

What is required in the Fifth Commandment? *Answer*: The Fifth Commandment requires that we preserve the honor of others and fulfill our responsibility to them whether they are superior, inferior, or equal in their relationship to us.

Theme verse: 'Honor your father and your mother, so that you may live long in the land the Lord your God is giving you' (Exod. 20:12).

No matter who we are, most of our relationships, whether directly or indirectly, are to those in authority over us. The Apostle Peter urged followers of Jesus to honour all authority figures, whether those superiors were Christians or not. 'Submit yourselves for the Lord's sake to every authority instituted among men: whether to the king, as the supreme authority, or to governors' (1 Peter 2:13-14). Peter even told slaves to submit to masters who were cruel to them for 'if you suffer for doing good and you endure it, this is commendable before God' (1 Peter 2:20). Peter pointed us to Christ's example of unjust suffering to encourage all of us to patiently endure during times of unfair treatment. Christ entrusted himself to a higher authority, to his Father 'who judges justly' (1 Peter 2:23). God ordains who is over us, whether that person is a government official or a boss. If we are unfairly treated, remember that trials are sent by God as his means of strengthening Christian character in us. When we disobey or dishonour a human authority we are indirectly disobeying God who ordained human institutions. We should remember that when Peter wrote to his fellow believers Nero was the brutal, godless Roman emperor. 'Show proper respect to everyone: Love the brotherhood of believers, fear God, honor the king' (1 Peter 2:17).

SCRIPTURE READING: 1 PETER 2:13-25

August 5

Honour to Christ alone

Honouring our parents

Westminster Catechism Question #64:

What is required in the Fifth Commandment? *Answer*: The Fifth
Commandment requires that we preserve the honor of others
and fulfill our responsibility to them whether they are superior,
inferior, or equal in their relationship to us.

Theme verse: 'Honor your father and your mother, so that you
may live long in the land the Lord your God is giving you'
(Exod. 20:12).

The first four commandments deal with our relationship to God.
This commandment, then, is the first to address our relationship
with people. It is first because God knows that if we honour our
parents it greatly facilitates looking up in reverence and honour to
the Lord. Jesus said, 'The one who sent me is with me; he has not
left me alone, for I always do what pleases him' (John 8:28). And
when the Pharisees were hurling their insults at Christ he replied:
'I am not possessed by a demon, but I honor my Father and you
dishonor me' (John 8:49). Ultimately, honour belongs to Christ
alone. He alone is our Saviour, he alone is perfect and sinless,
he alone is righteous and he alone is worshiped and honoured in
heaven. The wise men not only bowed the knee before the newborn king, but they also presented him expensive gifts (Matt.
2:11). We should do the same, offering the Lord our gifts of praise
and lives of gratitude and reverence. We honour Christ by advo-
cating his cause and standing up for his truth in a world that has
rejected him as their King. We show honour to the Lord when we
are dishonoured for his sake. And we honour Jesus because he is
worthy and we want to join the hosts in heaven who sing: 'To him
who sits on the throne and to the Lamb be praise and honor and
glory and power, for ever and ever!' (Rev. 5:14). Amen.

Scripture reading: Matthew 2:1-12

August 6

DO NOT MURDER

(WEEK 32: DAY 1)

Do not murder

Westminster Catechism Question #68:

What is required in the Sixth Commandment? *Answer*: The Sixth Commandment requires all lawful efforts to preserve our own life and the life of others.

Theme verse: 'You shall not murder' (Exod. 20:13).

The sixth commandment prohibits murder. God hates the wicked act of shedding another person's blood and he requires justice to be carried out against such evil. 'Whoever sheds the blood of man, by man shall his blood be shed; for in the image of God has God made man' (Gen. 9:6). Therefore, a legitimate government is required to exercise its biblical authority to punish murderers. God also will personally demand every murderer to account for the life of his fellow man (Gen. 9:5). Behind the act of murder lies the anger and malice of a person who shows no regard that human beings are made in the image of God. In killing a human being, a murderer demonstrates contempt both for God and for men and women. The sixth commandment is not only saying 'do not murder', but it is also requiring that we actively pursue the preservation of life. Working to stop abortion and euthanasia, helping the victims of abuse and counselling friends, caring for our own health and counselling those who struggle with anger are just a few of many practical ways we can promote the saving of human life. 'The acts of the sinful nature are obvious: hatred, discord, jealousy, fits of rage ... But the fruit of the Spirit is love, joy, peace, patience ... gentleness and self-control' (Gal. 5:19-23).

SCRIPTURE READING: GALATIANS 5:13-26

August 7

PRESERVING LIFE

(WEEK 32: DAY 2)

Do not murder

Westminster Catechism Question #68:

What is required in the Sixth Commandment? *Answer*: The Sixth Commandment requires all lawful efforts to preserve our own life and the life of others.

Theme verse: 'You shall not murder' (Exod. 20:13).

Ahab and Jezebel were the wicked rulers in Israel at the time of Elijah. Believing that it would please Baal, and that her false god would then send rain, Jezebel was killing off the Lord's prophets. But Obadiah, a devout believer in the Lord, was a servant for Ahab and Jezebel in the palace. At great personal risk, he hid one hundred of the Lord's prophets in caves and cared for them, bringing them food and water during this period of drought and severe famine (1 Kings 18:2-4). Out of a heart of love Obadiah was fulfilling the requirements of the sixth commandment by seeking to preserve God's people. In another instance, the Apostle Paul and Silas had been thrown into jail for preaching the gospel (Acts 16:16-40). The Lord sent an earthquake that opened the prison doors. In those days if any prisoners escaped the jailer would be executed. The jailer assumed the prisoners had all escaped and was about to commit suicide. But Paul preserved the life of the Philippian jailer by telling him that no one had escaped. The jailer recognized Paul's Christian faith as being supernatural and asked how he could be saved. Paul then led him and his family to Christ. One of the clearest demonstrations of our love for Jesus Christ is when people see our efforts to promote the well-being of others and to preserve human life.

SCRIPTURE READING: 1 KINGS 18:1-16

August 8

Do not murder

Westminster Catechism Question #68:

What is required in the Sixth Commandment? *Answer*: The Sixth Commandment requires all lawful efforts to preserve our own life and the life of others.

Theme verse: 'You shall not murder' (Exod. 20:13).

In the Old Testament, if a person killed someone involuntarily, he could flee to a designated place of safety in order to avoid being killed in revenge. But if the sixth commandment was broken, where a person killed in a pre-meditated fashion, there was no place of safety. 'If a man schemes and kills another man deliberately, take him away from my altar and put him to death' (Exod. 21:14). The act of killing another human being is so heinous in God's sight that Jesus, in the Sermon on the Mount, prohibited all sins and attitudes of the heart that might lead a person to murder. 'I tell you that anyone who is angry with his brother will be subject to judgment' (Matt. 5:22). Here Jesus is condemning the anger that so easily rises up in us. Instead of giving vent to our anger, the Lord wants us to go to the person who has offended us and seek reconciliation. Anger is potentially so dangerous that we should set aside everything, even our religious activities, and seek reconciliation immediately. This action should be taken as quickly as possible, before our anger spirals out of control. Anger is not the only emotion that causes a person to consider striking or killing another, but it is the most obvious one. Christians must be like their God, who is 'slow to anger, abounding in love and faithfulness' (Exod. 34:6).

SCRIPTURE READING: MATTHEW 5:21-26

August 9
Envy's target
(week 32: day 4)

Do not murder

Westminster Catechism Question #68:

What is required in the Sixth Commandment? *Answer*: The Sixth Commandment requires all lawful efforts to preserve our own life and the life of others.

Theme verse: 'You shall not murder' (Exod. 20:13).

Cain's slaying of his brother, Abel, is the first recorded murder in the Bible. His motivation was a mixture of jealousy and anger. Abel's sacrifice had been accepted by the Lord, but Cain's sacrifice was not accepted because it had been made without thought or proper devotion. Cain lured his brother out to an open field and killed him. It was an especially monstrous act as it was pre-meditated and committed against a godly man who was his own flesh and blood. The sin of anger and envy mastered Cain and controlled him. Anger can quickly rise and then wane, but envy is often deep-rooted. 'Anger is cruel and fury overwhelming, but who can stand before jealousy?' (Prov. 27:4). There are many examples of the dangers of envy in the Bible. Satan envied the special relationship Adam and Eve enjoyed with God. He did not rest until he had robbed them of it (Gen. 3). Joseph's brothers were envious of the favour his father bestowed on him, so they sold him into slavery (Gen. 37). Envy begins with a feeling of being wronged by God and ends in injury inflicted on men and women. The Apostle Paul lists 'envy' and 'factions' side by side as activities of the sinful nature (Gal. 5:21). When we are envious we are telling God that he has been unfair to us. Avoid this bitter root.

Scripture reading: Genesis 4:1-16

August 10

Do not murder

Westminster Catechism Question #68:

What is required in the Sixth Commandment? *Answer*: The Sixth Commandment requires all lawful efforts to preserve our own life and the life of others.

Theme verse: 'You shall not murder' (Exod. 20:13).

Hatred is another emotion that serves as a catalyst for murder. 'What causes fights and quarrels among you? Don't they come from your desires that battle within you? You want something but don't get it. You kill and covet, but you cannot have what you want. You quarrel and fight' (James 4:1-2). The world loses interest in the Christian faith when they see God's people quarrelling and divided. Paul was deeply concerned about this in the Corinthian church. 'You are still worldly. For since there is jealousy and quarreling among you, are you not worldly?' (1 Cor. 3:3). Paul was afraid to even visit the church as he feared he would find anger, factions and slander within the divided body of believers. Scripture teaches that hatred has no place within our lives or the church. We must be especially careful in this area if we are interested in preserving our own soul and preparing it for heaven. How can we hate when the Lord endured hatred, slander and death in order to free us from sin? 'And do not grieve the Holy Spirit of God, with whom you were sealed for the day of redemption. Get rid of all bitterness, rage and anger, brawling and slander, along with every form of malice. Be kind and compassionate to one another, forgiving each other, just as in Christ God forgave you' (Eph. 4:30-32).

SCRIPTURE READING: JAMES 3:13 – 4:3

August 11

Do not murder

Westminster Catechism Question #68:

What is required in the Sixth Commandment? *Answer*: The
Sixth Commandment requires all lawful efforts to preserve our
own life and the life of others.

Theme verse: 'You shall not murder' (Exod. 20:13).

The sixth commandment requires that we preserve our own life.
We should take care of our bodies through proper eating habits,
diet, exercise and recreation. We must exert our bodies through
work but then make sure we get enough rest. The Bible teaches
that we should care for our bodies: 'After all, no one ever hated
his own body, but he feeds and cares for it, just as Christ does the
church' (Eph. 5:29). The reason we are to care for our bodies is
because Christ purchased us, body and soul, when he died for us.
Our bodies belong to him and 'you were bought at a price. Therefore honor God with your body' (1 Cor. 6:20). Paul's argument is
that the Holy Spirit has taken up residence in our bodies. They
belong to God, and therefore, we are to be good stewards of the
bodies that now belong to another. Caring for ourselves becomes
an act of worship to God. When our bodies work well we are more
alert and receptive to the spiritual maintenance of our souls. And
nothing is more important than the care and preservation of our
souls. The Apostle Paul gave us the proper perspective: 'For physical training is of some value, but godliness has value for all things,
holding promise for both the present life and the life to come' (1
Tim. 4:8). Therefore, praise God with your soul and body!

SCRIPTURE READING: 1 TIMOTHY 4:1-16

August 12

THE MURDER OF JESUS
(WEEK 32: DAY 7)

Do not murder

Westminster Catechism Question #68:

What is required in the Sixth Commandment? *Answer*: The Sixth Commandment requires all lawful efforts to preserve our own life and the life of others.

Theme verse: 'You shall not murder' (Exod. 20:13).

Jesus was murdered. Of course, the envy and rage, the hatred and torture that Jesus experienced is beyond our comprehension. Jesus endured the onslaught of the demons of hell as well as the enmity and malice of the people. The people who were directly involved in the crucifixion hated Christ for many reasons. Pilate was annoyed at Jesus for putting him in a political bind. Judas was bitterly disappointed in Christ for not implementing a political kingdom that would place Judas in a position of power. Herod hated Christ's purity in the face of his own adultery and wickedness. The Pharisees envied his popularity. They recognized that 'God had anointed Jesus of Nazareth with the Holy Spirit and power, and how he went around doing good and healing all who were under the power of the devil' (Acts 10:38). Also, they saw Jesus as a political and spiritual opponent and despised him for rebuking them publicly for their spiritual hypocrisy. None of these people was content until Jesus was nailed to a cross and his life taken away. 'When they hurled their insults at him, he did not retaliate; when he suffered, he made no threats' (1 Peter 2:23). The sixth commandment was never so violently broken, but never did God turn evil into so much blessing for the world, and particularly, the children of God.

SCRIPTURE READING: ACTS 10:34-43

August 13
TAKING DRASTIC MEASURES
(WEEK 33: DAY 1)

Sexual purity

Westminster Catechism Question #71:

What is required in the Seventh Commandment? *Answer*: The Seventh Commandment requires the preservation of our own and our neighbor's chastity, in heart, speech, and behavior.

Theme verse: 'You shall not commit adultery' (Exod. 20:14).

The Bible prohibits both adultery and fornication. Adultery is the act of being unfaithful to one's spouse by voluntarily having sexual intercourse with someone else. Fornication is the act of voluntary sexual intercourse by unmarried people. The Lord Jesus declares that people who participate in these activities will not inherit the kingdom of God (Rev. 22:15). The catechism answer explains the biblical command. The seventh commandment requires more than just refraining from the physical acts of adultery or fornication. Jesus calls us to be chaste in our heart, speech and behavior towards others: 'Anyone who looks at a woman lustfully has already committed adultery with her in his heart' (Matt. 5:28). Although Jesus uses hyperbole, the message is clear that we must take drastic measures in dealing with temptation: 'If your right eye causes you to sin, gouge it out and throw it away' (Matt. 5:29). Through God's grace and power we can win this battle against sexual temptation. Victory requires a work of divine grace in the soul and a willingness to fight hard against the inclinations of our sinful nature. Our own happiness, our desire to please God and our witness that we belong to Christ demand that we enjoy a clear conscience with regards to the use of our bodies.

SCRIPTURE READING: MATTHEW 5:27-30

August 14
DAVID'S REBELLION
(WEEK 33: DAY 2)

Sexual purity

Westminster Catechism Question #71:

What is required in the Seventh Commandment? *Answer*: The Seventh Commandment requires the preservation of our own and our neighbor's chastity, in heart, speech, and behavior.

Theme verse: 'You shall not commit adultery' (Exod. 20:14).

In 2 Samuel we read of the steps that led to David's adultery with Bathsheba. Rather than being with his troops, David was in the king's palace enjoying reports of the victory gained by his army. He was headstrong and believed that he could do whatever he wished because of his vast power. By calling Bathsheba into his palace, he made his act of adultery an arrogant display of rebellion against God. After his adultery, David sent for Bathsheba's husband, Uriah. He hoped that he would return to his wife, so that the impression could be given that Uriah was the father of the unborn child. When this plan failed, David arranged for Uriah to be murdered in the front line of battle. The seventh commandment is never broken in isolation. Adulterers must live a lie, constantly attempting to cover their tracks. David boldly broke the sixth, seventh, ninth and tenth commandments. But he did eventually recognize his sins and confess them to God. When Nathan exposed David's sin we read his words of repentance in the fifty-first psalm: 'Against you, you only, have I sinned and done what is evil in your sight' (Ps. 51:4). In addition to the enormity of his sin against Bathsheba and Uriah, David rightly acknowledged and confessed that the sin of adultery is a sin against the Holy One.

SCRIPTURE READING: 2 SAMUEL 11:1-27

August 15

Sexual purity

Westminster Catechism Question #71:

What is required in the Seventh Commandment? *Answer*: The Seventh Commandment requires the preservation of our own and our neighbor's chastity, in heart, speech, and behavior.

Theme verse: 'You shall not commit adultery' (Exod. 20:14).

David's sin of adultery with Bathsheba carried immediate consequences. First, his sin was exposed. David said to Nathan, 'I have sinned against the Lord' (2 Sam. 12:13). Through Nathan the prophet, God announced that his private sin would become public: 'You did it in secret, but I will do this thing in broad daylight before all Israel' (2 Sam. 12:12). Secondly, violence became part of his family heritage (2 Sam. 12:10). Thirdly, David's wives were violated by Absalom (2 Sam. 12:11). Fourthly, the son born through Bathsheba died in infancy (2 Sam. 12:18). As a result of his engineering Uriah's death, David lost four of his sons. Throughout his years, David's murder of Uriah and adultery with Bathsheba became permanent stains on an otherwise godly life. The punishment in Israel for adultery was death by stoning. David was a blessed man, however, because the Lord, in his grace, forgave David's sin. Nathan was able to comfort the king: 'The Lord has taken away your sin. You are not going to die' (2 Sam. 12:13). None the less, David experienced the pain of a tortured conscience: 'let the bones you have crushed rejoice' (Ps. 51:8). There is a high price to pay for immoral behaviour. The better route is to remember that you have been bought with the price of the Saviour's blood. Therefore, 'honor God with your body' (1 Cor. 6:20).

SCRIPTURE READING: 2 SAMUEL 12:1-23

August 16

Sexual purity

Westminster Catechism Question #71:

What is required in the Seventh Commandment? *Answer*: The Seventh Commandment requires the preservation of our own and our neighbor's chastity, in heart, speech, and behavior.

Theme verse: 'You shall not commit adultery' (Exod. 20:14).

Sometimes we assume that a spiritual question needs a flowery spiritual answer. When dealing with temptation, with the lusts of the flesh, how often have we been told to take the matter to the Lord in prayer? Of course, we should do that. But the Bible, at this point, is very practical. Its advice is simply to stop entertaining lustful thoughts. Peter wrote: 'Dear friends, I urge you, as aliens and strangers in the world, to abstain from sinful desires' (1 Peter 2:11). In other words, stop lusting. Or Paul states directly: 'Flee from sexual immorality' (1 Cor. 6:18). What could be clearer? The Bible's answer to dealing with the problem of lust is to stop entertaining lustful thoughts. Put them to death. Peter does not prescribe a program of therapy or say that sin should be treated as an addiction. He simply states that we should abstain. Paul tells us to flee. The Bible is telling us that we have no business indulging these sinful thought patterns. If sexual temptation is getting us down we must not resort to 'handing it all over to Jesus' as a spiritual quick-fix. If you have been justified by his blood, you have graciously received freedom from sin. That means you have power to abstain from sinning. 'We died to sin, how can we live in it any longer?' (Rom. 6:2). And again, 'Resist the devil, and he will flee from you' (James 4:7).

SCRIPTURE READING: JAMES 4:1-12

August 17
FLEEING TEMPTATION
(WEEK 33: DAY 5)

Sexual purity

Westminster Catechism Question #71:

What is required in the Seventh Commandment? *Answer*: The Seventh Commandment requires the preservation of our own and our neighbor's chastity, in heart, speech, and behavior.

Theme verse: 'You shall not commit adultery' (Exod. 20:14).

Mrs Potiphar's approach to Joseph was bold and confrontational: 'Come to bed with me!' (Gen. 39:7). But Joseph refused. His understanding of the matter was biblically clear: 'How then could I do such a wicked thing and sin against God?' (Gen. 39:9). When Potiphar's wife became even more direct, grabbing him by his clothes, Joseph responded correctly. He ran. The Bible tells us that running is an excellent way to deal with temptation! Joseph knew God and realized that adultery was a wicked thing, a sin against God. But Joseph paid a price for his moral purity. Mrs Potiphar's slander against him caused her husband to throw Joseph into prison. Even there, the Bible stresses that 'the Lord was with him' (Gen. 39:20). Though Joseph's situation changed drastically, God sustained him and drew near to him. God blessed Joseph, even in prison, and gave him a position of authority over all the other prisoners. We see him finally raised up among the Egyptians as the one who, because the Lord was with him, held their future and lives in his hands. Joseph was blessed because he had, at an early age, made a conscious decision to honour God with his life. He chose a way of life that throttled sin and crushed it, sapping sin's strength, rooting it out and depriving it of its influence. Blessing always follows such godly choices.

SCRIPTURE READING: GENESIS 39:1-23

August 18
MARITAL LOVE
(WEEK 33: DAY 6)

Sexual purity

Westminster Catechism Question #71:

What is required in the Seventh Commandment? *Answer*: The Seventh Commandment requires the preservation of our own and our neighbor's chastity, in heart, speech, and behavior.

Theme verse: 'You shall not commit adultery' (Exod. 20:14).

God invented sex, and sexual desire is a good thing. It is a gift of God. God made man male and female and it was God who instituted marriage (Gen. 2:24). Marriage not only involves the separation of a husband and wife from their previous families but it also involves a sexual relationship: two people becoming one flesh in the eyes of God. The Old Testament *Song of Songs* speaks profoundly of sexual love as a normal part of marital life, something good that God has created for humanity's enjoyment. The Lord rejoices with his creation in his gift of marital and sexual love. The *Song* powerfully portrays the beauty and delights of sex and its exclusive nature within marriage: 'My lover is mine and I am his' (Song of Solomon 2:16). Marital love is spoken of as precious: 'If one were to give all the wealth of his house for love, it would be utterly scorned' (Song of Solomon 8:7). God wants such intimacy and sexual love within marriage because he wants what is best for us. Marriage shields and protects such intense and honourable love where trust and mutual submission can express themselves fully and unashamedly. Such love and its delights are scorned, abused and distorted today and solid examples of it are increasingly rare. But to those who choose God's way of love, they discover it to be 'more delightful than wine' (Song of Solomon 1:2).

SCRIPTURE READING: SONG OF SOLOMON 8

August 19
THE BIBLICAL STANDARD
(WEEK 33: DAY 7)

Sexual purity

Westminster Catechism Question #71:

What is required in the Seventh Commandment? *Answer*: The
Seventh Commandment requires the preservation of our own
and our neighbor's chastity, in heart, speech, and behavior.

Theme verse: 'You shall not commit adultery' (Exod. 20:14).

'But among you there must not be even a hint of sexual immorality, or of any kind of impurity' (Eph. 5:3). The struggle with
sexual temptation is fierce. To maintain sexual purity can be difficult, even for people who live in a setting where the biblical ideal
is upheld and, to a large degree, maintained. We battle not only
with our old sin nature, but we also live in a culture that encourages sexual immorality. A person trying to live a morally pure
life before God is bombarded daily with a different message than
what he reads in the Bible. In the face of secular pressure to accept sex outside of marriage as normal, too few churches today
encourage members to follow the Bible's standards of sexual mo-
rality. An unbiblical and unhealthy laxity prevails, offering forgiveness without the need of repentance. Yet God calls us to a
higher and better life. God's law has not changed. The seventh
commandment calls us to sexual purity. The city of Corinth was
known throughout the ancient world as a place of grotesque sexual immorality. Temple prostitution was openly practiced by the
masses. Yet Paul, when speaking to the church at Corinth, did
not compromise the biblical standard: 'Flee sexual immorality …
your body is a temple of the Holy Spirit' (1 Cor. 6:18-19). We are
called to that same standard.

SCRIPTURE READING: 1 CORINTHIANS 6:12-20

August 20
USING MONEY WISELY
(WEEK 34: DAY 1)

Do not steal

Westminster Catechism Question #74:

What is required in the Eighth Commandment? *Answer*: The Eighth Commandment requires that we obtain and increase our wealth and the wealth of others lawfully.

Theme verse: 'You shall not steal' (Exod. 20:15).

The eighth commandment has two components: 1) robbery and theft are sins, and 2) any accumulation of wealth must be acquired through lawful means. Implied in this commandment is the exhortation to not envy our neighbours' lawful efforts to obtain wealth for themselves. Rather than being envious of our neighbours' good fortunes, we should rejoice with them and seek to protect their property as well as our own. And what does God require of people who have accumulated wealth? It is not to simply spend on themselves: 'He who has been stealing must steal no longer, but must work, doing something useful with his own hands, that he may have something to share with those in need' (Eph. 4:28). Paul's admonition is more than 'stop stealing'. He is calling former thieves to do good by working in order to meet the needs of others. The vast majority of people go to work in order to acquire wealth for themselves. But the Christian is called to make work an act of worship by acquiring wealth to bless others. If you have been blessed with God's abundance, glorify God with it, using money as currency to live on and also to alleviate spiritual and physical misery. Wise Christians send their treasure on ahead, 'where moth and rust do not destroy, and where thieves do not break in and steal' (Matt. 6:20).

SCRIPTURE READING: EPHESIANS 4:25-32

August 21
THE CAUSES FOR STEALING
(WEEK 34: DAY 2)

Do not steal

Westminster Catechism Question #74:

What is required in the Eighth Commandment? *Answer*: The Eighth Commandment requires that we obtain and increase our wealth and the wealth of others lawfully.

Theme verse: 'You shall not steal' (Exod. 20:15).

There are really only two internal reasons for stealing. The first is unbelief, a lack of trust in God to provide for us. After the people of Israel left Egypt, God supernaturally provided streams of water from a rocky crag. Yet the people continued to demand more. They spoke against God, saying, 'Can God spread a table in the desert?' (Ps. 78:19). They simply did not believe God would provide for them and so they felt they had to fend for themselves. The same lack of trust is embedded in the heart of every thief. The second internal reason for stealing is covetousness. King Ahab coveted Naboth's vineyard (1 Kings 21) and was willing to kill Naboth in order to have it. David desired Bathsheba and stole her away from her husband. Since neither the vineyard nor Bathsheba could be acquired lawfully, theft was the only recourse. There also is an external cause for stealing. It is Satan's deceitful counsel. For instance, Judas was a thief (John 12:6) who was controlled by the evil one (John 13:27). And Satan robbed Adam and Eve of their innocence. He has been stealing from us ever since. If we are not careful, Satan will rob us of eternal life: 'Those along the path are the ones who hear, and then the devil comes and takes away the word from their hearts, so that they may not believe and be saved' (Luke 8:12).

SCRIPTURE READING: LUKE 8:1-15

August 22
ACHAN'S SIN
(WEEK 34: DAY 3)

Do not steal

Westminster Catechism Question #74:

What is required in the Eighth Commandment? *Answer*: The
Eighth Commandment requires that we obtain and increase our
wealth and the wealth of others lawfully.

Theme verse: 'You shall not steal' (Exod. 20:15).

The Israelites gained a great victory at the battle of Jericho, but
soon after were defeated at Ai. They were defeated, in part, because of arrogance, believing that they could conquer the inhabitants of Ai without the Lord's help. But they were also defeated
because a man named Achan had stolen some of the riches of Ca-
naan that had been devoted to the Lord. This act of stealing was
a serious matter because it broke covenant with God; 'He who is
caught with the devoted things shall be destroyed by fire' (Josh.
7:15). Achan was enraptured by all the plunder, stealing and hiding 'a beautiful robe from Babylon, two hundred shekels of silver
and a wedge of gold' (Josh. 7:21). When the people recovered the
stolen items they spread them out before the Lord, not wanting
to hide anything from the great Judge. They were eager to deal
with this terrible sin that had infected the camp of Israel. Only
after Achan and his family had been put to death did the Lord
turn from his fierce anger. The application is obvious. The eighth
commandment is to be obeyed. God is rightfully angered when we
selfishly hoard what he has given us in abundance or when we rob
him of what rightfully belongs to him. This is particularly true
when we offer indifferent praise and worship, and fail to give him
the glory due his name.

SCRIPTURE READING: JOSHUA 7:1-26

August 23
MASTERY OVER MONEY
(WEEK 34: DAY 4)

Do not steal

Westminster Catechism Question #74:

What is required in the Eighth Commandment? *Answer*: The Eighth Commandment requires that we obtain and increase our wealth and the wealth of others lawfully.

Theme verse: 'You shall not steal' (Exod. 20:15).

Money is a dangerous commodity. The Apostle Paul warned us that it can destroy: 'People who want to get rich fall into temptation and a trap and into many foolish and harmful desires that plunge men into ruin and destruction' (1 Tim. 6:9). But money can also be used to powerfully demonstrate a person's love for God and longing for heaven: 'Command them to do good, to be rich in good deeds, and to be generous and willing to share. In this way they will lay up treasure for themselves as a firm foundation for the coming age, so that they may take hold of the life that is truly life' (1 Tim. 6:19). These verses teach us to use our money wisely, investing in what will bring the best return. When we give generously we demonstrate that money does not control us. It is not an idol. We have mastery over it and the possibility of stealing in order to acquire money or possessions is a ridiculous notion. 'Money is a root for all kinds of evil' (1 Tim. 6:10) because people are content with loving money rather than loving God. The Lord loves when his people are 'cheerful givers' (2 Cor. 9:7). It proves that they are content with the abundance that the Lord has provided them. Wise people pursue 'godliness with contentment', knowing that 'we brought nothing into the world, and we can take nothing out of it' (1 Tim. 6:6-7).

SCRIPTURE READING: 2 CORINTHIANS 9:6-15

August 24
WANTING LESS, GETTING MORE
(WEEK 34: DAY 5)

Do not steal

Westminster Catechism Question #74:

What is required in the Eighth Commandment? *Answer*: The Eighth Commandment requires that we obtain and increase our wealth and the wealth of others lawfully.

Theme verse: 'You shall not steal' (Exod. 20:15).

Christian happiness is puzzling to the non-Christian because it comes not from getting more but from wanting less of what this world offers. People think that the more material things they possess the happier they will be. That is why thieves make a living out of stealing. Christians find that what really makes them happy is wanting only the things God chooses to give them. Their happiness arises not from the size of their bank balances, but from their willingness to be satisfied with what God gives them. A person who has many things but wants more will be miserable. A person who has a few things but does not want anything else will be happy. 'Keep your lives free from the love of money and be content with what you have, because God has said, "Never will I leave you; never will I forsake you"' (Heb. 13:5). This is an important lesson for us to learn since it so clearly testifies that we have set our affection on greater things. The Bible promises that placing our hope in God is the source of real happiness. 'Command those who are rich in this present world not to be arrogant nor to put their hope in wealth, which is so uncertain, but to put their hope in God, who richly provides us with everything for our enjoyment' (1 Tim. 6:17). Do not settle for anything less than the riches that are in Christ Jesus.

SCRIPTURE READING: I TIMOTHY 6:11-21

August 25

Do not steal

Westminster Catechism Question #74:

What is required in the Eighth Commandment? *Answer*: The Eighth Commandment requires that we obtain and increase our wealth and the wealth of others lawfully.

Theme verse: 'You shall not steal' (Exod. 20:15).

'If you see your brother's ox or sheep straying, do not ignore it but be sure to take it back to him' (Deut. 22:1). This verse gives us a clear directive as to how a Christian responds when a wallet drops out of a man's pocket or a woman misplaces her purse. The eighth commandment requires that we should not just be concerned about our own economic well-being but also the financial needs of others. As we have opportunity, we are to actively assist fellow believers to earn money or find employment. We also must be concerned for the possessions of others and that the potential for stealing them is reduced. The eighth commandment is a law intended not only as a basis for punishing criminal behaviour but also to express our concern for people and their possessions. Followers of Christ long for economic justice, especially for the poor among us. 'Do not take advantage of a hired man who is poor and needy, whether he is a brother Israelite or an alien living in one of your towns. Pay him his wages each day before sunset, because he is poor and is counting on it. Otherwise, he may cry to the Lord against you, and you will be guilty of sin' (Deut. 24:14-15). Christian employers pay their employees fairly and on time. And followers of Christ show mercy to the needy, remembering that they have been shown mercy.

SCRIPTURE READING: DEUTERONOMY 22:1-4; 24:5-22

August 26
THE GOOD SHEPHERD
(WEEK 34: DAY 7)

Do not steal

Westminster Catechism Question #74:

What is required in the Eighth Commandment? *Answer*: The Eighth Commandment requires that we obtain and increase our wealth and the wealth of others lawfully.

Theme verse: 'You shall not steal' (Exod. 20:15).

John 10 asks us to picture a sheepfold, a walled enclosure where sheep are kept at night. There are two people in this story vitally interested in the sheep. The first person is a thief. He is willing to climb over the wall and find his way to the sheep in order to steal or kill them. In contrast, there is the true shepherd, who enters by the legal and correct way, through the one gate. The sheep hear the true shepherd's voice (John 10:3) and happily follow him, comforted by his love and care of them. The true shepherd leads the sheep to green pasture; he knows each sheep by name and they know him. Jesus is that Good Shepherd. He comes into our world to fulfil the eighth commandment. Far from stealing from us or demanding from us, this Good Shepherd gives generously to us, even laying down his life for the sheep. There are others, unlike Jesus, who are nothing more than thieves and robbers (John 10:8), seeking how they might get their hands on God's people for their own evil purposes, 'coming only to steal, kill and destroy' (John 10:10). Jesus has not come to steal but to 'give them eternal life, and they shall never perish; no one can snatch them out of my hand' (John 10:28). Have you come to the Good Shepherd to find eternal life? He came that you 'may have life, and have it to the full' (John 10:10).

SCRIPTURE READING: JOHN 10:1-18

Telling the truth

Westminster Catechism Question #77:

What is required in the Ninth Commandment? *Answer*: The Ninth Commandment requires that we maintain and promote truth between persons, upholding our own and our neighbor's good name, especially in witness-bearing.

Theme verse: 'You shall not give false testimony against your neighbor' (Exod. 20:16).

The ninth commandment requires that we tell the truth, especially when we are speaking about another person or testifying about an incident which has occurred. Telling the truth can be hard because so often it is costly. When a mother discovers a broken cookie jar, the guilty child is tempted to blame the younger brother or sister. The Chief Executive Officer will deny embezzling corporation funds though the money trail leads directly to him. Some people go through life living a lie, keeping secrets they are afraid to disclose. Others become so good at lying that it becomes second nature to them. Our Saviour always told the truth. Even when confronted by angry mobs who sought to take his life, our perfect Lord spoke clearly and truthfully: 'My Father, whom you claim as your God, is the one who glorifies me. Though you do not know him, I know him. If I said I did not, I would be a liar like you, but I do know him and keep his word' (John 8:54-55). The devil and the sinful nature which we possess have no hold on Christ (John 14:30), and therefore, Jesus always told the truth. Telling the truth is a fruit of the Spirit which should increasingly be seen in us as we progress in the Christian life: 'Speaking the truth in love, we will in all things grow up into him who is the Head, that is, Christ' (Eph. 4:15).

SCRIPTURE READING: JOHN 14:15-31

August 28
SLANDERING ANOTHER
(WEEK 35: DAY 2)

Telling the truth

Westminster Catechism Question #77:

What is required in the Ninth Commandment? *Answer*: The Ninth Commandment requires that we maintain and promote truth between persons, upholding our own and our neighbor's good name, especially in witness-bearing.

Theme verse: 'You shall not give false testimony against your neighbor' (Exod. 20:16).

The ninth commandment forbids disparaging our neighbour, or slandering another person. Just as a scorpion carries poison in its tail, the slanderer carries poison in his tongue. King David appealed to the Lord to come to his defence when he was being maliciously slandered by those whom he had considered friends: 'Ruthless witnesses come forward; they question me on things I know nothing about. They repay me evil for good and leave my soul forlorn' (Ps. 35:11-12); 'they slandered me without ceasing' (Ps. 35:15). As a follower of Christ grows in holiness and Christlikeness it is not unusual for slander against a believer to increase. The Apostle Paul testified that he was the subject of a slanderous report (Rom. 3:8). Slanderers claimed John the Baptist was demon-possessed (Matt. 11:18). Jesus was accused of being 'a glutton and a drunkard, a friend of tax collectors and sinners' (Matt. 11:19). Later, Jesus was also accused of being demon-possessed (John 8:48). Slander robs people of their good name and dignity, and once begun, it is nearly impossible to stamp out. It is essential that we not initiate gossip or slander others, nor receive malicious reports about others until the information has been carefully examined. 'The Lord detests lying lips, but he delights in men who are truthful' (Prov. 12:22).

SCRIPTURE READING: PSALM 35

254

August 29
ONE WITH THE FATHER
(WEEK 35: DAY 3)

Telling the truth

Westminster Catechism Question #77:

What is required in the Ninth Commandment? *Answer*: The Ninth Commandment requires that we maintain and promote truth between persons, upholding our own and our neighbor's good name, especially in witness-bearing.

Theme verse: 'You shall not give false testimony against your neighbor' (Exod. 20:16).

The Pharisees accused Jesus of breaking the ninth commandment, along with the first and third commandments. The Pharisees denounced his testimony as blasphemous because Jesus claimed to be God: 'I and the Father are one' (John 10:30). The charge of blasphemy here was much more serious than simply reviling or speaking irreverently about God. Jesus was claiming to be equal with God, and stated clearly that he is God. Such a claim is, of course, totally unacceptable from any person other than the Lord Jesus himself. Unable to believe his words, the Pharisees picked up stones in order to kill him. They were intent on literally taking the law into their own hands, although without due process. The law required the death penalty for blasphemy: 'Anyone who blasphemes the name of the Lord must be put to death. The entire assembly must stone him. Whether an alien or native-born, when he blasphemes the Name, he must be put to death' (Lev. 24:16). Jesus never backed away from his claim that he was God in the flesh. In fact, he asks us to take a good look at both his words and his miracles: 'that you may know and understand that the Father is in me, and I in the Father' (John 10:32,37-38). Jesus claimed to be God in the flesh. If he told us the truth, then it is right to worship him. No other response makes sense.

SCRIPTURE READING: JOHN 10:22-39

August 30

Telling the truth

Westminster Catechism Question #77:

What is required in the Ninth Commandment? *Answer*: The Ninth Commandment requires that we maintain and promote truth between persons, upholding our own and our neighbor's good name, especially in witness-bearing.

Theme verse: 'You shall not give false testimony against your neighbor' (Exod. 20:16).

In the short letter of 3 John, the Apostle John writes to a dear friend named Gaius. John's purpose in writing was to thank Gaius for showing hospitality to fellow believers who had been sent into Asia as missionaries. He also wrote to warn Gaius and the believers in Asia about a man named Diotrephes. Diotrephes was a church leader who held dictatorial power in the church. To maintain his grip on power and enhance his own reputation, he lied about the Apostle John and other faithful Christians: 'Diotrephes, who loves to be first, will have nothing to do with us. So if I come, I will call attention to what he is doing, gossiping maliciously about us' (3 John vv. 9-10). Discerning Christians, such as John, could see that Diotrephes was a person who could not be trusted to tell the truth. He had no difficulty attacking the Apostle John whom Jesus loved. He would even stop people from welcoming missionaries into their home. In contrast, Gaius and a man named Demetrius, feared God and were concerned about honesty in speech; 'Demetrius is well spoken of by everyone — and even by the truth itself' (3 John v. 12). The unity and love that are to be the hallmarks of the church require commitment to the truth, honesty in speech, carefulness in speaking about others, and a conscious desire to honour God by keeping the ninth commandment.

SCRIPTURE READING: 3 JOHN

August 31

Telling the truth

Westminster Catechism Question #77:

What is required in the Ninth Commandment? *Answer*: The Ninth Commandment requires that we maintain and promote truth between persons, upholding our own and our neighbor's good name, especially in witness-bearing.

Theme verse: 'You shall not give false testimony against your neighbor' (Exod. 20:16).

King David asked an extremely important question: 'Lord, who may dwell in your sanctuary? Who may live on your holy hill?' (Ps. 15:1). David asked what the requirements were for being welcomed into God's presence as his special guest. Then the Lord gave the answer: 'He whose walk is blameless and who does what is righteous, who speaks the truth from his heart and has no slander on his tongue, who does his neighbor no wrong and casts no slur on his fellowman' (Ps. 15:2-3). Access into the presence of the Lord is not based on sacrifices or purification ceremonies. It is based on moral righteousness and truth-telling. David and the other psalmists often wrote about their experience of being the recipients of slander and malicious talk: 'His speech is smooth as butter, yet war is in his heart; his words are more soothing than oil, yet they are drawn swords' (Ps. 55:21). The comfort for David, and for us, is that we can appeal to God during times when we are the subject of malicious gossip. In God's courtroom a person finds a sympathetic Judge who will redress such attacks. The person who loves the truth and 'keeps his oath even when it hurts' (Ps. 15:4) is the kind of person who can fall asleep at night with a clear conscience, comforted by the reality that God's sanctuary is open to him now and for eternity.

SCRIPTURE READING: PSALM 15

September 1

Telling the truth

Westminster Catechism Question #77:

What is required in the Ninth Commandment? *Answer*: The Ninth Commandment requires that we maintain and promote truth between persons, upholding our own and our neighbor's good name, especially in witness-bearing.

Theme verse: 'You shall not give false testimony against your neighbor' (Exod. 20:16).

The book of Proverbs emphasizes the damage done by false witnesses: 'A truthful witness gives honest testimony, but a false witness tells lies. Reckless words pierce like a sword, but the tongue of the wise brings healing' (Prov. 12:17-18). In Proverbs 6:16-19 are listed seven things the Lord detests. Four of them bear directly on the ninth commandment: 'a lying tongue … a heart that devises wicked schemes … a false witness who pours out lies and a man who stirs up dissension among brothers.' In Deuteronomy 19:15-21 the Lord gave directions for handling criminal cases and the possibility of false witnesses. More than one witness was needed to convict anyone of a criminal act. And should a malicious witness take the stand the two people involved in the dispute 'must stand in the presence of the Lord before the priests and the judges' (Deut. 19:17). The consequences of such an act are clear. Not only was earthly justice to be meted out against a false witness or the accused, but both men were stating, on oath, that they were willing to stand one day before God as their Judge. Eternity was weighed in the balance based on God's judgement of who was or was not telling the truth. Because eternity is in view for us as well, the ninth commandment requires that we promote truth between persons, especially in witness-bearing.

SCRIPTURE READING: DEUTERONOMY 19:15-21;
PROVERBS 12:14-22

September 2

Telling the truth

Westminster Catechism Question #77:

What is required in the Ninth Commandment? *Answer*: The Ninth Commandment requires that we maintain and promote truth between persons, upholding our own and our neighbor's good name, especially in witness-bearing.

Theme verse: 'You shall not give false testimony against your neighbor' (Exod. 20:16).

Had it been possible for Jesus to compromise his statements and soften the requirements of the ninth commandment, he could have avoided a great deal of pain. During the course of his earthly ministry, he was subjected to many attempts on his life because of his steadfast truthfulness. When Jesus proclaimed his deity as the great 'I Am' (John 8:58) the Pharisees picked up stones to kill him. When Jesus preached in his hometown synagogue and declared that the Scriptures were fulfilled in their hearing, the citizens of Nazareth were enraged by his words, and attempted to throw him down a cliff. Before Pilate, Jesus declared: 'For this reason I was born, and for this I came into the world, to testify to the truth. Everyone on the side of truth listens to me' (John 18:37). When the 'Word became flesh' and lived among us, the two distinguishing characteristics of Jesus were his graciousness and his truthfulness (John 1:14). 'For the law was given through Moses; grace and truth came through Jesus Christ' (John 1:17). In the Garden of Gethsemane Jesus prayed for our spiritual progress: 'Sanctify them by the truth; your word is truth' (John 17:17). Nothing demonstrates so profoundly our freedom from sin and the power of Christ's life within us, than when we obey the truth of God's Word, and 'speak the truth in love' (Eph. 4:15).

SCRIPTURE READING: JOHN 18:28-40

September 3
A MORE EXCELLENT POSSESSION
(WEEK 36: DAY 1)

Do not covet

Westminster Catechism Question #80:

What is required in the Tenth Commandment? *Answer*: The Tenth Commandment requires full contentment with our own condition, with a charitable frame of spirit towards our neighbor, and all that is his.

Theme verse: 'You shall not covet your neighbor's house. You shall not covet your neighbor's wife, or his manservant or maidservant, his ox or donkey, or anything that belongs to your neighbor' (Exod. 20:17).

The tenth commandment forbids a covetous spirit. To 'covet' means to have an eager desire for something, particularly something that belongs to someone else. Rather than coveting, the Bible teaches us to seek the contentment which is found in a vital relationship with God. The Lord promises that if we seek first his kingdom and his righteousness, he will provide all our needs. The Lord offers us himself as a more excellent possession than our puny desires for something less than God, and he chides us for our sinful feelings of jealousy over other people's possessions. Being content with what we have makes our lives peaceful and fulfilling. Paul could testify: 'I have learned to be content whatever the circumstances. I know what it is to be in need, and I know what it is to have plenty. I have learned the secret of being content in any and every situation, whether well fed or hungry, whether living in plenty or in want. I can do everything through him who gives me strength' (Phil. 4:11-13). The tenth commandment also requires that we adopt a favourable attitude towards our neighbours and what belongs to them. If we can have such an attitude we will be conforming to Christ's own attitude of love: 'Each of you should look not only to your own interests, but also to the interests of others' (Phil. 2:4).

SCRIPTURE READING: PHILIPPIANS 4:10-20

September 4

Do not covet

Westminster Catechism Question #80:

What is required in the Tenth Commandment? *Answer*: The Tenth Commandment requires full contentment with our own condition, with a charitable frame of spirit towards our neighbor, and all that is his.

Theme verse: 'You shall not covet your neighbor's house. You shall not covet your neighbor's wife, or his manservant or maidservant, his ox or donkey, or anything that belongs to your neighbor' (Exod. 20:17).

In the early days of the Church the Apostle Philip traveled to a city in Samaria and proclaimed Christ there. The crowds listened attentively to Philip and saw the miraculous signs he performed. Many people were converted and there was great joy in that region. Someone who closely watched the movements of Philip was a man named Simon. He was a magician who had attracted great crowds to watch his sorcery. He claimed he was someone great, a true representative of God. When Simon witnessed the power of the apostles when they laid hands on the people, he offered the disciples money and said: 'Give me also this ability so that everyone on whom I lay my hands may receive the Holy Spirit' (Acts 8:19). But Peter answered him: 'May your money perish with you, because you thought you could buy the gift of God with money! You have no part or share in this ministry, because your heart is not right before God' (Acts 8:20-21). Peter called on Simon to repent of his covetousness because Simon's longing was not for the glory of God, but for the personal glory that would come from showing off his skills. Covetousness is never so ugly and objectionable than when the gracious gifts of the Holy Spirit are improperly used to exalt a person or church rather than honouring the Lord.

SCRIPTURE READING: ACTS 8:9-24

September 5

Do not covet

Westminster Catechism Question #80:

What is required in the Tenth Commandment? *Answer*: The Tenth Commandment requires full contentment with our own condition, with a charitable frame of spirit towards our neighbor, and all that is his.

Theme verse: 'You shall not covet your neighbor's house. You shall not covet your neighbor's wife, or his manservant or maidservant, his ox or donkey, or anything that belongs to your neighbor' (Exod. 20:17).

The Lord most likely placed 'Do not covet' as the final commandment because it encapsulates all the others. A heart freed from covetousness expresses love to Christ by keeping all the commands. But a covetous heart breaks them all. Notice how this plays itself out with each commandment: *The first*: The covetous heart has other gods, whether it is money, a job, alcohol, a relationship, or other obsessions. *The second*: The covetous heart is committed in time and resources to these 'gods', and makes an idol of them. *The third*: A person who covets makes false promises to God to try to fulfil cravings. *The fourth*: There is simply no interest in setting aside a day to worship Christ when the coveted object beckons. *The fifth*: Proper respect for parents and the protection of family relationships lose priority due to covetousness. *The sixth*: A covetous heart tramples on anyone or anything to obtain the object of desire. *The seventh*: An adulterous heart covets what belongs to another. *The eighth*: The covetous heart will rob, steal or cheat to get what it wants. *The ninth*: The covetous heart will lie and slander another in order to gain power, money or advantage. *The tenth*: The covetous heart is jealous of his neighbour's wealth. But in contrast, 'love does no harm to its neighbor. Therefore love is the fulfillment of the law' (Rom. 13:10).

SCRIPTURE READING: EXODUS 20:1-21

262

September 6

Do not covet

Westminster Catechism Question #80:

What is required in the Tenth Commandment? *Answer*: The Tenth Commandment requires full contentment with our own condition, with a charitable frame of spirit towards our neighbor, and all that is his.

Theme verse: 'You shall not covet your neighbor's house. You shall not covet your neighbor's wife, or his manservant or maidservant, his ox or donkey, or anything that belongs to your neighbor' (Exod. 20:17).

God gave us the Ten Commandments to show us what sin looks like. Anyone who scans down the list of these commandments knows that he has broken every one of them. The Apostle Paul tells us that one of the main purposes of the Ten Commandments is for us to realize that we are sinners: 'I would not have known what coveting really was if the law had not said, "Do not covet"' (Rom. 7:7). In fact, Paul goes on to say that knowing the law only makes matters worse: 'But sin, seizing the opportunity afforded by the commandment, produced in me every kind of covetous desire' (Rom. 7:8). If the tenth commandment and all the commands of God actually fan the flames of sin, should we throw them out? Of course not, since we know that the Law of God is spiritual and holy and given to us by God himself. For the sensitive Christian, the law is a constant reminder that we are not like God. He is holy. We are sinners. Paul had a tender heart. He felt the weight of looking at the command, 'do not covet' and it forced him to confess that he was full of covetousness. When the sin of covetousness is so powerful in us, having had a long growing season in our souls, what could ever stamp it out? Praise God, 'because through Christ Jesus the law of the Spirit of life' sets us free 'from the law of sin and death' (Rom. 8:2).

SCRIPTURE READING: ROMANS 7:7 – 8:4

September 7
OVERCOMING TEMPTATIONS
(WEEK 36: DAY 5)

Do not covet

Westminster Catechism Question #80:

What is required in the Tenth Commandment? *Answer*: The Tenth Commandment requires full contentment with our own condition, with a charitable frame of spirit towards our neighbor, and all that is his.

Theme verse: 'You shall not covet your neighbor's house. You shall not covet your neighbor's wife, or his manservant or maidservant, his ox or donkey, or anything that belongs to your neighbor' (Exod. 20:17).

After his fourth missionary journey, Paul was imprisoned once again under Nero, the diabolical emperor at Rome. In his first imprisonment he had lived in a rented house, but now he was chained in a cold dungeon. His friends had difficulty finding him and Paul knew his earthly life was nearly over. In this setting, Paul wrote his second letter to Timothy, asking him to come quickly to see him. Paul was lonely and longed for the Christian fellowship of the devoted Timothy. In the midst of the fires of persecution a number of people had deserted Paul. One such person was a man named Demas. To Timothy the Apostle Paul would write: 'Do your best to come to me quickly, for Demas, because he loved this world, has deserted me and has gone to Thessalonica' (2 Tim. 4:9-10). Demas had been at one time a faithful assistant to Paul (Col. 4:14; Philem. v. 24), but he quickly abandoned Paul when persecution arose. We would like to think well of Demas, but Paul's words are uncompromising. Demas looked at the two options: 1) devotion to Christ and his kingdom (with persecution), or 2) the bright lights of Thessalonica and earthly pleasures. We are compelled to believe that love for Christ was sacrificed and that Demas coveted the world's comforts. This cut into Paul's lonely heart very deeply. Had you been Demas what choice would you have made?

SCRIPTURE READING: 2 TIMOTHY 4:6-22

September 8

Do not covet

Westminster Catechism Question #80:

What is required in the Tenth Commandment? *Answer*: The Tenth Commandment requires full contentment with our own condition, with a charitable frame of spirit towards our neighbor, and all that is his.

Theme verse: 'You shall not covet your neighbor's house. You shall not covet your neighbor's wife, or his manservant or maidservant, his ox or donkey, or anything that belongs to your neighbor' (Exod. 20:17).

One of the warning signs that we are entertaining covetous thoughts is if we find our conversations revolving around finances, possessions, our jobs, or 'shopping 'til we drop'. Jesus warned us that life consists of more than these (Matt. 6:25). When our minds are taken up with earthly things we should recognize that we are in danger. One time when Jesus was speaking before a crowd a man shouted to Jesus: 'Teacher, tell my brother to divide the inheritance with me' (Luke 12:13). Jesus not only refused the man's request, but he also warned him and the gathered crowd to guard against all kinds of covetousness, informing them that a person's life 'does not consist in the abundance of his possessions' (Luke 12:15). Jesus then went on to tell them the parable of the rich fool, who built larger barns to hold his crops, but gave no thought to his eternal soul. Jesus applied his parable to any of us who 'stores up things for himself' but is not rich toward God' (Luke 12:21). Jesus told us, rather, to 'provide purses for yourselves that will not wear out, a treasure in heaven that will not be exhausted, where no thief comes near and no moth destroys. For where your treasure is, there your heart will be also' (Luke 12:33-34). A solid devotional exercise is to make a habit of asking: 'What have my conversations consisted of today?' and 'Where is my treasure?'

SCRIPTURE READING: LUKE 12:13-34

September 9
THE CURE FOR COVETOUSNESS
(WEEK 36: DAY 7)

Do not covet

Westminster Catechism Question #80:

What is required in the Tenth Commandment? *Answer*: The Tenth Commandment requires full contentment with our own condition, with a charitable frame of spirit towards our neighbor, and all that is his.

Theme verse: 'You shall not covet your neighbor's house. You shall not covet your neighbor's wife, or his manservant or maid-servant, his ox or donkey, or anything that belongs to your neighbor' (Exod. 20:17).

What is the cure for covetousness? Here is the Bible's answer: 'This is the victory that has overcome the world, even our faith' (1 John 5:4). The root of covetousness is distrust of God's providence. But faith believes that God will provide, that he who feeds the birds will also feed his children, and that he who clothes the lilies will also clothe us. If we claim that our longing is for heaven but we are constantly feeding at the pig trough, people will see our hypocrisy and we make a mockery of our faith. True faith is the cure for anxious hearts that would worry about tomorrow's cares or jealously covet another person's possessions. True faith not only purifies the heart but satisfies it, because God becomes our delight. 'Lord, you have assigned me my portion and my cup; you have made my lot secure. The boundary lines have fallen for me in pleasant places; surely I have a delightful inheritance' (Ps. 16:5-6). And what an inheritance! But the Word of God is clear: 'no immoral, impure or greedy person — such a man is an idola-ter — has any inheritance in the kingdom of Christ and of God' (Eph. 5:5). What would a covetous person do in heaven? What kind of conversation could he hold with God or those who live there? Faith, then, overcomes love for the world and replaces it with love for Christ. Lord, increase our faith.

SCRIPTURE READING: 1 JOHN 5:1-12

September 10

Keeping the commandments

Westminster Catechism Question #82:

Is anyone able to keep the commandments of God perfectly?
Answer: No one since the fall of Adam and Eve is able to keep
the commandments of God perfectly, but daily breaks them in
thought, word, and deed.

Theme verse: 'If we claim to be without sin, we deceive ourselves
and the truth is not in us' (1 John 1:8).

This week's catechism question and answer explains God's purpose in giving us the Ten Commandments. The Lord is aware
of our inability to keep the commands. We break them daily in
thought, word and deed. The Law was given to show us our sinfulness and drive us to a Saviour who frees us from the condemnation of the Law. Our theme verse (1 John 1:8) reaffirms what we
know internally, that we are sinners in need of rescue. The Bible
tells us to run in faith to the Redeemer and rejoice in his atoning sacrifice for us on the cross. He has removed the penalty for
lawbreakers such as we are. The catechism answer also reminds
us of the doctrine of justification. Since we are unable to keep the
commandments, God needs to justify saving us. The justification
for his pardoning our sins is that he sent Christ to pay the penalty
for sin in our place. We are justified by grace through faith, not
by keeping the law. Now that we have been set free from the condemnation of the law, we rejoice in the Ten Commandments. By
Christ's Spirit, we are able to live according to their standard, not
because we must in order to gain salvation, but because we want
to please him who has rescued us from sin and death. In view of
God's mercy, 'offer your bodies as living sacrifices, holy and pleasing to God — this is your spiritual act of worship' (Rom. 12:1).

SCRIPTURE READING: 1 JOHN 1:5 – 2:6

September 11

No one is righteous

(week 37: day 2)

Keeping the commandments

Westminster Catechism Question #82:

Is anyone able to keep the commandments of God perfectly?
Answer: No one since the fall of Adam and Eve is able to keep
the commandments of God perfectly, but daily breaks them in
thought, word, and deed.

Theme verse: 'If we claim to be without sin, we deceive ourselves
and the truth is not in us' (1 John 1:8).

Probably because we are so prone to minimize the awfulness and
gravity of sin, large portions of the Bible are devoted to explain-
ing it. For instance, in Romans 3:10-18, the Apostle Paul pulls
together quotations from the Old Testament that condemn us,
stating that both Jews and Gentiles are under the power and dom-
ination of sin. The extent of our depravity is total. Every part of
our being is polluted. Not one person is righteous (Rom. 3:10).
Our minds do not comprehend the nature of God and no one is
interested in seeking after God (Rom. 3:11). Absolutely everyone
is inclined towards evil (Rom. 3:12). Our speech is full of either
cursing or slander, and our words are full of deadly poison (Rom.
3:13-14). With vicious schemes formulated in our minds, we rush
to carry out our evil intentions (Rom. 3:17). Paul's conclusion,
drawn from Psalm 36:1, summarizes the sad appraisal of our condition: 'There is no fear of God before their eyes.' The Scriptures
paint a sombre picture. It is not that we are as bad as we could
possibly be; it is simply that every part of our being is polluted.
We have a sin nature that leaves us hopelessly short of God's standard of perfect righteousness and required holiness. God wants
us to recognize our sin nature so that we will be more appreciative
of the greatness of his deliverance, and that we will respond with
grateful hearts.

Scripture reading: Romans 3:9-20

268

September 12

Keeping the commandments

Westminster Catechism Question #82:

Is anyone able to keep the commandments of God perfectly?
Answer: No one since the fall of Adam and Eve is able to keep
the commandments of God perfectly, but daily breaks them in
thought, word, and deed.

Theme verse: 'If we claim to be without sin, we deceive ourselves
and the truth is not in us' (1 John 1:8).

When Jesus was instructing Nicodemus on the need to believe
in him for salvation he gave this judgment: 'This is the verdict:
Light has come into the world, but men loved darkness instead of
light because their deeds were evil' (John 3:19). Jesus was telling
us that by nature we love darkness rather than light; we love sin
rather than holiness. When we are freed from this natural love
for darkness we become lovers of the light and of the commandments of God at the same time. But the Word of God as well
as our own personal experience testifies that 'the sinful mind is
hostile to God. It does not submit to God's law, nor can it do so.
Those controlled by the sinful nature cannot please God' (Rom.
8:7-8). Sometimes people try to alleviate their own sense of guilt
by making charitable contributions, volunteering their time, making a New Year's resolution, or some other personal sacrifice. But
on our own we can never get rid of our guilt and shame. Only the
Lord can show us the way to freedom from guilt and bring fulfilment. The Bible provides us the light that reveals the dangers in
our path and also opens before us a pathway to hope. Jesus said,
'It is not the healthy who need a doctor, but the sick … For I have
not come to call the righteous, but sinners' (Matt. 9:12-13).

SCRIPTURE READING: MATTHEW 9:1-13

September 13
PARTIAL OBEDIENCE PROHIBITED
(WEEK 37: DAY 4)

Keeping the commandments

Westminster Catechism Question #82:

Is anyone able to keep the commandments of God perfectly?
Answer: No one since the fall of Adam and Eve is able to keep
the commandments of God perfectly, but daily breaks them in
thought, word, and deed.

Theme verse: 'If we claim to be without sin, we deceive ourselves
and the truth is not in us' (1 John 1:8).

People will not enter heaven by trying to keep the Law in their
own strength. The Ten Commandments require perfect and perpetual obedience, and nothing less will do. The commandments
are not ten suggestions; they are commands that are obligatory. If
we conclude that merely making an effort to keep them is sufficient, the Ten Commandments and all other scriptural commands
lose their authority. God is not interested in partial obedience. His
verdict on keeping fifty or seventy per cent of his commands is:
'Cursed is everyone who does not continue to do everything written in the Book of the Law' (Gal. 3:10). In other words, we either
obey completely or we accept that we are condemned law-break-
ers. It is better if we accept the obvious and recognize that we are
powerless to keep God's holy law since 'no one will be declared
righteous in his sight by observing the law; rather, through the
law we become conscious of sin' (Rom. 3:20). Our calling, then, is
to rest in God's plan of rescuing us from condemnation. Clearly,
it is not a plan we would have devised. The blueprint was a display of wisdom beyond the intelligence of human beings. It was
God's design to send his own Son in human flesh. What a wonder!
It challenges the admiration of angels, and demands gratitude,
praise, and joyful acceptance from every human being.

SCRIPTURE READING: GALATIANS 3:1-14

September 14

Keeping the commandments

Westminster Catechism Question #82:

Is anyone able to keep the commandments of God perfectly?
Answer: No one since the fall of Adam and Eve is able to keep
the commandments of God perfectly, but daily breaks them in
thought, word, and deed.

Theme verse: 'If we claim to be without sin, we deceive ourselves
and the truth is not in us' (1 John 1:8).

Jesus knows all things in advance. Nothing catches him by surprise. So we can be assured that Jesus was not caught off guard
by the movements of those who plotted his death. In fact, we can
go further and say that the Lord charted the course of events that
would lead to his death: 'Indeed Herod and Pontius Pilate met
together with the Gentiles and the people of Israel in this city
to conspire against your holy servant Jesus, whom you anointed. They did what your power and will had decided beforehand
should happen' (Acts 4:27-28). Two things are at work here. First,
the Lord gave up his life voluntarily and submitted to the agony
of the cross because it was his will to do so. The Lord set the
date, time and place for the cataclysmic event of the cross. But
secondly, the major role-players who participated in the death of
Christ were not robots. Jesus 'did not need man's testimony about
man, for he knew what was in a man' (John 2:25). He did not
have to manipulate their evil hearts to move in a direction against
their will. Herod, Pilate, Judas, the Romans and the Jewish leaders simply followed their own sinful nature in making their decisions. Breaking the commandments of God was instinctive. The
Saviour's sacrifice broke the power of the sin nature in believers so
that our new nature can now make God-honouring choices.

Scripture reading: John 2:12-25

September 15
THE DOWNWARD SPIRAL
(WEEK 37: DAY 6)

Keeping the commandments

Westminster Catechism Question #82:

Is anyone able to keep the commandments of God perfectly?
Answer: No one since the fall of Adam and Eve is able to keep
the commandments of God perfectly, but daily breaks them in
thought, word, and deed.

Theme verse: 'If we claim to be without sin, we deceive ourselves
and the truth is not in us' (1 John 1:8).

After Adam and Eve sinned in the Garden of Eden the downward
spiral of humankind was shockingly rapid. Cain soon killed his
brother. Within just a few generations, Lamech, a descendant of
Cain, announced his complete independence from God, boldly
committing murder and claiming to be the master of his own des-
tiny: 'I have killed a man for wounding me, a young man for injur-
ing me. If Cain is avenged seven times, then Lamech seventy-seven
times' (Gen. 4:23-24). The downward spiral continued to the point
where the wickedness of mankind was so great 'that every inclination of the thoughts of his heart was only evil all the time' (Gen.
6:5). We are told that the Lord was grieved that he had made us:
'I will wipe mankind, whom I have created, from the face of the
earth' (Gen. 6:7). The Lord's judgement of the human heart is
that it is rebellious, and that we break his commandments daily in
thought, word and deed. Therefore, in judgement, the Lord sent
a flood that wiped out all but a few members of the human family. But in mercy, he spared the lineage of godly Noah. This act of
judgement and mercy was a foreshadowing of future events. One
day he is coming again in judgement to destroy his enemies. But
he also will show mercy and 'be marveled at among all those who
have believed' (2 Thess. 1:10).

SCRIPTURE READING: GENESIS 6:1-8

September 16
SUDDENLY PERFECT
(WEEK 37: DAY 7)

Keeping the commandments

Westminster Catechism Question #82:

Is anyone able to keep the commandments of God perfectly?
Answer: No one since the fall of Adam and Eve is able to keep
the commandments of God perfectly, but daily breaks them in
thought, word, and deed.

Theme verse: 'If we claim to be without sin, we deceive ourselves
and the truth is not in us' (1 John 1:8).

One day we will keep the Lord's commandments perfectly. Most
of us understand the concept but have a hard time envisioning the
reality. Everything in our earthly experience is flawed and imperfect. The Apostle Paul confirmed this when he wrote: 'the whole
creation has been groaning up to the present time. Not only so,
but we ourselves, who have the firstfruits of the Spirit, groan inwardly as we wait eagerly for our adoption as sons, the redemption of our bodies' (Rom. 8:22-23). But then the day of Christ's
return will come and what a day that will be! Suddenly, everything
will be made perfect. 'In a flash, in the twinkling of an eye ... we
will be changed' (1 Cor. 15:52). Pain, sorrow and the groaning of
creation will finally be no more. On that day 'the ransomed of the
Lord will return. They will enter Zion with singing; everlasting
joy will crown their heads. Gladness and joy will overtake them,
and sorrow and sighing will flee away' (Isa. 35:10). Keeping the
commands of God will come naturally to us, and our inclinations
will be to always uphold them. In a true sense, the Ten Commandments, and all the commands of God, will be loved inwardly and
practised outwardly and effortlessly. And this will be the reason:
'We know that when he appears, we shall be like him, for we shall
see him as he is' (1 John 3:2).

SCRIPTURE READING: ISAIAH 35:1-10

September 17
REMOVING CONDEMNATION FROM US
(WEEK 38: DAY 1)

The wrath of God

Westminster Catechism Question #84:

What does every sin deserve? *Answer*: Every sin deserves God's wrath and curse, both in this life, and that which is to come.

Theme verse: 'No immoral, impure, or greedy person — such a man is an idolater — has any inheritance in the kingdom of Christ and of God' (Eph. 5:5).

When we think of Christ giving up his life at Calvary's cross we normally view his victory as directed primarily on behalf of men and women. But the Bible teaches that Christ's work at the cross was directed, first of all, towards God the Father. The Father's anger for our sinful conduct must be assuaged if we are to escape his punishment for our sin. When we think of the cross and reflect on the Redeemer dying there for us, we should see as of first importance, not our salvation, but our condemnation being carried away by the Lord. The Apostle John puts it this way: 'He is the atoning sacrifice for our sins' (1 John 2:2). This means that Jesus is the one who turns aside God's wrath and takes away our sins, satisfying the Father's anger with regards to our sin. As our theme verse indicates, no person whose sins are not atoned for can inherit the kingdom of Christ and of God: 'Whoever believes in the Son has eternal life, but whoever rejects the Son will not see life, for God's wrath remains on him' (John 3:36). When Christ died he fully paid the penalty for our sin and covered the debt we had built up before God. He fully met the demands to satisfy his Father's offended holiness and justice. Jesus offered his blood as an atoning sacrifice for sin. His life, of infinite worth, was the price required to set condemned sinners free.

SCRIPTURE READING: JOHN 3:22-36

274

September 18
CONTROLLED WRATH
(WEEK 38: DAY 2)

The wrath of God

Westminster Catechism Question #84:

What does every sin deserve? *Answer*: Every sin deserves God's wrath and curse, both in this life, and that which is to come.

Theme verse: 'No immoral, impure, or greedy person — such a man is an idolater — has any inheritance in the kingdom of Christ and of God' (Eph. 5:5).

God's righteous anger against sin is a controlled wrath. The Lord is not enraged like some irrational madman. Nor is God vindictive, unfeeling or spiteful. God's wrath is simply his holy indignation against sin. Because our Lord is righteous he expresses his hatred and personal revulsion to evil and his opposition to it by judging and condemning it. Therefore, before anything else, it is this demand in God himself — that his offended holiness must be satisfied — that necessitated the cross where Jesus made himself a perfect sin offering. Without the cross, it is our responsibility to fully meet the demands of the Ten Commandments, a demand that is too great for us. Without the cross, we remain objects of God's wrath, fully deserving of hell. However, at the cross, Jesus makes himself a perfect sin offering. Now, rather than being cast into hell, believers are covered by Christ's atoning sacrifice. For the believer in Jesus, the Father no longer demonstrates his anger for our sin. Instead, he displays his love towards us who are covered by the righteousness of Christ. 'This is how God showed his love among us: He sent his one and only Son into the world that we might live through him. This is love, not that we loved God, but that he loved us and sent his Son as an atoning sacrifice for our sins' (1 John 4:9-10).

SCRIPTURE READING: 1 JOHN 4:7-21

September 19

The wrath of God

Westminster Catechism Question #84:

What does every sin deserve? *Answer*: Every sin deserves God's wrath and curse, both in this life, and that which is to come.

Theme verse: 'No immoral, impure, or greedy person — such a man is an idolater — has any inheritance in the kingdom of Christ and of God' (Eph. 5:5).

From the human perspective, the world has all kinds of people from various backgrounds. But 'the Lord does not look at the things man looks at. Man looks at the outward appearance, but the Lord looks at the heart' (1 Sam. 16:7). The Lord, who looks only at the heart, sees only two kinds of people. John the Baptist used an analogy of 'wheat' and 'chaff' to explain the difference between these two groups. 'His winnowing fork is in his hand, and he will clear his threshing floor, gathering his wheat into the barn and burning up the chaff with unquenchable fire' (Matt. 3:12). The 'wheat' refers to all men and women who are believers in the Lord Jesus: people who are led by the Holy Spirit, who have known themselves as sinners, and have fled for refuge to the salvation offered in the gospel. The 'wheat' love and serve the Lord and they are his delight. The 'chaff' refers to all men and women who have no saving faith in Christ. Such people can be atheists or indifferent towards Christ, or even 'Christian', but in name only. They do not live for Christ and therefore bring him no glory or honour. They neglect the salvation that has been offered to them and live as if their time on earth is more important than eternity. The weighty question is neglected only at one's peril: are you wheat or are you chaff?

SCRIPTURE READING: 1 SAMUEL 16:1-13

September 20
HUMAN DEPRAVITY
(WEEK 38: DAY 4)

The wrath of God

Westminster Catechism Question #84:

What does every sin deserve? *Answer*: Every sin deserves God's wrath and curse, both in this life, and that which is to come.

Theme verse: 'No immoral, impure, or greedy person — such a man is an idolater — has any inheritance in the kingdom of Christ and of God' (Eph. 5:5).

The Scriptures make it clear that God's wrath against sin is not limited to end-time judgement of the wicked. In Romans 1, the Apostle Paul describes people who receive God's judgement here and now. 'The wrath of God is being revealed from heaven against all the godlessness and wickedness of men who suppress the truth by their wickedness' (Rom. 1:18). Paul identifies such people as those who intentionally suppress the obvious; for instance, that God has created all things (Rom. 1:20). Such people also refuse to glorify God or give thanks to the Lord for all his goodness (Rom. 1:21). They are proud, and in their foolishness exchange worship of God for worship of that which he has made (Rom. 1:23). As the wicked become more entrenched in their sin, God gives them over to their sinful desires, to sexual impurity and to shameful lusts (Rom. 1:24-27). Finally, the Lord abandons the wicked to 'a depraved mind, to do what ought not to be done' (Rom. 1:28), inventing ways of doing evil and encouraging others to do the same (Rom. 1:30-32). Such unspeakable conduct is not done ignorantly. Evil practice only finds its satisfaction when it is done in direct rebellion against God and his holy Law. God, of course, is not mocked. 'The Lord takes vengeance on his foes and maintains his wrath against his enemies' (Nahum 1:2).

SCRIPTURE READING: ROMANS 1:18-32

September 21

The wrath of God

Westminster Catechism Question #84:

What does every sin deserve? *Answer*: Every sin deserves God's wrath and curse, both in this life, and that which is to come.

Theme verse: 'No immoral, impure, or greedy person — such a man is an idolater — has any inheritance in the kingdom of Christ and of God' (Eph. 5:5).

When Paul wrote to the Ephesians he reminded them of what they were like before their conversion. 'As for you, you were dead in your transgressions and sins, in which you used to live when you followed the ways of this world' (Eph. 2:1-2). Paul does not leave it at that; he reminds his fellow believers that they had followed Satan and obeyed Satan's voice rather than Christ's (Eph. 2:2). He includes himself in this indictment: 'all of us also lived among them at one time, gratifying the cravings of our sinful nature' (Eph. 2:3). These evil practices are the evidence, for Paul, that 'we were by nature objects of wrath' (Eph. 2:4). God's wrath is the unchanging reaction of his holiness and righteousness against all that is sinful. It is like fire when it touches tinder, full of power and energy to destroy that which is doomed to destruction. But then the wonderful contrast: 'But because of his great love for us, God, who is rich in mercy, made us alive with Christ even when we were dead in transgressions' (Eph. 2:4-5). God sees our deadness and is moved to bring us to life. This divine, infinite love will ever remain the most wondrous and glorious mystery in the universe, far too deep for our finite minds to comprehend. One of heaven's great occupations will be to fathom more fully the depth of such love. Let us fall down before him and adore him.

SCRIPTURE READING: EPHESIANS 2:1-10

The wrath of God

Westminster Catechism Question #84:

What does every sin deserve? *Answer*: Every sin deserves God's wrath and curse, both in this life, and that which is to come.

Theme verse: 'No immoral, impure, or greedy person — such a man is an idolater — has any inheritance in the kingdom of Christ and of God' (Eph. 5:5).

Throughout the book of Hebrews the author warns his readers of the danger of leaving the fellowship of the Christian community. The mainly Jewish believers were enduring physical threats and other forms of persecution. Many were living in hiding. Under such circumstances many were wondering if following Christ was really worth all the pain. At first, the author simply warns his fellow believers against drifting away (Heb. 2:1). Then he warns them not to harden their hearts (Heb. 3:8). Further on, his admonitions become stronger, declaring that falling away from the faith is 'crucifying the Son of God all over again' (Heb. 6:6). By Hebrews 10 the author places before his readers the possibility of eternal judgement and speaks of abandoning the faith as the worst kind of sin: 'If we deliberately keep on sinning after we have received the knowledge of the truth, no sacrifice for sins is left, but only a fearful expectation of judgment and of raging fire that will consume the enemies of God' (Heb. 10:26-27). The author had his listeners take a good look around to see if there was any other person who could save them other than Jesus. He warned them that to reject the Lord Jesus was to place themselves in great jeopardy. 'It is a dreadful thing to fall into the hands of the living God' (Heb. 10:31).

SCRIPTURE READING: HEBREWS 10:19-39

September 23
FINAL JUDGEMENT
(WEEK 38: DAY 7)

The wrath of God

Westminster Catechism Question #84:

What does every sin deserve? *Answer*: Every sin deserves God's wrath and curse, both in this life, and that which is to come.

Theme verse: 'No immoral, impure, or greedy person — such a man is an idolater — has any inheritance in the kingdom of Christ and of God' (Eph. 5:5).

At the end of human history Jesus will return as the great Warrior-Messiah-King. The image of Christ that is revealed in Revelation 19 is vivid and awe-inspiring. His eyes are like blazing fire (Rev. 19:12). The armies of heaven follow him, also riding on white horses and dressed in fine linen (Rev. 19:14). The Apostle John describes Jesus as a great warrior with a sharp sword 'with which to strike down the nations ... He treads the winepress of the fury of the wrath of God almighty' (Rev. 19:15-16). An angel summons the wild birds to the immense slaughter that is about to take place (Rev. 19:17). All the anti-Christian powers are now to meet their doom. Satan's followers are 'killed with the sword that came out of the mouth of the rider on the horse' (Rev. 19:21). Satan himself is 'thrown into the lake of burning sulfur' (Rev. 20:10). Finally, all who have ever lived on the earth are gathered before King Jesus. Each person is 'judged according to what he had done' (Rev. 20:13), and, 'If anyone's name was not found written in the book of life, he was thrown into the lake of fire' (Rev. 20:15). At the end of time every force opposed to the rule and will of God will be crushed by Christ in this final, great judgement. 'For the wages of sin is death, but the gift of God is eternal life in CHRIST JESUS OUR LORD' (ROM. 6:23).

SCRIPTURE READING: REVELATION 19:11-21

PART 4:

THE MEANS OF GRACE

September 24

Faith

Westminster Catechism Question #86:

What is faith in Jesus Christ? *Answer*: Faith in Jesus Christ is a saving grace by which we receive and rest upon him alone for salvation, as he is offered to us in the gospel.

Theme verse: 'Yet to all who received him, to those who believed in his name, he gave the right to become children of God' (John 1:12).

Faith in Christ is necessary for salvation and is something God gives us in order to respond to him. The Bible explains what faith is. First, faith is a firm conviction which causes a person to acknowledge fully that what the Bible teaches is true: 'Now faith is being sure of what we hope for and certain of what we do not see' (Heb. 11:1). Secondly, faith is a personal surrender to Jesus Christ. 'Yet to all who received him, to those who believed in his name, he gave the right to become children of God' (John 1:12). Thirdly, faith is a life inspired to serve Christ with joy, having surrendered to him. 'Consider it pure joy, my brothers, whenever you face trials of many kinds, because you know that the testing of your faith develops perseverance. Perseverance must finish its work so that you may be mature and complete, not lacking anything' (James 1:2-4). The Scriptures explain that true faith is not just an intellectual opinion about God and the Christian faith. True faith perseveres and matures during times of trial, temptation and difficulty. Faith motivates us to seek with all our hearts the things that are unseen, including Christ himself, rather than becoming preoccupied with things that we see. True faith unites God's people and God in a relationship of love which lasts for eternity.

SCRIPTURE READING: HEBREWS 11:1-7

September 25

Faith

Westminster Catechism Question #86:

What is faith in Jesus Christ? *Answer*: Faith in Jesus Christ is a saving grace by which we receive and rest upon him alone for salvation, as he is offered to us in the gospel.

Theme verse: 'Yet to all who received him, to those who believed in his name, he gave the right to become children of God' (John 1:12).

The Apostle Paul longed to see his fellow Jews come to faith in the Lord Jesus Christ. But Israel's problem, according to Paul, was that they sought God's approval through their own efforts. They pursued a law of righteousness 'not by faith but as if it were by works' (Rom. 9:32). Such attempts always end in futility, because we can never merit God's favour by trying to keep God's commands in our own strength. God has told us how we can gain access to him and receive his righteousness. It is through faith in his Son. Israel rejected God's appointed means of salvation and therefore God rejected Israel. Paul's heart longed for the people of Israel to correct their thinking and prayed for the day the Lord would give them faith to accept their Messiah: 'My heart's desire and prayer to God for the Israelites is that they may be saved ... Since they did not know the righteousness that comes from God and sought to establish their own, they did not submit to God's righteousness' (Rom. 10:1,3). Paul could empathize with his fellow Jews. He had also had zeal for God, but like their zeal, it was based on a flawed understanding of God's way of salvation. Now that he had been shown mercy by God, Paul knew salvation came by grace 'through faith — and this not from yourselves, it is the gift of God — not by works, so that no one can boast' (Eph. 2:8-9).

SCRIPTURE READING: ROMANS 9:30 – 10:13

September 26
ABRAHAM'S FAITH
(WEEK 39: DAY 3)

Faith

Westminster Catechism Question #86:

What is faith in Jesus Christ? *Answer*: Faith in Jesus Christ is a saving grace by which we receive and rest upon him alone for salvation, as he is offered to us in the gospel.

Theme verse: 'Yet to all who received him, to those who believed in his name, he gave the right to become children of God' (John 1:12).

People with true faith demonstrate a consistent walk with God on a daily basis. Hebrews 11 provides three instances of Abraham's humble confidence in the Lord. First, Abraham left his secure home and journeyed to an unknown destination. He lived in tents as a foreigner in a new land, which required fresh faith for each new day. The reason that he lived in tents was because he believed God was preparing a secure home for him in heaven: a 'city with foundations, whose architect and builder is God' (Heb. 11:10). Secondly, Abraham believed that he and Sarah would have descendants: 'even though he was past age — and Sarah herself was barren' (Heb. 11:11). Abraham believed God could be counted on to keep his promise of a child. Thirdly, when God required Abraham to sacrifice Isaac, he believed God would miraculously resurrect Isaac. Abraham knew that God had made a covenant vow that through Isaac his offspring would come and that God cannot lie. With that firm faith conviction as bedrock for his thinking, Abraham proceeded to offer his son as a sacrifice. 'Abraham reasoned that God could raise the dead, and figuratively speaking, he did receive Isaac back from death' (Heb. 11:19). God is seeking men and women who possess Abrahamic faith, people who confidently trust the one who is always faithful.

SCRIPTURE READING: HEBREWS 11:8-19

September 27

Faith

Westminster Catechism Question #86:

What is faith in Jesus Christ? *Answer*: Faith in Jesus Christ is
a saving grace by which we receive and rest upon him alone for
salvation, as he is offered to us in the gospel.

Theme verse: 'Yet to all who received him, to those who believed
in his name, he gave the right to become children of God'
(John 1:12).

Lydia lived in the city of Thyatira, but through the providential
leading of God, she was in Philippi at the opportune time, where
she heard the preaching of the Apostle Paul. Although Lydia was
not familiar with Jesus, she was a Jewish woman, and therefore
had an excellent background for receiving Paul's proclamation.
On the Sabbath she went outside the city to a place of prayer.
There, 'the Lord opened her heart to respond to Paul's message'
(Acts 16:14). Lydia was given faith to receive the preaching as true.
It was not her prayers or Paul's powers of persuasion that opened
her heart to Jesus. It was the Holy Spirit who opened Lydia's heart
to receive the salvation offered to her in the gospel. The first outward evidence of saving faith was that Lydia and her believing
household were baptized. Paul obviously preached about the necessity of making an outward declaration of new faith and Lydia
willingly submitted to baptism as a sign that she now belonged
to the Lord. This was an opportunity for the family to publicly
demonstrate their new faith. The next evidence of Lydia's faith is
seen in her love, manifesting itself in hospitality: 'If you consider
me a believer in the Lord come and stay at my house' (Acts 16:15).
Love for fellow believers is a true mark of saving faith. Lord, open
our hearts as you did Lydia's.

SCRIPTURE READING: ACTS 16:6-15

September 28
CENTURION FAITH
(WEEK 39: DAY 5)

Faith

Westminster Catechism Question #86:

What is faith in Jesus Christ? *Answer*: Faith in Jesus Christ is
a saving grace by which we receive and rest upon him alone for
salvation, as he is offered to us in the gospel.

Theme verse: 'Yet to all who received him, to those who believed
in his name, he gave the right to become children of God'
(John 1:12).

One day Jesus entered the town of Capernaum, in Galilee. A Roman centurion, a man in charge of one hundred troops, was head-
quartered there. The centurion had a servant who was sick and
about to die. He sent Jewish elders to Jesus, requesting that Jesus
heal his servant. The elders were earnest in their request because
the centurion, though he was a Roman, was loved by the Jewish
community. He was concerned for the welfare of the people and
had even built the local synagogue. The striking thing about this
commander was his humility and complete trust in the power of
Jesus. When he learned that Jesus was on his way and knowing
Jewish laws concerning defilement by entering a Gentile home,
he sent friends to Jesus to say: 'Lord, don't trouble yourself, for I
do not deserve to have you come under my roof' (Luke 7:6). He
simply was asking that Jesus 'say the word and my servant will be
healed' (Luke 7:7). The greatness of the centurion's faith was apparent in his humility. Though the man was a high military officer
and great benefactor of the Jews he considered himself utterly
unworthy. Also this man's faith was centred on the *word* of Jesus.
Merely from what this man had heard about Jesus, without further experience and teaching, he showed absolute trust in Jesus'
word and its power. Lord, grant us such faith, where your word
is enough.

SCRIPTURE READING: LUKE 7:1-10

September 29

Faith

Westminster Catechism Question #86:

What is faith in Jesus Christ? *Answer*: Faith in Jesus Christ is a saving grace by which we receive and rest upon him alone for salvation, as he is offered to us in the gospel.

Theme verse: 'Yet to all who received him, to those who believed in his name, he gave the right to become children of God' (John 1:12).

Other than the centurion, the only other recorded time that Jesus publicly recognized a person's great faith was that of the Canaanite woman. Although she was a pagan woman, living outside of Israel, she understood that Jesus was claiming to be the Messiah of Israel: 'Lord, Son of David, have mercy on me!' (Matt. 15:22). Her daughter was suffering under the bondage of demon-possession. The disciples wanted Jesus to send her away, since it is apparent she was a nuisance, dogging their every move. Jesus turned to her and initially refused her request: 'It is not right to take the children's bread and toss it to their dogs' (Matt. 15:26). It appears that Jesus was unwilling to help someone outside the community of Israel. But in reality, the Messiah was simply drawing out her greater reserves of faith. The Saviour was not disappointed. This humble woman responded: 'Yes, Lord, but even the dogs eat the crumbs that fall from their masters' table' (Matt. 15:27). Jesus responded to the Canaanite woman: 'Woman, you have great faith! Your request is granted' (Matt. 15:28). Sometimes we wonder why the Lord doesn't answer our prayers immediately. Often it is because he wants to stretch our faith, causing us to seek him repeatedly and with increasing earnestness. The Lord challenges us to keep on asking, keep on seeking and keep on knocking.

SCRIPTURE READING: MATTHEW 15:21-28

September 30
FAITH'S DIVINE ORIGIN
(WEEK 39: DAY 7)

Faith

Westminster Catechism Question #86:

What is faith in Jesus Christ? *Answer*: Faith in Jesus Christ is a saving grace by which we receive and rest upon him alone for salvation, as he is offered to us in the gospel.

Theme verse: 'Yet to all who received him, to those who believed in his name, he gave the right to become children of God' (John 1:12).

Faith is the spiritual eye of the soul. It is the key that unlocks the door to a relationship with Jesus. Faith sees Christ, and as Christ is seen he becomes the object of delight, the pearl of great price. Saving faith has only one object and when we place our faith in Christ we can say: 'I know whom I have believed, and am convinced that he is able to guard what I have entrusted to him for that day' (2 Tim. 1:12). Faith sees majesty in Christ's words, dignity in the way he lived his earthly life and glory in his cross. The reason Peter would define it as 'precious faith' (2 Peter 1:1) and as 'of greater worth than gold' (1 Peter 1:7) is because of its divine origin. It comes from above; it is a free gift of God and a heavenly kindness. We place faith in all sorts of things: our car to get us from point A to point B, the chair to support our weight, the grocery store to provide uncontaminated food, gravity to keep dishes in the cupboard, and friends to keep confidences. But saving faith is supernatural, graciously given to us by God. Without faith, 'it is impossible to please God' (Heb. 11:6). It believes God's Word, trusts in Jesus for salvation, accepts the invisible Spirit as real, embraces tests and trials as essential for deepening faith, and is 'sure of what we hope for and certain of what we do not see' (Heb. 11:1).

SCRIPTURE READING: 2 TIMOTHY 1:1-14

October 1

Repentance

Westminster Catechism Question #87:

What is repentance? *Answer*: Repentance is a saving grace, by which a sinner, out of a true sense of his sin, and a realization of the mercy of God in Christ, with grief and hatred of his sin, turns from it to God, fully intending to endeavor to live a life of new obedience.

Theme verse: "'Return, faithless people; I will cure you of back-sliding.' 'Yes, we will come to you, for you are the Lord our God'" (Jer. 3:22).

Repentance occurs when an individual becomes aware of his or her spiritual poverty and sinfulness. Repentance subdues pride, producing a sense of personal unworthiness which leads to surrender to God in genuine humility. It is a profound change of the mind, heart and will. First, a change of *mind* causes a person to recognize the sinfulness of sin and the attractiveness of living a life of obedience to God. The sinner sees God's commandments as perfect and binding, and knows that he or she falls far short of what God requires. Secondly, a change of *heart* causes a person to hate sin because it dishonours God and destroys lives. Thirdly, a change of *will* causes a person to strive to be holy in order to please God. The outcome of repentance is a sanctified life. Jesus spoke about this at the outset of his ministry when he preached the Beatitudes. The first four Beatitudes (Matthew 5:3-6) record the steps which take a repentant sinner from death to life: 'Blessed are the poor in spirit', rather than proud and self-sufficient; 'Blessed are those who mourn', rather than those who never come to a place of sadness over their sins; 'Blessed are the meek', a humble spirit before God rather than a haughty, rebellious spirit; 'Blessed are those who hunger and thirst for righteousness', who long to be like Jesus, rather than like the world.

SCRIPTURE READING: MATTHEW 5:1-12

October 2
GODLY SORROW
(WEEK 40: DAY 2)

Repentance

Westminster Catechism Question #87:

What is repentance? *Answer*: Repentance is a saving grace, by which a sinner, out of a true sense of his sin, and a realization of the mercy of God in Christ, with grief and hatred of his sin, turns from it to God, fully intending to endeavor to live a life of new obedience.

Theme verse: "'Return, faithless people; I will cure you of backsliding.' 'Yes, we will come to you, for you are the Lord our God'" (Jer. 3:22).

At one point, the Apostle Paul had to write a very strongly-worded letter to the Corinthian church. His rebuke was very sharp, but it had good effect. The people responded with true, godly sorrow for their sinful practices: 'Even if I caused you sorrow by my letter, I do not regret it … not because you were made sorry, but because your sorrow led you to repentance' (2 Cor. 7:8-9). Paul went on to mention two kinds of sorrow. There is sorrow that leads to repentance and there is also sorrow that leads only to remorse. Some people are sad about their sin because they have been caught, or have been hurt by making poor choices. This type of sorrow is not real repentance and brings no spiritual change. But true repentance involves recognition of the heinousness of sin and a desire to be forgiven by God and to avoid such sins in the future. Thankfully, this was the type of sorrow the Corinthian church displayed. Paul noted that it produced earnestness to have their names cleared, longing to be made right with God, and alarm that they had strayed so far from obedience to God. 'Godly sorrow brings repentance that leads to salvation and leaves no regret, but worldly sorrow brings death' (2 Cor. 7:10). Instead of a self-centred sorrow that only regrets being caught, ask God for a repentant heart that pleads for heavenly grace.

SCRIPTURE READING: 2 CORINTHIANS 7:2-16

October 3
Repent or Perish
(week 40: day 3)

Repentance

Westminster Catechism Question #87:

What is repentance? *Answer*: Repentance is a saving grace, by which a sinner, out of a true sense of his sin, and a realization of the mercy of God in Christ, with grief and hatred of his sin, turns from it to God, fully intending to endeavor to live a life of new obedience.

Theme verse: "'Return, faithless people; I will cure you of backsliding.' 'Yes, we will come to you, for you are the Lord our God'" (Jer. 3:22).

One day some people who were gathered around Jesus asked him about the Galileans who had died at the hands of Pilate. Apparently, while these Galileans were worshiping in the temple, Pilate ordered them to be killed and their blood to be mixed with the blood of their animal sacrifices. Such an act of defilement was an unspeakable offence to faithful Jews. Most Jews would assume that these poor Galileans were guilty of a major transgression for God to have allowed their deaths to occur in such a horrific manner. But Jesus cleared up their theological confusion by answering: 'Do you think that these Galileans were worse sinners than all the other Galileans because they suffered this way? I tell you, no! But unless you repent, you too will all perish' (Luke 13:3). The Lord informed his listeners that these poor Galileans were not worse sinners than the rest of us. In fact, we have no right to consider ourselves out of danger of death if we are strangers to true repentance. It will not suffice to simply be alarmed about our sin. Genuine repentance must be felt and known inwardly; it is an abiding sense of sin, and a turning away from it with grief that we have loved it in the past. This sense of sin should drive us to Christ who possesses power to cleanse and forgive. Jesus urges us to come to him. He is able to save repentant sinners from a dreadful end.

Scripture reading: Luke 13:1-9

October 4
OUR FIRST DUTY
(WEEK 40: DAY 4)

Repentance

Westminster Catechism Question #87:

What is repentance? *Answer*: Repentance is a saving grace, by which a sinner, out of a true sense of his sin, and a realization of the mercy of God in Christ, with grief and hatred of his sin, turns from it to God, fully intending to endeavor to live a life of new obedience.

Theme verse: '"Return, faithless people; I will cure you of backsliding." "Yes, we will come to you, for you are the Lord our God"' (Jer. 3:22).

There is no command to repent in the Ten Commandments. That summary of our duties to God and others was given to us by God as our moral responsibility. The commands were not designed to restore us to favour with God. They were used by God to show us our sin and our need of rescue. But when the gospel began to be preached by John the Baptist, his first proclamation was: 'Repent, for the kingdom of heaven is near' (Matt. 3:2). Repentance is the first duty that God requires of us. Without it, not a single step can be taken that would return us to a relationship with God, and there is no possibility of obtaining favour with God. We must understand that God has a right to be displeased with us, that he has made no mistake in his view of us, and that every attempt of ours to excuse ourselves will fall on deaf ears. When the Pharisees and Sadducees came to where John the Baptist was baptizing, he cried out to them: 'You brood of vipers! Who warned you to flee the coming wrath? Produce fruit in keeping with repentance' (Matt. 3:7-8). The Pharisees and Sadducees relied on their lineage as descendants of Abraham and felt comfortable that salvation was theirs as a birthright. But John warned them that judgement was very near and that the fruit of repentance was essential if they were to escape the fire of hell.

SCRIPTURE READING: MATTHEW 3:1-12

October 5

Repentance

Westminster Catechism Question #87:

What is repentance? *Answer*: Repentance is a saving grace, by which a sinner, out of a true sense of his sin, and a realization of the mercy of God in Christ, with grief and hatred of his sin, turns from it to God, fully intending to endeavor to live a life of new obedience.

Theme verse: "'Return, faithless people; I will cure you of backsliding.' 'Yes, we will come to you, for you are the Lord our God'" (Jer. 3:22).

In the Parable of the Lost Sheep, Jesus was speaking to a diverse group. There were tax collectors and other 'sinners' following him, delighting in his message of hope. There were also Pharisees, who muttered among themselves about the Saviour's willingness to mingle with 'sinners'. In his parable, Jesus tells the Pharisees and scribes that they would have no difficulty leaving ninety-nine of their sheep in order to retrieve one lost sheep. If a Pharisee would do that for a lost sheep, should not Jesus do that for a lost human being, one of the outcast 'sinners' of society? In contrast to the murmuring and sour faces of the Pharisees is the delight and 'rejoicing in heaven' of the angels over 'one sinner who repents' (Luke 15:7). One of the marked features of Christ's ministry was the attraction of society's outcasts to him and his preaching. He condemned sin in no uncertain terms but at the same time opened the way of forgiveness through repentance and faith. But Jesus also reached out in love to the Pharisees who were self-righteous and aloof. If only they, too, would see their need of repentance! If they would repent, then the joy of forgiveness would be theirs and the angels in heaven would further rejoice that more sinners had come home.

SCRIPTURE READING: LUKE 15:1-10

October 6
TWO LOST SONS
(WEEK 40: DAY 6)

Repentance

Westminster Catechism Question #87:

What is repentance? *Answer*: Repentance is a saving grace, by which a sinner, out of a true sense of his sin, and a realization of the mercy of God in Christ, with grief and hatred of his sin, turns from it to God, fully intending to endeavor to live a life of new obedience.

Theme verse: '"Return, faithless people; I will cure you of backsliding." "Yes, we will come to you, for you are the Lord our God"' (Jer. 3:22).

In the Parable of the Lost Son the scene is very dramatic. Here, the heavenly Father is pictured as having two sons. The older son is a picture of the Pharisees, begrudgingly serving the Father. The younger son typifies open sinners, living a life of sinful recklessness. Both are sinners, yet the younger son typifies the sinner who turns from God and runs into open worldliness whereas the older son typifies a self-righteous sinner who is outwardly in the church, but inwardly without faith. Both are lost and both must return. The younger son took his inheritance money and squandered it in riotous living before being confronted by personal sin, poor choices and independence from God. But 'he came to his senses' (Luke 15:17) and in that moment of contrition and repentance he was justified in his Father's sight. He became rational and balanced in his thinking. He returned to his Father and exclaimed: 'Father, I have sinned against heaven and against you' (Luke 15:21). In humility he gave up every claim of personal righteousness and received grace and pardon. But the older son was arrogant and self-righteous. So bitter was his hatred that he would not recognize the younger son as his own brother. There was no appreciation of God's love or God's joy when a sinner repents. What applications can we find in this parable for our own lives?

SCRIPTURE READING: LUKE 15:11-32

October 7

Repentance

Westminster Catechism Question #87:

What is repentance? *Answer*: Repentance is a saving grace, by which a sinner, out of a true sense of his sin, and a realization of the mercy of God in Christ, with grief and hatred of his sin, turns from it to God, fully intending to endeavor to live a life of new obedience.

Theme verse: "'Return, faithless people; I will cure you of backsliding.' 'Yes, we will come to you, for you are the Lord our God'" (Jer. 3:22).

The presentation of the gospel can sometimes consist of entreaties to 'accept Jesus as Saviour', 'ask Jesus into your heart' or 'make a decision for Christ'. Many have been conditioned into thinking that because they have recited a prayer, made a commitment, signed a card, or walked down an aisle in response to a call for decision, they are now Christians. But we must be careful that we are not deceiving ourselves by merely giving intellectual assent to Christ and the validity of the gospel and yet doing nothing about it. In salvation, repentance and faith are inextricably bound together. Repentance is a change of mind that leads to action. The prodigal son of Luke 15 left his life of sin and returned to his Father, believing by faith that his Father would receive him. On the day of Pentecost, Peter's instruction was: 'Repent then, and turn to God, so that your sins may be wiped out, that times of refreshing may come from the Lord' (Acts 3:19). His call was to turn from their former way of thinking and to begin living, by faith, for the Lord. So then, repentance is the necessary change of mind and will that arises from sorrow for sin that leads to a transformed life by turning to God in faith. Those who repent keep right on repenting, forsaking the old life on a daily basis and clinging to the new, reconciled life that is joyfully theirs in Jesus Christ.

SCRIPTURE READING: ACTS 3:11-26

October 8

Preaching the Word

Westminster Catechism Question #89:

How is the Word made effective in salvation? *Answer*: The Spirit of God makes the reading, but especially the preaching of the Word, an effective means of convincing and converting sinners, and of building them up in holiness and comfort, through faith, to salvation.

Theme verse: 'This is what we speak, not in words taught us by human wisdom but in words taught by the Spirit, expressing spiritual truths in spiritual words' (1 Cor. 2:13).

Most people come to faith in Jesus Christ through hearing the preached Word. The Holy Spirit has chosen the 'foolishness of preaching' to bring sinners to God: 'For the message of the cross is foolishness to those who are perishing, but to us who are being saved it is the power of God' (1 Cor. 1:18). Preaching the message of the cross brings one of two responses. Either a person hears it and it makes no sense, or the Holy Spirit plants the Word in a person's heart where it is embraced and loved. Some people try to make sense of the message of the cross by putting their own twist to it, or as Paul would say, their own 'wisdom' to it, but this ends up nullifying it. Once Jesus becomes no more than a great moral teacher, or his cross is nothing more than a beautiful example of self-giving love, the gospel has been robbed of its power. If the preaching of the cross sounds ridiculous and unworthy of serious consideration, a person has removed the only possible means to be saved. 'Has not God made foolish the wisdom of the world? For since in the wisdom of God the world through its wisdom did not know him, God was pleased through the foolishness of what was preached to save those who believe' (1 Cor. 1:20-21). Paul left the results of his preaching up to God and the hearer, but he was steadfast to preach nothing other than 'Christ crucified' (1 Cor. 1:23).

SCRIPTURE READING: 1 CORINTHIANS 1:18-31

October 9
COMMUNICATING THE GOSPEL
(WEEK 41: DAY 2)

Preaching the Word

Westminster Catechism Question #89:

How is the Word made effective in salvation? *Answer*: The Spirit of God makes the reading, but especially the preaching of the Word, an effective means of convincing and converting sinners, and of building them up in holiness and comfort, through faith, to salvation.

Theme verse: 'This is what we speak, not in words taught us by human wisdom but in words taught by the Spirit, expressing spiritual truths in spiritual words' (1 Cor. 2:13).

In the Old Testament the Lord would give a message through one of his prophets who would then proclaim: 'Thus saith the Lord!' The prophet was forbidden to alter the message in any way. In the same way, today's messenger of the gospel is to transmit God's Word exactly as he has received it. In Luke 10, Jesus sent out seventy-two disciples as heralds of his message. Their task was to announce the good news about Jesus, making sure they did not alter the message. When they returned from their missionary journey they were overjoyed: 'Lord, even the demons submit to us in your name' (Luke 10:17). Satan was defeated when the good news of the gospel was proclaimed clearly and powerfully. That message from the early church still rings throughout the world today. All of our enemies: Satan, sin, death and hell, are overcome by the power of the cross. Therefore, communicating the gospel message clearly is essential if the saving work of Christ is to be known, understood and loved. Jesus said, 'He who listens to you listens to me; he who rejects you rejects me; but he who rejects me rejects him who sent me' (Luke 10:16). If that is the case, that people are held responsible before God for what they have heard preached, it is critical that we communicate the gospel clearly and passionately.

SCRIPTURE READING: 2 KINGS 1:1-17

October 10
THE FLAWLESS WORD
(WEEK 41: DAY 3)

Preaching the Word

Westminster Catechism Question #89:

How is the Word made effective in salvation? *Answer*: The Spirit of God makes the reading, but especially the preaching of the Word, an effective means of convincing and converting sinners, and of building them up in holiness and comfort, through faith, to salvation.

Theme verse: 'This is what we speak, not in words taught us by human wisdom but in words taught by the Spirit, expressing spiritual truths in spiritual words' (1 Cor. 2:13).

The Spirit of God uses the proclamation of the Word to convert sinners to belief in Jesus Christ. But what is so special about the Bible over other books of wisdom? First, the Bible is infallible. There are no mistakes in it as it was originally given to us. 'The law of the Lord is perfect' (Ps. 19:7). It is flawless because it was authored by God, and he is flawless. Secondly, the Bible is authoritative. Since the God who wrote the Bible speaks only truth, the Word of God is our ultimate authority. 'Every word of God is flawless; he is a shield to those who take refuge in him. Do not add to his words, or he will rebuke you and prove you a liar' (Prov. 30:5-6). Thirdly, the Bible is complete. Nothing needs to be added. There are no spiritual experiences by individual believers or churches which should be tacked on to the end of the Bible, nor can anyone claim to possess a prophetic message that carries biblical authority. The book of Revelation ends with a warning not to add to or subtract from it: 'If anyone adds anything to them, God will add to him the plagues described in this book. And if anyone takes words away from this book of prophecy, God will take away from him his share in the tree of life' (Rev. 22:18-19). The Holy Spirit uses the Bible to change hearts because it is infallible, authoritative and complete.

SCRIPTURE READING: PROVERBS 30:1-6

October 11

Preaching the Word

Westminster Catechism Question #89:

How is the Word made effective in salvation? *Answer*: The Spirit of God makes the reading, but especially the preaching of the Word, an effective means of convincing and converting sinners, and of building them up in holiness and comfort, through faith, to salvation.

Theme verse: 'This is what we speak, not in words taught us by human wisdom but in words taught by the Spirit, expressing spiritual truths in spiritual words' (1 Cor. 2:13).

Not only is the Bible infallible, authoritative and complete, it is also effective. It produces results. The Scriptures tell us how to become Christians and prepare us for a life of faith. Some people have the blessing of knowing the Bible from an early age. 'From infancy you have known the holy Scriptures which are able to make you wise for salvation through faith in Christ Jesus' (2 Tim. 3:15). Whether you grew up with the Scriptures or not, when you read and hear the Word of God you learn how to live as a Christian. The Scriptures are 'useful for teaching, rebuking, correcting and training in righteousness, so that the man of God may be thoroughly equipped for every good work' (2 Tim. 3:16-17). The Bible teaches us what we need to know about God and his purposes, helps us recognize our sin and the right way to respond to it, and shows us how to walk in the path of salvation. In other words, the Good News is used to accomplish the Lord's desire to bring worshipers to him, taking them from darkness to light and from death to life, so that he may be glorified among his people in every land and culture group. 'So is my word that goes out from my mouth: It will not return to me empty, but will accomplish what I desire and achieve the purpose for which I sent it' (Isa. 55:11).

SCRIPTURE READING: ISAIAH 55:1-13

October 12
THE BIBLE'S COMFORT
(WEEK 41: DAY 5)

Preaching the Word

Westminster Catechism Question #89:

How is the Word made effective in salvation? *Answer*: The Spirit of God makes the reading, but especially the preaching of the Word, an effective means of convincing and converting sinners, and of building them up in holiness and comfort, through faith, to salvation.

Theme verse: 'This is what we speak, not in words taught us by human wisdom but in words taught by the Spirit, expressing spiritual truths in spiritual words' (1 Cor. 2:13).

The Bible shows us our sinfulness, but it is also our source for hope, comfort and blessing. During difficult times the Scriptures become God's vehicle to encourage us and instil hope within us. 'For everything that was written in the past was written to teach us, so that through endurance and the encouragement of the Scriptures we might have hope' (Rom. 15:4). The Psalms are filled with words of comfort when we are weighed down with problems and concerns: 'My flesh and my heart may fail, but God is the strength of my heart and my portion forever' (Ps. 73:26). And God uses his Word to bless us as we are shaped and moulded into a lifestyle that is pleasing to him. 'But the man who looks intently into the perfect law that gives freedom, and continues to do this, not forgetting what he has heard, but doing it — he will be blessed in what he does' (James 1:25). When we read the Word of God, receive its message, and the Spirit of God is shaping us by it, we are blessed people. The Spirit of God is accomplishing his work in us, applying the Word to our lives. Blessing comes to those who 'humbly accept the word planted in you, which can save you' (James 1:21). When we receive the Word of God, we not only receive salvation from death, but also the gift of God's hope, comfort and blessing.

SCRIPTURE READING: PSALM 73:1-28

October 13

Preaching the Word

Westminster Catechism Question #89:

How is the Word made effective in salvation? *Answer*: The Spirit of God makes the reading, but especially the preaching of the Word, an effective means of convincing and converting sinners, and of building them up in holiness and comfort, through faith, to salvation.

Theme verse: 'This is what we speak, not in words taught us by human wisdom but in words taught by the Spirit, expressing spiritual truths in spiritual words' (1 Cor. 2:13).

To understand the Bible, a person must be a believer in Jesus Christ: 'so that your faith might not rest on men's wisdom, but on God's power' (1 Cor. 2:5). The Apostle Paul was speaking to the Corinthian church about the ignorance of the philosophers of the world. Paul's argument was that he spoke 'a message of wisdom among the mature, but not the wisdom of this age or of the rulers of this age' (1 Cor. 2:6). Without the aid of the Holy Spirit, people cannot understand the Word or love it because the message of the Bible cannot be grasped on a human level; the eye cannot see it, the ear cannot hear it and the mind cannot conceive it (1 Cor. 2:9). But the Christian can receive the message of the Bible because 'God has revealed it to us by his Spirit' (1 Cor. 2:10). We do not depend on human reason; we depend on the Holy Spirit to make the Scriptures clear to us: 'We have not received the spirit of the world but the Spirit who is from God, that we may understand what God has freely given us' (1 Cor. 2:12). When God is gracious to us he makes us open to his Word by the power of the Holy Spirit. We begin the quest of searching for the truth and longing to know the Lord. When that occurs we eagerly respond to the gospel invitation, words not 'taught us by human wisdom but in words taught by the Spirit, expressing spiritual truths in spiritual words' (1 Cor. 2:13).

SCRIPTURE READING: 1 CORINTHIANS 2:1-16

October 14

Preaching the Word

Westminster Catechism Question #89:

How is the Word made effective in salvation? *Answer*: The Spirit of God makes the reading, but especially the preaching of the Word, an effective means of convincing and converting sinners, and of building them up in holiness and comfort, through faith, to salvation.

Theme verse: 'This is what we speak, not in words taught us by human wisdom but in words taught by the Spirit, expressing spiritual truths in spiritual words' (1 Cor. 2:13).

One of the great needs of our age is for sound and powerful preaching of the gospel. Throughout the world there is a hunger for the Word of God with few preachers to declare it effectively. 'Jesus went through all the towns and villages, teaching in their synagogues, preaching the good news of the kingdom' (Matt. 9:35). He noticed during his preaching that the people were 'harassed and helpless, like sheep without a shepherd' (Matt. 9:36). He then challenged us to pray for more preachers of the good news: 'The harvest is plentiful but the workers are few. Ask the Lord of the harvest, therefore, to send out workers into his harvest field' (Matt. 9:37-38). Paul amplified on the same concern: 'How, then, can they call on the one they have not believed in? And how can they believe in the one of whom they have not heard? And how can they hear without someone preaching to them?' (Rom. 10:14). Paul saw the need for sending out preachers of the gospel to every part of the world. How critical it is that people hear of Jesus, for how will anyone believe in a person who is unknown? 'Go,' Jesus said, 'disciple the nations' (Matt. 28:18). Get your feet dirty running everywhere with the gospel that brings freedom from sin because 'faith comes from hearing the message, and the message is heard through the word of Christ' (Rom. 10:17).

SCRIPTURE READING: MATTHEW 9:35-38; ROMANS 10:8-18

October 15
MEDITATING ON THE WORD
(WEEK 42: DAY 1)

Receiving the Word

Westminster Catechism Question #90:

How is the Word to be read and heard, that it may become effective in salvation? *Answer*: That the Word may become effective in salvation, we must attend to it with diligence, preparation and prayer; receive it with faith and love, hide it in our hearts and practice it in our lives.

Theme verse: 'I have hidden your Word in my heart that I might not sin against you' (Ps. 119:11).

The psalmist wrote: 'I have hidden your Word in my heart that I might not sin against you' (Ps. 119:11), and a few verses later: 'I meditate on your precepts and consider your ways. I delight in your decrees; I will not neglect your Word' (Ps. 119:15-16). The psalmist understood how important it is to know the Scriptures and to understand what God requires of us, so he made it his ambition to engage his mind and heart in a prayerful way when he read the Word or heard it preached. Knowing God's Word is not something passive. The catechism lesson explains that we must not merely hear Scripture, but must also act on what we learn. Followers of Christ are eager to drink in God's Word, finding the teaching to be life and health to the soul. The Bible gives us specific guidance on how to respond — instructing us, for example, to set aside the Lord's Day for worshiping God, hearing his Word, and hiding it in our hearts. When we listen diligently to the Word being preached or meditate on it during our devotional time, seeking to apply its contents to our lives, we please God and are blessed by him (Ps. 119:2). We should prepare ourselves as individuals by studying the Bible with a pure heart, and by receiving its teaching with faith and a genuine love for its truth. Only then will the Word become part of us, and manifest its truth in the way we live.

SCRIPTURE READING: PSALM 119:1-16

303

October 16

Receiving the Word

Westminster Catechism Question #90:

How is the Word to be read and heard, that it may become effective in salvation? *Answer*: That the Word may become effective in salvation, we must attend to it with diligence, preparation and prayer; receive it with faith and love, hide it in our hearts and practice it in our lives.

Theme verse: 'I have hidden your Word in my heart that I might not sin against you' (Ps. 119:11).

After years of neglect, the Book of the Law of Moses was re-discovered in the temple. When King Josiah, one of the few godly kings of Israel, heard the words of the Law, he tore his robes: 'Great is the Lord's anger that is poured out on us because our fathers have not kept the word of the Lord, they have not acted in accordance with all that is written in this book' (2 Chron. 34:22). Josiah proceeded to rectify matters. He gathered the elders of Judah together and went up to the temple of the Lord. There, the king read all the words of the covenant in their hearing. In the presence of the Lord and the people the king renewed the covenant 'to follow the Lord and keep his commands, regulations and decrees with all his heart and all his soul, and to obey the words of the covenant written in this book' (2 Chron. 34:31). The young king was a godly leader who brought the people of Israel back to the Lord, providing a powerful example of how to live according to God's Word. He removed the idols from all Israel, and instituted both the celebration of the Passover as well as burnt offerings at the temple. He was greatly respected by the surrounding nations and the Lord blessed his reign. Josiah made a covenant with the Lord to obey and live by the Scriptures. Are you willing to make such a covenant with the Lord?

SCRIPTURE READING: 2 CHRONICLES 34:14-33

October 17
THE NOBLE BEREANS
(WEEK 42: DAY 3)

Receiving the Word

Westminster Catechism Question #90:

How is the Word to be read and heard, that it may become effective in salvation? *Answer*: That the Word may become effective in salvation, we must attend to it with diligence, preparation and prayer; receive it with faith and love, hide it in our hearts and practice it in our lives.

Theme verse: 'I have hidden your Word in my heart that I might not sin against you' (Ps. 119:11).

After preaching in Thessalonica, the Apostle Paul travelled south to Berea. Upon arriving there, he and his travelling companions went to the Jewish synagogue. He discovered that 'the Bereans were of more noble character than the Thessalonians; for they received the message with great eagerness and examined the Scriptures every day to see if what Paul said was true' (Acts 17:11). Many were converted to Jesus. Here were open minds ready to receive the teaching of Scripture. Many of the converts were Old Testament saints who knew the Lord under the terms of the Old Testament. Their hearts were wide open to receive the gospel because they already understood their Old Testament Scriptures. Paul could convince the Bereans that Jesus was the fulfilment of messianic prophecies because his preaching was backed up by the Old Testament. The Bereans were noble because they gave the preaching of the gospel a fair hearing and thoroughly investigated the Scriptures to see if the good news of Jesus was really true. This kind of earnestness and pursuit of the truth yielded exciting results, for many of the people of Berea believed on the Lord Jesus. The Bereans are an excellent reminder that we must never study the Scriptures in a haphazard, careless fashion. The Lord always 'rewards those who earnestly seek him' (Heb. 11:6).

SCRIPTURE READING: ACTS 17:1-15

October 18

Receiving the Word

Westminster Catechism Question #90:

How is the Word to be read and heard, that it may become
effective in salvation? *Answer*: That the Word may become
effective in salvation, we must attend to it with diligence,
preparation and prayer; receive it with faith and love, hide it in
our hearts and practice it in our lives.

Theme verse: 'I have hidden your Word in my heart that I might
not sin against you' (Ps. 119:11).

The Apostle Paul admonished the younger Timothy to devote
himself 'to the public reading of Scripture, to preaching and to
teaching' (1 Tim. 4:13). He was told to 'be diligent in these matters; give yourself wholly to them, so that everyone may see your
progress' (1 Tim. 4:15). Progress is realized when we take hold
of what is called 'the means of grace', particularly the study of
the Bible and prayer. Near the end of his life, Paul would again
exhort Timothy to present himself to God 'as one approved, a
workman who does not need to be ashamed and who correctly
handles the word of truth' (2 Tim. 2:15). Paul was a tentmaker,
making tents out of goatskins. He would cut the hides carefully
so they would fit together correctly. Paul used that example to inform Timothy that he needed to correctly handle every portion of
Scripture if he was to make sense of the entire Word of God. We
cannot understand the whole unless we know what to do with the
parts of the Bible. In the same way, our study of the Word must be
done earnestly and thoroughly so that we are not ignorant of the
Bible's message or what is required of us while we live on earth.
The Scriptures must be a flowing, cohesive and systematic Word
in our lives. We are called, as was Timothy, to watch our lives and
doctrine closely (1 Tim. 4:16).

SCRIPTURE READING: 2 TIMOTHY 2:14-26

October 19
CRAVING SPIRITUAL MILK
(WEEK 42: DAY 5)

Receiving the Word

Westminster Catechism Question #90:

How is the Word to be read and heard, that it may become effective in salvation? *Answer*: That the Word may become effective in salvation, we must attend to it with diligence, preparation and prayer; receive it with faith and love, hide it in our hearts and practice it in our lives.

Theme verse: 'I have hidden your Word in my heart that I might not sin against you' (Ps. 119:11).

The Word of God brings people to Christ but that's just the start of its work in our lives. Once we become believers, the Bible, empowered by the Holy Spirit, transforms us into increasing Christlikeness. The apostle Peter informed us that the Bible provides 'spiritual milk' that helps us grow in our salvation: 'Like newborn babies, crave pure spiritual milk, so that by it you may grow up in your salvation, now that you have tasted that the Lord is good' (1 Peter 2:2). A baby desires just one thing – milk! It really doesn't care about anything else. An infant is not interested in the house it lives in, the color of the curtains or the score at the football game. A baby is single-minded in its craving for milk. Peter exhorts us to develop a similarly single-minded devotion to the Word. We are to put other interests aside, attending to the Scriptures with diligence, preparation and prayer; receiving it with faith and love, and hiding it in our hearts so that we will practice it in our lives. When we became followers of Christ, the Lord gave us the gift of his holy Word. The Word is eternal and will be with us in heaven. It is imperishable. While we live out our Christian lives that imperishable word continues to sanctify us, renewing the image of God in us. 'For the word of God is living and active, sharper than any double-edged sword' (Hebrews 4:12).

SCRIPTURE READING: 1 PETER 1:13 – 2:3

October 20
THE GIFT OF WISDOM
(WEEK 42: DAY 6)

Receiving the Word

Westminster Catechism Question #90:

How is the Word to be read and heard, that it may become effective in salvation? *Answer*: That the Word may become effective in salvation, we must attend to it with diligence, preparation and prayer; receive it with faith and love, hide it in our hearts and practice it in our lives.

Theme verse: 'I have hidden your Word in my heart that I might not sin against you' (Ps. 119:11).

Paul was in prison when he received news that the church at Ephesus was thriving because its members had hidden God's Word in their hearts and were practising it in their lives. Paul was thrilled with the news and it must have lightened the weight of his captivity. His thankfulness for this good news led him into intercession for the Ephesians. 'I have not stopped giving thanks for you, remembering you in my prayers. I keep asking that the God of our Lord Jesus Christ, the glorious Father, may give you the Spirit of wisdom and revelation, so that you may know him better' (Eph. 1:16-17). Wisdom and revelation come from an understanding of the Word of God. Paul had planted the gospel seed in Ephesus, and now he was pleased to learn that the gospel was taking root in people's lives, making them wise in the Scriptures, and deepening believers in holiness and love. Having taken possession of such great spiritual blessings, Paul wanted to remind them of the greatness and the value of these gifts. We often take God's supreme gifts as a matter of course, which results in regarding the Word and prayer lightly. And when we put our Bibles away it is frightening how quickly we can forget the God of the Bible. May the Lord help us to look for wisdom 'as for silver and search for it as for hidden treasure' (Prov. 2:4).

SCRIPTURE READING: PROVERBS 2:1-22

October 21
DIVINE REVELATION
(WEEK 42: DAY 7)

Receiving the Word

Westminster Catechism Question #90:

How is the Word to be read and heard, that it may become effective in salvation? Answer: That the Word may become effective in salvation, we must attend to it with diligence, preparation and prayer; receive it with faith and love, hide it in our hearts and practice it in our lives.

Theme verse: 'I have hidden your Word in my heart that I might not sin against you' (Ps. 119:11).

The Christian's view of the Bible is that it is God's Word written, and that it is the final authority for all matters of Christian faith and practice. We look to the Scriptures for information about itself and we discover that the Bible has a *divine origin*: 'all Scripture is God-breathed' (2 Tim. 3:16); that is, God wrote the Scriptures while using human authors. Christians also believe in the *unity* of Scripture. A literary historian might see the Bible as some sort of library: a miscellaneous set of public records, history books, poetry, letters and sermons, put together over a thousand years or more. But it is more than a library of books by human authors; it is a single book with a single authority — God the Spirit — and a single theme — God the Son, and the Father's saving purposes, which all revolve around Jesus, the focal centre of the Bible. Christians, therefore, believe that the Bible is the *Word of God*, the sum total of divine revelation recorded in a God-breathed written form, and that every spiritual statement is to be received as a divine utterance. You may open the Scriptures confidently knowing the Bible is word for word God-given; its message is an organic unity, the infallible Word of an infallible God. Its message is centred on Jesus Christ and its meaning is grasped only by those who humbly seek and gladly receive the help of the Holy Spirit.

SCRIPTURE READING: PSALM 119:17-40

October 22

The Sacraments

Westminster Catechism Question #93:

What are the sacraments of the New Testament? *Answer*: The sacraments of the New Testament are baptism and the Lord's Supper.

Theme verse: 'For whenever you eat this bread and drink this cup, you proclaim the Lord's death until he comes' (1 Cor. 11:26).

There are at least five ways in which baptism and the Lord's Supper are similar. First, both sacraments were instituted by Christ. It was Jesus who said: 'Go and make disciples of all nations, baptizing them in the name of the Father and of the Son and of the Holy Spirit' (Matt. 28:19). It was also Jesus who said about the bread: 'This is my body,' and about the cup: 'This cup is the new covenant in my blood' (1 Cor. 11:24-25). Secondly, both sacraments are to be perpetually observed in the church by his followers (Matt. 28:20 and 1 Cor. 11:26). Thirdly, both sacraments use material elements (water for baptizing, bread and wine for eating and drinking). Fourthly, both are signs that we are part of the visible church of God. And fifthly, both sacraments are reminders that we belong to God, that 'you are not your own; you were bought at a price' (1 Cor. 6:19-20). Baptism and the Lord's Supper are dissimilar in that baptism is to be administered only once, by water, as a sign of our new birth and entrance into the family of God. The Lord's Supper is to be administered often, using the elements of bread and wine, to represent and openly declare that Jesus is our Saviour and the nourishment for our soul, and to confirm our desire to continue 'being transformed into his likeness with ever-increasing glory' (2 Cor. 3:18).

SCRIPTURE READING: MARK 14:12-26

October 23
THE OUTWARD SIGN
(WEEK 43: DAY 2)

The Sacraments

Westminster Catechism Question #93:

What are the sacraments of the New Testament? *Answer*: The sacraments of the New Testament are baptism and the Lord's Supper.

Theme verse: 'For whenever you eat this bread and drink this cup, you proclaim the Lord's death until he comes' (1 Cor. 11:26).

In the Old Testament, circumcision was the sign of the old covenant that God made with the children of Israel. The prophets predicted that the old covenant would be replaced with a new covenant, one that promised both forgiveness of sins and the power to live a holy life (Jer. 31:31-34; Ezek. 36:25-27). When Jesus came he inaugurated this promised new covenant through his death at the cross. He instituted baptism as the outward, visible sign that forgiven sinners were a part of the new covenant and now included in the family of God (Matt. 28:18-20). To be baptized, persons were required to confess and repent of sin (Acts 2:38) and receive by faith the Lord Jesus as their Messiah, the Son of God and the Saviour of the world (Mark 16:15-16; Acts 8:12). Baptism was to be administered in the name of the Trinity: Father, Son and Holy Spirit, an altogether new concept that was foreign to Jewish thought. Baptism was not a pledge of some future blessings (as was the case with John the Baptist's baptism), but of true spiritual blessings immediately available for the new believer in Jesus. The Lord Jesus fulfilled all the promises of John the Baptist's baptism. He had come! And by his death and resurrection he has secured the forgiveness of sins and the gift of the Holy Spirit (Acts 2:38) for all believers.

SCRIPTURE READING: EZEKIEL 36:24-38

311

October 24

The Sacraments

Westminster Catechism Question #93:

What are the sacraments of the New Testament? *Answer*: The sacraments of the New Testament are baptism and the Lord's Supper.

Theme verse: 'For whenever you eat this bread and drink this cup, you proclaim the Lord's death until he comes' (1 Cor. 11:26).

It is lamentable that some people have asserted that baptism no longer needs to be practised. While baptism, in itself, has no power to save us from sin, baptism is a necessity for all believers in Jesus if we are to take the Bible seriously. First, Christ commanded his disciples to be baptized (Matt. 28:18-20). His authority to require baptism from all his followers extends to every land in every age until he comes again. Our personal obedience to this command will be indicative of whether we 'make it our goal to please him' (2 Cor. 5:9). Secondly, Jesus himself submitted to baptism. The first recorded step Jesus took in his public ministry was to ask John the Baptist for baptism. It was so important to Jesus that he walked sixty miles from Nazareth to a place at the Jordan River near Jerusalem. Jesus submitted to baptism because he came into our world to identify with sinners and carry away our sin. Thirdly, it was practised by the apostles and they were men under divine orders. Peter 'ordered that they be baptized' (Acts 10:48). Whether it was 3,000 who were saved on the day of Pentecost (Acts 2:38,41), the Samaritans who believed under Philips' preaching (Acts 8:12) or the Ethiopian eunuch (Acts 8:38), they were all baptized 'immediately' (Acts 16:33). Have you followed the Lord into the waters of baptism?

SCRIPTURE READING: ACTS 8:26-40

A SIGN OF GRACE
(WEEK 43: DAY 4)

The Sacraments

Westminster Catechism Question #93:

What are the sacraments of the New Testament? *Answer*: The sacraments of the New Testament are baptism and the Lord's Supper.

Theme verse: 'For whenever you eat this bread and drink this cup, you proclaim the Lord's death until he comes' (1 Cor. 11:26).

Baptism, like the Lord's Supper, is a sacrament — a sacred pledge and sign of what God has done for every truly penitent believer in Christ. It signifies that God, on his own initiative, decided to show grace and favour towards sinners. We do not baptize ourselves; someone must baptize us. This is not an insignificant detail, because it demonstrates that salvation is by grace alone, something that is done for us and given to us by God. The minister who baptizes us does so in a representative capacity. He stands in for the Lord Jesus, for it is Christ alone who bestows the blessings of salvation on us. Baptism means that we are united to Christ both in his crucifixion and his resurrection: 'Don't you know that all of us who were baptized into Christ Jesus were baptized into his death? We were therefore buried with him through baptism into death in order that, just as Christ was raised from the dead through the glory of the Father, we too may live a new life' (Rom. 6:3-4). Baptism means that we have said 'good-bye' to the old life and 'hello' to the new life in Jesus. Therefore, while we know that baptism does not save, the Lord gave us this ordinance to signify that our sins have been forgiven: 'having our hearts sprinkled to cleanse us from a guilty conscience and having our bodies washed with pure water' (Heb. 10:22).

SCRIPTURE READING: ROMANS 6:1-14

October 26
Not forgetting
(week 43: day 5)

The Sacraments

Westminster Catechism Question #93:

What are the sacraments of the New Testament? *Answer*: The sacraments of the New Testament are baptism and the Lord's Supper.

Theme verse: 'For whenever you eat this bread and drink this cup, you proclaim the Lord's death until he comes' (1 Cor. 11:26).

The Lord's Supper was ordained for the purpose of always remembering the death of Christ and the benefits we receive from it. 'For whenever you eat this bread and drink this cup, you proclaim the Lord's death until he comes' (1 Cor. 11:26). The bread in the Lord's Supper is broken, given and eaten to remind us of Christ's body given on the cross for our sins. The wine that is poured out and received is meant to remind us of Christ's blood shed on the cross for our sins. When we partake of the bread and wine we are reminded, in the most striking manner, of the salvation Christ has obtained for our souls. If there was one thing Jesus did not want us to forget, it was his death. He died so that we could be redeemed and his sacrifice at the cross is the cornerstone and foundation of all our hopes for pardon and peace with God. The life Christ lived on earth — his teaching, preaching and miracles, were all important and essential to demonstrate his divinity and carry out his Father's will — but his death as a substitute for us was certainly his unspeakably gracious gift. His death was the payment of our debt to God, and the Lord's Supper is our reminder of his mighty work. Whenever God's people gather for the Lord's Supper they are to do this, Jesus said, 'In remembrance of me.'

Scripture reading: 1 Corinthians 11:17-26

October 27

The Sacraments

Westminster Catechism Question #93:

What are the sacraments of the New Testament? *Answer*: The sacraments of the New Testament are baptism and the Lord's Supper.

Theme verse: 'For whenever you eat this bread and drink this cup, you proclaim the Lord's death until he comes' (1 Cor. 11:26).

Not everyone should participate in the Lord's Supper. 'For anyone who eats and drinks without recognizing the body of the Lord eats and drinks judgment on himself' (1 Cor. 11:29). This verse is telling us that persons must first understand what the elements of bread and wine represent before coming to the Lord's Supper, namely, Christ's body and blood as an atoning sacrifice for sin. This verse also teaches that people who live in open sin, with no inclination to give up their disobedience, should not participate in the Lord's Supper. To do so is an insult to Christ, and shows contempt for what Christ accomplished for sinners. We cannot actually be remembering Christ's death if we continue to cling to the sins which he died to remove. Such a person shows no appreciation of Christ's offer of salvation. Also, self-righteous people should not come to the Lord's Supper. Anyone who thinks they can be saved by their own efforts rather than the justifying work of Jesus need not come. Such persons may be outwardly moral and respectable in their conduct, but if they trust in their own goodness for salvation they are entirely in the wrong place attending the Lord's Supper. Persons who should come to the Lord's Supper are those who have demonstrated repentance towards God, faith in the Lord Jesus, and practical love towards others.

SCRIPTURE READING: 1 CORINTHIANS 11:27-34

October 28
BENEFITS OF THE SUPPER
(WEEK 43: DAY 7)

The Sacraments

Westminster Catechism Question #93:

What are the sacraments of the New Testament? *Answer*: The sacraments of the New Testament are baptism and the Lord's Supper.

Theme verse: 'For whenever you eat this bread and drink this cup, you proclaim the Lord's death until he comes' (1 Cor. 11:26).

What are the benefits of partaking in the Lord's Supper? Some people are superstitious about the sacrament, believing that it somehow magically confers salvation, or that life will improve if God sees them taking the elements. But the benefit that true-hearted followers of Christ may expect to receive from the Lord's Supper is the strengthening and refreshment it brings to our souls (1 Cor. 10:16). Through the sacred meal we receive clearer views of Christ and his atonement and clearer views of all the offices which Christ fills as our Prophet, Priest and King. We see more clearly the redemption Christ has obtained for us by dying in our place, greater understanding of our full and perfect acceptance in Christ before God, and fresh reasons for deep repentance for sin and a more lively faith. Whoever eats the bread and drinks the wine in a right spirit will find himself drawn into closer communion with Christ, and will feel that he understands the Lord better. The Lord's Supper should always humble and yet encourage us, knowing that an enormous price has been paid for our redemption. The Supper should also sanctify us, reminding us that we belong to Christ and must always live to please him. Finally, it should cause us to praise Christ, give thanks to him and remind us of our obligation to live a consistently holy life before the Lord.

SCRIPTURE READING: JOHN 6:44-58

October 28
BENEFITS OF THE SUPPER
(WEEK 43: DAY 7)

The Sacraments

Westminster Catechism Question #93:

What are the sacraments of the New Testament? *Answer*: The sacraments of the New Testament are baptism and the Lord's Supper.

Theme verse: 'For whenever you eat this bread and drink this cup, you proclaim the Lord's death until he comes' (1 Cor. 11:26).

What are the benefits of partaking in the Lord's Supper? Some people are superstitious about the sacrament, believing that it somehow magically confers salvation, or that life will improve if God sees them taking the elements. But the benefit that true-hearted followers of Christ may expect to receive from the Lord's Supper is the strengthening and refreshment it brings to our souls (1 Cor. 10:16). Through the sacred meal we receive clearer views of Christ and his atonement and clearer views of all the offices which Christ fills as our Prophet, Priest and King. We see more clearly the redemption Christ has obtained for us by dying in our place, greater understanding of our full and perfect acceptance in Christ before God, and fresh reasons for deep repentance for sin and a more lively faith. Whoever eats the bread and drinks the wine in a right spirit will find himself drawn into closer communion with Christ, and will feel that he understands the Lord better. The Lord's Supper should always humble and yet encourage us, knowing that an enormous price has been paid for our redemption. The Supper should also sanctify us, reminding us that we belong to Christ and must always live to please him. Finally, it should cause us to praise Christ, give thanks to him and remind us of our obligation to live a consistently holy life before the Lord.

SCRIPTURE READING: JOHN 6:44-58

October 29
COMMUNION WITH GOD
(WEEK 44: DAY 1)

Prayer

Westminster Catechism Question #98:

What is prayer? *Answer*: Prayer is the offering up of our desires to God for things agreeable to his will, in the name of Christ, with confession of our sins and thankful acknowledgement of his mercies.

Theme verse: 'This is the confidence we have in approaching God: that if we ask anything according to his will, he hears us' (1 John 5:14).

Prayer is a recurring theme in the Bible, from Genesis through Revelation, and we are taught the importance and necessity of prayer by the countless examples of it. From the outset of the Bible we read, 'At that time men began to call on the name of the Lord' (Gen. 4:26). And at the end of Revelation there is this prayerful cry: 'Amen. Come, Lord Jesus' (Rev. 22:20). Instances of earnest prayer are plentiful. Jacob wrestled all night in prayer. Daniel prayed three times a day. David made prayer his constant companion and left us prayers that meet every need or circumstance in our lives. We are told that Elijah was just like us, and that we should be just like him, praying earnestly (James 5:17). Paul and Silas 'were praying and singing hymns to God, and the other prisoners were listening to them' (Phil. 16:25), when God sent an earthquake to free them. The many examples of prayer drive home commands of God and declare promises that he has made. Since God has made prayer prominent in his Word he intends for it to be conspicuous in our lives. So deep are our necessities that we should not cease to pray until we are in heaven. If we have nothing to pray about it is because we do not know our spiritual poverty. May we always heed the scriptural command to 'Devote yourselves to prayer' (Col. 4:2).

SCRIPTURE READING: JAMES 5:13-20

October 30
THE IMPORTANCE OF PRAYER
(WEEK 44: DAY 2)

Prayer

Westminster Catechism Question #98:

What is prayer? *Answer*: Prayer is the offering up of our desires
to God for things agreeable to his will, in the name of Christ,
with confession of our sins and thankful acknowledgement of
his mercies.

Theme verse: 'This is the confidence we have in approaching
God: that if we ask anything according to his will, he hears us'
(1 John 5:14).

One could convincingly argue that prayer is the most important
practice in the Christian life, even above other 'means of grace'
such as Bible reading or attending public worship. Consider, first-
ly, that we cannot come to Christ unless we repent of our sin and
our cry of repentance is a prayer for mercy and pardon. Secondly,
a habit of prayer is one of the surest marks of a true Christian.
The first act of a newborn infant is breathing and the first act of
new Christians is praying: 'Then Jesus told his disciples a parable
to show them that they should always pray and not give up' (Luke
18:1). The Holy Spirit, who makes us new creatures, also implants
this sense of adoption, and makes us cry 'Abba, Father' (Rom.
8:15). Thirdly, diligence in prayer is the secret of holiness. There
is an immense gap between Christians in this area. Believers who
earnestly pray fight a more valiant fight than the rest of us, and
run a more victorious race. And fourthly, prayer is one of the best
ways to acquire happiness and contentment. We are all subject
to trials and discouragements. The best way to overcome anxiety
and discouragement is to take everything to God in prayer. 'Call
upon me in the day of trouble; and I will deliver you, and you will
honor me' (Ps. 50:15). We can measure the health of our soul by
the earnestness and sincerity of our prayers.

SCRIPTURE READING: LUKE 18:1-8

October 31
THE NECESSITY OF PRAYER
(WEEK 44: DAY 3)

Prayer

Westminster Catechism Question #98:

What is prayer? *Answer*: Prayer is the offering up of our desires
to God for things agreeable to his will, in the name of Christ,
with confession of our sins and thankful acknowledgement of
his mercies.

Theme verse: 'This is the confidence we have in approaching
God: that if we ask anything according to his will, he hears us'
(1 John 5:14).

Prayer is communion with God. It is a spiritual transaction with
the Creator of heaven and earth. God is a Spirit, and our own
spirit within us, made alive by the Holy Spirit at our conversion,
now longs to commune with God, present our requests to him,
and receive from him answers that are according to his will. The
purpose of prayer is to honour God's name. It is not the utterance
of words, or even the expression of our feelings. It occurs when
our souls approach the throne of God by the power of the Holy
Spirit. Prayer should never be rote or distant; it should be a time
when we sincerely and affectionately pour out our hearts to God.
Prayer includes adoration, praise, confession, thanksgiving, intercession and making our requests known to God. We never have to
pray to inform God of our needs because he knows everything already. Rather, we pray to express our confidence in him and commune with him, confessing our sins and seeking his provision for
our daily needs as well as interceding for others. The Lord does
not grant our prayers when they fall outside his will. However,
'This is the confidence we have in approaching God: that if we ask
anything according to his will, he hears us. And if we know that
he hears us — whatever we ask — we know that we have what we
asked of him' (1 John 5:14).

SCRIPTURE READING: 1 JOHN 5:13-21

November 1

Prayer

Westminster Catechism Question #98:

What is prayer? *Answer*: Prayer is the offering up of our desires
to God for things agreeable to his will, in the name of Christ,
with confession of our sins and thankful acknowledgement of
his mercies.

Theme verse: 'This is the confidence we have in approaching
God: that if we ask anything according to his will, he hears us'
(1 John 5:14).

The act of prayer has two primary goals. One goal is the glory of
God. The other goal is to experience the joy of fellowship with
Christ. 'Until now you have not asked for anything in my name.
Ask and you will receive, and your joy will be complete' (John
16:24). Jesus invites us to pray to him in order that we might have
fellowship with him. And fellowship with Jesus never disappoints.
Prayerlessness is joylessness, but a humble and sincere prayer life
leads to fullness of joy. Prayer is the centre of our fellowship with
Jesus. In prayer we speak to him as if he was visibly standing in
front of us. 'Our fellowship is with the Father and with his Son,
Jesus Christ. We write this to make our joy complete' (1 John
1:3,4). Prayer is God's appointed means to bring contentment
to our lives because prayer is our way to respond to the Lord as
he speaks to us through his Word. Prayer draws us into the presence of God and blesses us with the assurance that we are united
to God, that our lives have rich meaning and purpose, and that
the Lord will one day take us to have fellowship with him face
to face. Fellowship with Jesus is essential to inner contentment.
Our prayers glorify God when we pursue our joy in him and not
in ourselves. So do not leave prayer out of your schedule today.
Make room for it — for the glory of God and that your joy might
be complete.

SCRIPTURE READING: JOHN 16:17-33

November 2

Prayer

Westminster Catechism Question #98:

What is prayer? *Answer*: Prayer is the offering up of our desires to God for things agreeable to his will, in the name of Christ, with confession of our sins and thankful acknowledgement of his mercies.

Theme verse: 'This is the confidence we have in approaching God: that if we ask anything according to his will, he hears us' (1 John 5:14).

The prophet Jeremiah had been cast into prison. While experiencing the discomforts of confinement, the Lord spoke to him: 'Call to me and I will answer you and tell you great and unsearchable things you do not know' (Jer. 33:3). God's directive to Jeremiah has three parts. First, God told his discouraged prophet to call out to him, to pray. If he would do so, the Lord would reveal to him his plans and purposes for Israel. God's people often discover the best truths about their God in the midst of trying circumstances. Serious illness or injury will motivate us to seek medical help in order to regain our health. Similarly, when we are discouraged we are motivated to call out to God for spiritual encouragement and peace. Secondly, in Jeremiah 33:3, God promised that if Jeremiah prayed he would answer him. Jesus has revealed himself in his Word as the God of love, full of grace and truth. He will not hide himself from those who seek his grace and favour but will surely answer our prayers according to his will. Thirdly, God promised Jeremiah that if he prayed, his faith would be greatly strengthened. We should fully expect to discover a deeper spiritual experience and know more of the higher spiritual life if we find ourselves much in prayer. Prayer is the instrument God uses to elevate our spirit and bring peace to troubled hearts.

SCRIPTURE READING: JEREMIAH 33:1-9

November 3
CHILDLIKE OBEDIENCE
(WEEK 44: DAY 6)

Prayer

Westminster Catechism Question #98:

What is prayer? *Answer*: Prayer is the offering up of our desires to God for things agreeable to his will, in the name of Christ, with confession of our sins and thankful acknowledgement of his mercies.

Theme verse: 'This is the confidence we have in approaching God: that if we ask anything according to his will, he hears us' (1 John 5:14).

One of the conditions for effective prayer is that we possess childlike obedience. This means that God's children respect their Father. It means that we should not expect every desire to be fulfilled, because parents who give their children everything they ask for are not acting in their children's best interests. We must be careful when we read John's words to his fellow believers: 'Dear friends, if our hearts do not condemn us, we have confidence before God and receive from him anything we ask, because we obey his commands and do what pleases him' (1 John 3:21-22). This promise assumes that we understand that our prayers must be in agreement with our Father's will and does not mean God will give us what we want whenever we want it. Our Father, like a good parent, will give us what is best for us, even if it is not what we desire at the time, and we need to learn to faithfully accept what God sends our way. Our Father disciplines his children as an act of love. If we do not keep God's commandments he will respond with a rebuke. If 'you do not accept my correction but continue to be hostile toward me, I will be hostile toward you' (Lev. 26:23-24). For us to possess real power and confidence that our prayers will be answered there must be childlike obedience, purity of heart, and a desire to obey God's Word.

SCRIPTURE READING: LEVITICUS 26:14-26

November 4

Prayer

Westminster Catechism Question #98:

What is prayer? *Answer*: Prayer is the offering up of our desires to God for things agreeable to his will, in the name of Christ, with confession of our sins and thankful acknowledgement of his mercies.

Theme verse: 'This is the confidence we have in approaching God: that if we ask anything according to his will, he hears us' (1 John 5:14).

Most of our times of prayer are solitary, whether we prefer praying alone or not. But when we are able, group prayer is a powerful way of meeting with God and strengthening the fellowship of believers. The Lord seems to particularly bless united prayer, when his people are humbly seeking his favour corporately, for we are told that whenever 'two of you on earth agree about anything you ask for, it will be done for you by my Father in heaven' (Matt. 18:19). The spiritual virtues of humility, meekness, faith and joy are dramatically strengthened in corporate prayer and the results are greater power and blessing for the Church of God. Peter was rescued from prison in response to united prayer because 'the church was earnestly praying to God for him' (Acts 12:5). Pentecost came when the disciples 'were all together in one place' (Acts 2:1). And when God answers united prayer there is nothing sweeter than God's people gathering for united praise. To praise God for mercies received benefits our fellow believers: 'Glorify the Lord with me; let us exalt his name together' (Ps. 34:8). Combined praise is an anticipation of heaven, for in that great assembly, there will be 'the roar of a great multitude in heaven shouting: "Hallelujah! Salvation and glory and power belong to our God"' (Rev. 19:1).

SCRIPTURE READING: ACTS 12:1-19

November 5

Our Father in heaven

Westminster Catechism Question #100:

What does the preface to the Lord's Prayer teach us? *Answer*:
The preface to the Lord's Prayer (which is 'Our Father in
heaven') teaches us to draw near to God with holy reverence and
confidence, as children to a father who is able and ready to help
us; and that we should pray with and for others.

Theme verse: 'But when you pray, go into your room, close the
door and pray to your Father, who is unseen. Then your Father,
who sees what is done in secret, will reward you' (Matt. 6:6).

The disciples asked Jesus to teach them how to pray, and the
writers of the Westminster Shorter Catechism thought that the
Saviour's answer (The Lord's Prayer: Matthew 6:9-13) was so
important that it merited eight separate questions and answers.
The Lord Jesus did not restrict his followers to using only the exact words of his prayer. Instead, he said, 'This, then, is *how* you
should pray' (Matt. 6:9). His words provide an outline for a short
but comprehensive prayer and our petitions should conform to
the Lord's outline. The preface of the Lord's Prayer is 'Our Father
in heaven'. Although the Father is the only person of the Trinity who is addressed in the Lord's Prayer, the Son and the Holy
Spirit are not excluded. The Father is mentioned because he is the
first person of the Trinity; the Son and Holy Spirit are included
because they are the same in essence. In that sense, when we pray
to the Father we are praying to all three persons of the Godhead.
Just as God gave Moses a blueprint of the tabernacle and told
him, 'Make this tabernacle and all its furnishings exactly like the
pattern I will show you' (Exod. 25:9), the Lord Jesus has given us
the Lord's Prayer as a pattern for our prayers. While we are not
tied to its words, make the Lord's Prayer the rule and model for all
your petitions, commended to you by its Author.

SCRIPTURE READING: MATTHEW 6:9-15

November 6

Our Father in heaven

Westminster Catechism Question #100:

What does the preface to the Lord's Prayer teach us? *Answer*:
The preface to the Lord's Prayer (which is 'Our Father in
heaven') teaches us to draw near to God with holy reverence and
confidence, as children to a father who is able and ready to help
us; and that we should pray with and for others.

Theme verse: 'But when you pray, go into your room, close the
door and pray to your Father, who is unseen. Then your Father,
who sees what is done in secret, will reward you' (Matt. 6:6).

Kings and presidents give themselves titles, such as 'Your Majesty', and God could have required the same from us when we
pray. Certainly when we pray there is nothing wrong with praising
God by offering titles that exalt the greatness of the Lord and the
excellence of his attributes. But in this model prayer the Lord Jesus told us simply to address God more intimately by saying: 'Our
Father in heaven'. Such a warm and inviting title is an expression
of God's love and condescension towards us which encourages us
to pray. It would be difficult to pray to a ruthless dictator, but it is
a joy to pray to one's loving Heavenly Father. There are many Hebrew names for God that speak to his might, power, sovereignty
and right to judge. The name 'Jehovah', for instance, carries majesty in it. But when Jesus tells us to simply pray to 'our Father', the
message it conveys is one of kindness, love, mercy and acceptance.
While everyone can say that God is their father because he has
made all of us, there is little comfort in such a thought. Real intimacy and joy with God comes from having 'received the Spirit of
sonship' and being able to cry 'Abba, Father' (Rom. 8:15). Those
who can say 'our Father' with real confidence are only those who
are born again. 'How great is the love the Father has lavished on
us, that we should be called children of God!' (1 John 3:1).

SCRIPTURE READING: ACTS 13:26-33

November 7
HAVING THE SAME FATHER
(WEEK 45: DAY 3)

Our Father in heaven

Westminster Catechism Question #100:

What does the preface to the Lord's Prayer teach us? *Answer*:
The preface to the Lord's Prayer (which is 'Our Father in
heaven') teaches us to draw near to God with holy reverence and
confidence, as children to a father who is able and ready to help
us; and that we should pray with and for others.

Theme verse: 'But when you pray, go into your room, close the
door and pray to your Father, who is unseen. Then your Father,
who sees what is done in secret, will reward you' (Matt. 6:6).

The Bible describes God the Father and Jesus as having a father-
son relationship, yet they are co-equals. They created the world
together. Jesus is eternally united with the Father as one God, and
he is 'the radiance of God's glory and the exact representation of
his being' (Heb. 1:3). Jesus could say to his disciples, 'If you really
knew me you would know my Father as well. From now on, you
do know him and have seen him' (John 14:7). A few verses later
he would say, 'I am in the Father and the Father is in me' (John
14:11). The Lord Jesus is a perfect Son because he has the same
nature and possesses all the same attributes as his perfect Father.
We, too, can say that we are sons and daughters of God and that
God is our Father, but not in the same way as the Lord Jesus. We
are adopted children who have been shown mercy and have entered into the family of God, not by any personal virtue, but by
God's pure grace. God sent his Son 'to redeem those under law,
that we might receive the full rights of sons' (Gal. 4:5). God has
sent his Holy Spirit into our hearts, freeing us from our slavery to
sin, and adopting us into his family, even blessing us with all the
rights and privileges of the children of God. So let us give thanks
for our adoption and that, though unworthy, we can call God our
Father and Christ our brother.

SCRIPTURE READING: GALATIANS 3:26 – 4:7

November 8
United by faith
(WEEK 45: DAY 4)

Our Father in heaven

Westminster Catechism Question #100:

What does the preface to the Lord's Prayer teach us? *Answer*:
The preface to the Lord's Prayer (which is 'Our Father in
heaven') teaches us to draw near to God with holy reverence and
confidence, as children to a father who is able and ready to help
us; and that we should pray with and for others.

Theme verse: 'But when you pray, go into your room, close the
door and pray to your Father, who is unseen. Then your Father,
who sees what is done in secret, will reward you' (Matt. 6:6).

Everyone may call God Creator and Judge, but having God as our
Father is reserved for those who are 'sons of God through faith in
Christ Jesus' (Gal. 3:26). Faith in Jesus is the gift from God that
makes us legitimate children. Faith unites us to Christ, making us
brothers and sisters to Jesus, and making the Heavenly Father our
Father. Christ entered our world and took on humanity in order
to identify himself with us and reconcile us to his Father by his
sacrificial death at the cross. He is our champion, who is willing
to die for us in order to bring us to his Father as restored people.
'Both the one who makes men holy and those who are made holy
are of the same family. So Jesus is not ashamed to call them brothers' (Heb. 2:11). But for Christ's work at the cross to have value for
us as individuals, and for us to be considered brothers and sisters
of Christ, we must receive him by faith. All the benefits of family membership, including the joy of heaven itself, are received by
faith. 'To all who received him, to those who believed in his name,
he gave the right to become children of God' (John 1:12). Pray for
saving faith, the kind of faith that moves beyond God being only
your Creator and Judge. Pray for faith that allows you to approach
the throne of grace with confidence crying, 'Abba, Father.'

SCRIPTURE READING: HEBREWS 2:5-18

November 9

THE BEST FATHER
(WEEK 45: DAY 5)

Our Father in heaven

Westminster Catechism Question #100:

What does the preface to the Lord's Prayer teach us? *Answer*:
The preface to the Lord's Prayer (which is 'Our Father in
heaven') teaches us to draw near to God with holy reverence and
confidence, as children to a father who is able and ready to help
us; and that we should pray with and for others.

Theme verse: 'But when you pray, go into your room, close the
door and pray to your Father, who is unseen. Then your Father,
who sees what is done in secret, will reward you' (Matt. 6:6).

It is impossible to have a better father than our Heavenly Father.
First, he is described in the Bible as 'The Ancient of Days', which
means that from the beginning of time he has been present for
us. Secondly, Jesus told us that his Father is our heavenly role-
model and we should aim to be perfect 'as your heavenly Father
is perfect' (Matt. 5:48). Thirdly, our Father is perfectly wise and
he knows how to make things turn out best for us (Rom. 8:28).
Fourthly, he is the Father of love. 'God is love' (1 John 4:16). There
is no parent who can match the love and delight of God for the
children he has redeemed. 'He will take great delight in you, he
will quiet you with his love, he will rejoice over you with singing'
(Zeph. 3:17). Fifthly, our Heavenly Father promises to 'meet all
your needs according to his glorious riches in Christ Jesus' (Phil.
4:19). Sixthly, God is an excellent Father because he disciplines
us for our good, changing our hearts, and setting us on a better course. 'Our fathers disciplined us for a little while as they
thought best; but God disciplines us for our good, that we may
share in his holiness' (Heb. 12:10). And seventhly, God 'who alone
is immortal, and who lives in unapproachable light' (1 Tim. 6:16)
is the best Father because he never dies. Should we not run into
the arms of a Father such as this?

SCRIPTURE READING: ZEPHANIAH 3:14-20

November 10

Our Father in heaven

Westminster Catechism Question #100:

What does the preface to the Lord's Prayer teach us? *Answer*:
The preface to the Lord's Prayer (which is 'Our Father in
heaven') teaches us to draw near to God with holy reverence and
confidence, as children to a father who is able and ready to help
us; and that we should pray with and for others.

Theme verse: 'But when you pray, go into your room, close the
door and pray to your Father, who is unseen. Then your Father,
who sees what is done in secret, will reward you' (Matt. 6:6).

Just before the Lord gave us the Lord's Prayer as our model prayer,
he warned us not to make a show of our praying. 'But when you
pray, go into your room, close the door and pray to your Father,
who is unseen. Then your Father, who sees what is done in secret,
will reward you' (Matt. 6:6). Jesus was not talking about prohibiting public prayer in the congregation since in the Lord's Prayer he
teaches us to pray to '*our* Father', and for '*our* daily bread'. In fact,
we are encouraged to pray with and for others: 'And pray in the
Spirit on all occasions with all kinds of prayers and requests. With
this in mind, be alert and always keep on praying for all the saints'
(Eph. 6:18). What Jesus was prohibiting was hypocritical praying.
In the time of Christ the Pharisees would actually have a servant
blowing a trumpet ahead of them as they walked to the temple
to pray. They wanted everyone to notice their piety and that they
were on their way to pray and give alms. But Jesus commends private prayer where there is no intrusion and the worshiper is alone
with God. True praying must start in secret since its very nature
is personal communion of the soul with God. Prayers that are intended to impress others rather than communicate with God are
offensive to the Lord. One measure of our spiritual health is our
eagerness to pray to the Lord when we are alone.

SCRIPTURE READING: MATTHEW 6:1-8

November 11
Our Father in heaven
(week 45: day 7)

Our Father in heaven

Westminster Catechism Question #100:

What does the preface to the Lord's Prayer teach us? *Answer*:
The preface to the Lord's Prayer (which is 'Our Father in
heaven') teaches us to draw near to God with holy reverence and
confidence, as children to a father who is able and ready to help
us; and that we should pray with and for others.

Theme verse: 'But when you pray, go into your room, close the
door and pray to your Father, who is unseen. Then your Father,
who sees what is done in secret, will reward you' (Matt. 6:6).

It is vital when we pray to God, and call him our Father, that we
remind ourselves that he is 'our Father *in heaven*'. He is majestic
and his greatness is beyond knowledge. 'God is in heaven and you
are on earth' (Eccles. 5:2). It is because we are weak and sinful
that we humbly drop to our knees before God, remembering that
he knows all about us. 'Nothing in all creation is hidden from
God's sight. Everything is uncovered and laid bare before the eyes
of him to whom we must give account' (Heb. 4:13). If we want to
receive God's blessing when we pray we must be completely honest with him. He knows everything, and there is nothing hidden
from him. We must remember also that he has the right to punish
and the power to bless us. He is able to save or destroy. Remember, too, the Father's holiness and justice. When we approach our
Father in prayer we must do so 'with reverence and awe, for our
God is a consuming fire' (Heb. 12:28-29). So, whenever we pray,
we must take these two truths and place them at the beginning of
all our prayers: 1) that God is 'our Father' — the almighty, eternal, unchangeable, gracious and holy God, and 2) that our Father
is 'in heaven', above us, who knows all about us as a father who
knows what is best for his child. His arms are outstretched to bless
you with all the blessings of his heaven.

Scripture reading: Ecclesiastes 5:1-7

November 12

HALLOWING GOD'S NAME
(WEEK 46: DAY 1)

God's holy name

Westminster Catechism Question #101:

What do we pray for in the first petition? *Answer*: In the first petition (which is 'hallowed be your name') we pray that God would enable us and others to glorify him for who he is, and that he would work all things for his own glory.

Theme verse: 'Let them know that you, whose name is the Lord — that you alone are the Most High over all the earth' (Ps. 83:18).

The first petition of the Lord's Prayer commands us to pray that God's name will be glorified in all things, and that he would empower us to honour and bless his great name by the way we live and speak. There is a reason why this petition comes first: the hallowing of God's name is the most important calling and responsibility of the Christian. When we speak of God's name we are referring to his essence, those characteristics that make him truly God. All of his attributes, such as his wisdom, power, holiness, justice, goodness and truth, are characteristics that make God known to us. To hallow God's name is to set it apart from common use, to protect his name from abuse and profanity, and to use it in a holy and reverent way ourselves. God's name is sacred. We cannot add anything to God's glory, or make him greater than he already is, but we can exalt and honour his name in our world, and make him more attractive in the eyes of others. We especially hallow God's name when we trust in him: 'In him our hearts rejoice, for we trust in his holy name' (Ps. 33:21). Our calling is to exalt the name of the Father, Son and Holy Spirit in worship, evangelism, service and the use of our time and money. In short, all of life is lived to glorify and honour the sacred name of God the Father, Son and Holy Spirit.

SCRIPTURE READING: PSALM 33:1-22

November 13

God's holy name

Westminster Catechism Question #101:

What do we pray for in the first petition? *Answer*: In the first petition (which is 'hallowed be your name') we pray that God would enable us and others to glorify him for who he is, and that he would work all things for his own glory.

Theme verse: 'Let them know that you, whose name is the Lord — that you alone are the Most High over all the earth' (Ps. 83:18).

The Apostle Peter described followers of Christ in lofty terms, using honorifics such as 'a chosen people, a royal priesthood, a holy nation, a people belonging to God' (1 Peter 2:9). These grand titles inform us that we have a magnificent purpose: to 'declare the praises of him who called you out of darkness into his wonderful light' (1 Peter 2:9). Our calling is to declare the worthiness of God's name. This makes it obvious why 'hallowed be your name' is the first petition in the Lord's Prayer since our chief end is 'to glorify God and to enjoy him forever'. Peter's description serves as a reminder that Christians occupy a position of honour. No one stands between us and God and no person rules over us except the Lord himself, so we function as royal priests. We are part of a 'holy nation', people completely separated from non-believers, and dedicated solely to God. We are a 'people belonging to God', a special treasure that is precious to God. We should not let these exalted honours become a source of pride. The dignity and honour God bestows on his people is not for the purpose of meditating on ourselves or gloating in our self-worth. Peter's titles to describe the people of God have an undertone of admonition in them since that is the Lord's purpose: 'The people I formed for myself … may proclaim my praise' (Isa. 43:21).

SCRIPTURE READING: I PETER 2:4-12

November 14

God's holy name

Westminster Catechism Question #101:

What do we pray for in the first petition? *Answer*: In the first petition (which is 'hallowed be your name') we pray that God would enable us and others to glorify him for who he is, and that he would work all things for his own glory.

Theme verse: 'Let them know that you, whose name is the Lord — that you alone are the Most High over all the earth' (Ps. 83:18).

God revealed himself to the children of Israel under various names. Sometimes the Lord would call himself 'El' or 'Elohim' which means his 'strength' and his 'power'. Later God revealed himself in that great and wonderful name 'Jehovah' which means 'the self-existent one'. He used this name to make himself known to Moses at the burning bush as the eternally self-existent God. When Moses asked him for his name, God told him: '"I AM WHO I AM." That is what you are to say to the Israelites: "I AM" has sent me to you' (Exod. 3:14). There are other names in the Old Testament to describe God: 'The Lord will provide' (Jehovah-jireh), 'the Lord who heals' (Jehovah-rapha), 'the Lord our Banner' (Jehovah-nissi), 'the Lord our peace' (Jehovah-Shalom), 'the Lord our Righteousness' (Jehovah-tsidkenu), and 'the Lord is present' (Jehovah-shammah). These names reveal to us God's nature, being, character and attributes. When we pray 'hallowed be your name' we are declaring that all these names describe our great God. In the Lord's Prayer, Jesus is teaching us to pray that the whole world may come to know God in the fullness of his glory, and that the whole world may honour God for who he is. To pray 'hallowed by your name' is to have a deep and burning desire for the honour and glory of God.

SCRIPTURE READING: EXODUS 3:1-15

November 15

God's holy name

Westminster Catechism Question #101:

What do we pray for in the first petition? *Answer*: In the first petition (which is 'hallowed be your name') we pray that God would enable us and others to glorify him for who he is, and that he would work all things for his own glory.

Theme verse: 'Let them know that you, whose name is the Lord — that you alone are the Most High over all the earth' (Ps. 83:18).

The consuming passion of the Lord Jesus was his desire to honour and exalt the name of his Father. In his high priestly prayer, Jesus prayed: 'I have brought you glory on earth by completing the work you gave me to do' (John 17:4). As followers of Christ we are to ask God to show us more of his greatness and majesty. Too often we speak glibly about God, forgetting that we are talking about the eternal, absolute and almighty God. If we speak glibly about God we then fail to appreciate the goodness and kindness of God or his providential leading in our lives. The psalmist delighted in celebrating God as our rock (Ps. 18), as our shepherd who leads us (Ps. 23), and as our righteousness (Ps. 35). The psalmist's exuberance for God's holy name is particularly apparent in Psalm 34: 'Glorify the Lord with me; let us exalt his name together' (Ps. 34:3). At first glance, the exhortation to join him in glorifying the Lord seems quite ridiculous. How can we add to the greatness of God or more highly exalt the name that is exalted over all? What the psalmist is requesting is that followers of Jehovah join him in making our great God more attractive and better known among the peoples of the world. And when we think of it, hallowing God's name then becomes the springboard for missions as we seek to exalt his name among the nations.

SCRIPTURE READING: PSALM 34

November 16
HE MUST INCREASE
(WEEK 46: DAY 5)

God's holy name

Westminster Catechism Question #101:

What do we pray for in the first petition? *Answer*: In the first petition (which is 'hallowed be your name') we pray that God would enable us and others to glorify him for who he is, and that he would work all things for his own glory.

Theme verse: 'Let them know that you, whose name is the Lord — that you alone are the Most High over all the earth' (Ps. 83:18).

We are called to do everything for the glory of God (1 Cor. 10:31), and we hallow God's name when we ascribe the honour of all we do to him alone. But pride sometimes makes us want to put ourselves in a position of honour rather than enthroning Christ in our hearts. When King Herod became so prideful that he began to think of himself as godlike, he was struck down by an angel of the Lord (Acts 12:23). On the other hand, John the Baptist was fully committed to exalting Christ, and transferred all the honours he was receiving to Jesus. He said that the one who deserved worship was the Son of God and noted that 'He who comes after me (Jesus) has surpassed me because he was before me' (the Word at the beginning of time) (John 1:15). John recognized that he was a mere man, baptizing with available water. But Jesus was coming to baptize us in the Holy Spirit. The Apostle Paul spoke in the same humble language as John the Baptist: 'I am the least of the apostles and do not even deserve to be called an apostle' (1 Cor. 15:9). Paul recognized that his ministry was possible only because of 'the grace of God that was with me' (1 Cor. 15:10). Both John and Paul are solid reminders to us that our privilege and high calling is to hallow God's name, and that all of life is to be lived 'for the praise of *his* glory' (Rom. 1:12) and not for ours.

SCRIPTURE READING: JOHN 1:15-28

November 17
Honouring God by obedience
(week 46: day 6)

God's holy name

Westminster Catechism Question #101:

What do we pray for in the first petition? *Answer*: In the first petition (which is "hallowed be your name") we pray that God would enable us and others to glorify him for who he is, and that he would work all things for his own glory.

Theme verse: 'Let them know that you, whose name is the Lord — that you alone are the Most High over all the earth' (Ps. 83:18).

We hallow and sanctify God's name when we obey him. Jesus is our perfect example of honouring the Father's name through an obedient life. His death at the cross greatly honoured his Father, for 'it was the Lord's will to crush him and cause him to suffer' (Isa. 53:10). Jesus did not shrink back from glorifying his Father through obedient suffering. 'When you have lifted up the Son of Man, then you will know that I am the one I claim to be … The one who sent me is with me; he has not left me alone, for I always do what pleases him' (John 8:28-29). In heaven, the angels are pictured as creatures that hallow God's name through perfect obedience. 'Praise the Lord, you his angels, you mighty ones who do his bidding, who obey his word' (Ps. 103:20). And the angels in the book of Revelation have 'encircled the throne and … in a loud voice they sang: "Worthy is the Lamb who was slain, to receive power and wealth and wisdom and strength and honor and glory and praise!"' (Rev. 5:11-12). If we want to join the Lord Jesus and the angels in hallowing God's name we can look to Abraham as a solid example. When God required the sacrifice of Isaac, Abraham was prepared to obediently offer the Lord his miracle child (Gen. 22:12), 'for to obey is better than sacrifice, and to heed is better than the fat of rams' (1 Sam. 15:22).

Scripture reading: Psalm 103

November 18

God's holy name

Westminster Catechism Question #101:

What do we pray for in the first petition? *Answer*: In the first petition (which is 'hallowed be your name') we pray that God would enable us and others to glorify him for who he is, and that he would work all things for his own glory.

Theme verse: 'Let them know that you, whose name is the Lord — that you alone are the Most High over all the earth' (Ps. 83:18).

We hallow and sanctify God's name when we lift up his name in our praises. God has given us voices for a reason: 'My mouth is filled with your praise, declaring your splendor all day long' (Ps. 71:8). In heaven God's name is constantly praised by angels and glorified saints. They are perpetually singing their hallelujahs: 'To him who sits on the throne and to the Lamb be praise and honor and glory and power, for ever and ever!' (Rev. 5:13). God calls us to prepare for heaven by beginning our praises of him here on earth. If our souls are filled with thanksgiving they will burst forth in praise to God's holy name. King David was called 'Israel's singer of songs' (2 Sam. 23:1) because he loved to sing praises to the Lord. The Psalms are filled with his praise music: 'I will exalt you, my God the King; I will praise your name for ever and ever' (Ps. 145:1). Praising God hallows his name, spreads the Lord's fame, and verbalizes the excellence of our Saviour while exalting him in the eyes of others. Certainly praise is one of the highest and purest acts of our religion. Someone has said that in prayer we act like humans, but in praise we act like angels. Hallowing God's name is not only the great work of the Christian but also of the church of God: 'Sing to the Lord a new song, his praise in the assembly of the saints' (Ps. 149:1).

SCRIPTURE READING: PSALM 149

November 19

The coming kingdom

Westminster Catechism Question #102:

What do we pray for in the second petition? *Answer*: In the second petition (which is 'Your kingdom come') we pray that Satan's kingdom may be destroyed; and that the kingdom of Christ may be advanced, ourselves and others brought into it and kept in it; and that Christ may return soon.

Theme verse: 'Behold, I am coming soon! My reward is with me, and I will give to everyone according to what he has done' (Rev. 22:12).

The petition 'Your kingdom come' teaches us that God is a great and exalted King. He is not great because his subjects have made him great; he is great in and of himself. So we sing our praises 'to him who rides the ancient skies above, who thunders with mighty voice' (Ps. 68:33). The Lord Jesus is also pictured as being the king of a righteous kingdom: 'Your throne, O God, will last forever and ever, and righteousness will be the scepter of your kingdom' (Heb. 1:8). It is wise for us to serve such a king because he easily defeats his enemies, and will come one day to establish his kingdom in the new heavens and new earth. When we pray 'Your kingdom come,' we are asking two things. First, we desire to see God's kingdom established in our lives. This means that we want to see our consciences being ruled by Christ and our hearts becoming more subject to him. Secondly, we are asking the Lord to return soon in order to establish his kingdom in the new heavens and new earth. This will be his final victory over Satan, sin and hell. In this triumphant kingdom we shall reign with Christ and enjoy the blessings of eternal fellowship with God. This kingdom has already come in the person of Jesus Christ and will be fulfilled when he comes again to establish his kingdom. Jesus would have you pray for his soon return.

SCRIPTURE READING: PSALM 68:20-35

November 20

The coming kingdom

Westminster Catechism Question #102:

What do we pray for in the second petition? *Answer*: In the second petition (which is 'Your kingdom come') we pray that Satan's kingdom may be destroyed; and that the kingdom of Christ may be advanced, ourselves and others brought into it and kept in it; and that Christ may return soon.

Theme verse: 'Behold, I am coming soon! My reward is with me, and I will give to everyone according to what he has done' (Rev. 22:12).

The petitions in the Lord's Prayer have a divine order to them. The Lord has us pray 'Hallowed be your name' in the first petition. But the moment we pray that prayer we are reminded of the fact that God's name is not hallowed in our world. We live in a world of sin and profanity. We then wonder about why this is the case. Why don't people bow before the Lord to exalt and praise him? The answer is, of course, because of sin that separates humanity from God. There is a satanic kingdom that opposes our Saviour's kingdom that must and will be destroyed. As the Apostle Paul states it: 'The god of this age has blinded the minds of unbelievers, so that they cannot see the light of the gospel of the glory of Christ' (2 Cor. 4:4). Our desire as followers of Christ is that God's name will be glorified and that the kingdom of Christ will be advanced. Therefore, Jesus challenges us to pray for this advancement of the heavenly kingdom, first in our own hearts, and then in the hearts of others throughout the world. We must proclaim the good news to the entire world that there is a much better kingdom that they can join through repentance and faith in Christ. Satan may have entered this world for the moment, and humanity is under his dominion now, but Christ will one day turn this world and all its kingdoms into his own glorious kingdom.

SCRIPTURE READING: 2 CORINTHIANS 4:1-18

November 21
ESTABLISHING THE KINGDOM
(WEEK 47: DAY 3)

The coming kingdom

Westminster Catechism Question #102:

What do we pray for in the second petition? *Answer*: In the second petition (which is 'Your kingdom come') we pray that Satan's kingdom may be destroyed; and that the kingdom of Christ may be advanced, ourselves and others brought into it and kept in it; and that Christ may return soon.

Theme verse: 'Behold, I am coming soon! My reward is with me, and I will give to everyone according to what he has done' (Rev. 22:12).

When we pray 'Your kingdom come' we are actually praying that God would rule the earth rather than Satan. We are praying that his laws would be established and that peace and righteousness would replace all the hatred and discord we live with now. In one sense, the kingdom has already come. It came when the Lord Jesus was here. He said, 'If I drive out demons by the finger of God, then the kingdom of God has come to you' (Luke 11:20). Jesus was informing us that the kingdom has already arrived and that he is exercising his power and majesty now. And the kingdom of God is also at work in each one of us who knows Jesus as Saviour and Lord. The kingdom of God is present in his Church, in all who confess and love the Lord Jesus. But the day is yet to come when Christ's kingdom will be fully established here upon the earth. The whole message of the Bible looks forward to that. Christ came down from heaven to earth to establish and bring us this glorious kingdom. He is still engaged in that task and will continue to be engaged in it until history runs its course and the Father hands over the kingdom of this world to his Son. So when Christ taught his disciples to pray 'Your kingdom come,' he was asking us to pray for the kingdom to be established in our own hearts, in the hearts of others, and ultimately, throughout the world.

SCRIPTURE READING: LUKE 11:14-28

November 22
LONGING FOR CHRIST'S RETURN
(WEEK 47: DAY 4)

The coming kingdom

Westminster Catechism Question #102:

What do we pray for in the second petition? *Answer*: In the second petition (which is 'Your kingdom come') we pray that Satan's kingdom may be destroyed; and that the kingdom of Christ may be advanced, ourselves and others brought into it and kept in it; and that Christ may return soon.

Theme verse: 'Behold, I am coming soon! My reward is with me, and I will give to everyone according to what he has done' (Rev. 22:12).

When we pray 'Your kingdom come,' it indicates that 'we are looking forward to a new heaven and a new earth, the home of righteousness' (2 Peter 3:13). God has promised that we can anticipate a day when all sin and evil and wrong and everything that is opposed to God will finally have been routed. This prayer promotes the longings in our hearts for the time when the Lord will come back again, when all that is against him will be cast into the lake of fire, and the kingdoms of this world will have become the kingdoms of our God. At the very end of the Bible we are told that the Holy Spirit and the bride of Christ, his church, are saying, 'Come!' and whoever thirsts for God is also saying, 'Come!' There is a tremendous longing for the Saviour's return for all those who are tired of the world as it is and who long for the new heavens and new earth. The Lord promises us that he will not delay: 'Yes, I am coming soon.' Our reply is: 'Amen. Come, Lord Jesus' (Rev. 22:17,20). The Lord's Prayer teaches us that before we begin to think about our own personal needs and desires, or even the urgent needs of family and friends, we should have a burning desire within us for the coming of Christ's kingdom, and that the name of God would be glorified and exalted throughout our hurting world.

SCRIPTURE READING: 2 PETER 3:1-18

November 23

The coming kingdom

Westminster Catechism Question #102:

What do we pray for in the second petition? *Answer*: In the second petition (which is 'Your kingdom come') we pray that Satan's kingdom may be destroyed; and that the kingdom of Christ may be advanced, ourselves and others brought into it and kept in it; and that Christ may return soon.

Theme verse: 'Behold, I am coming soon! My reward is with me, and I will give to everyone according to what he has done' (Rev. 22:12).

During his earthly ministry, Jesus sent out seventy-two of his followers on a missionary journey. Their assignment was to spread the good news that the kingdom of God had come. When they returned from their mission trip they were elated and reported to Jesus that even the demons were submitting to them in his name. The joy of these disciples was not so much because they were received with open arms, or because their message found ready acceptance, or even because they were counted worthy to be the missionaries of Jesus. They were excited because the kingdom of darkness was being overthrown by the kingdom of light. These disciples did not use the name of Jesus as a lucky charm. The kingdom of darkness is not overthrown by superstitious chanting of the name of the deity. Instead, what the disciples witnessed was the fall of Satan himself by the power of Christ when the good news of the kingdom was preached. Jesus told his followers that he 'saw Satan fall like lightning from heaven' (Luke 10:18). In the supernatural world Jesus could see Satan's power, exalted as high as heaven, falling to terrible defeat. Satan has been crushed by our all-conquering Saviour and he continues to suffer defeat wherever the powerful gospel of the kingdom is proclaimed by the messengers of Jesus.

SCRIPTURE READING: LUKE 10:1-24

November 24
PROTECTIVE ARMOUR
(WEEK 47: DAY 6)

The coming kingdom

Westminster Catechism Question #102:

What do we pray for in the second petition? *Answer*: In the second petition (which is 'Your kingdom come') we pray that Satan's kingdom may be destroyed; and that the kingdom of Christ may be advanced, ourselves and others brought into it and kept in it; and that Christ may return soon.

Theme verse: 'Behold, I am coming soon! My reward is with me, and I will give to everyone according to what he has done' (Rev. 22:12).

Because of Christ's great triumph at the cross, believers in Jesus fight on the side of a victorious leader. The Lord has us stand with him against all his and our enemies until they are completely destroyed. He has given us some strength because we have received new life in Christ, but we always need fresh supplies of the Lord's inexhaustible power. We are admonished to 'put on the full armor of God so that you can take your stand against the devil's schemes' (Eph. 6:11). The imagery is of a soldier on the front line of battle, putting on his protective armour. What military equipment will we need to fight against the kingdom of darkness? The devil is an expert opposing commander and we will need to be well-equipped in order to battle effectively. This is spiritual warfare and we will need the strong, disciplined characteristics of Christ. We will need to have the truth of the Word of God shaping our thinking, the righteousness of Christ that is received by faith and the peace of God in our hearts that makes us ready for battle! Throughout this lifelong conflict we will need to trust the Lord moment by moment, reflecting on God's Word to us, praying in the power of the Spirit, and keeping alert against enemy attack upon our souls and the souls of others. In so doing, God's people move forward victoriously on behalf of Christ's kingdom.

SCRIPTURE READING: EPHESIANS 6:10-20

November 25

TWO KINGDOMS

(WEEK 47: DAY 7)

The coming kingdom

Westminster Catechism Question #102:

What do we pray for in the second petition? *Answer*: In the second petition (which is 'Your kingdom come') we pray that Satan's kingdom may be destroyed; and that the kingdom of Christ may be advanced, ourselves and others brought into it and kept in it; and that Christ may return soon.

Theme verse: 'Behold, I am coming soon! My reward is with me, and I will give to everyone according to what he has done' (Rev. 22:12).

While Jesus was on earth he told a number of parables that help us understand the nature of his kingdom as opposed to Satan's kingdom. In one such parable Jesus described the kingdom of heaven as similar to 'a man who sowed good seed in his field. But while everyone was sleeping, his enemy came and sowed weeds among the wheat, and went away' (Matt. 13:24-25). Jesus later explained the parable to his disciples. Jesus came to sow the good seed of the gospel into our souls, producing true believers who 'shine like the sun in the kingdom of their Father' (Matt. 13:43). The devil sows weeds that produce 'sons of the evil one' (Matt. 13:38). Christ is informing us that right up until the end of the age these two kingdoms will grow side by side. But when he comes to judge the world there will be a separation of the good seed from the bad, a separation of the righteous from the unrighteous. The wicked will be thrown 'into the fiery furnace, where there will be weeping and gnashing of teeth' (Matt. 13:42), but the righteous will enter the joy of the kingdom of Christ. In this parable, as with so many others, Jesus is asking us to ask ourselves, 'What kind of soil and what kind of seed am I? Am I a child of the kingdom of Christ or the kingdom of darkness? How will it go for me at the final judgement?' How do you answer?

SCRIPTURE READING: MATTHEW 13:24-43

November 26
ANGELIC OBEDIENCE
(WEEK 48: DAY 1)

The will of God

Westminster Catechism Question #103:

What do we pray for in the third petition? *Answer*: In the third petition (which is 'Your will be done on earth as it is in heaven') we pray that God, by his grace, would make us able and willing to know, obey and submit to his will in all things, as the angels do in heaven.

Theme verse: 'I desire to do your will, O God; your law is within my heart' (Ps. 40:8).

The third petition consists of two parts, doing God's will ('your will be done on earth') and how to do God's will ('as it is done in heaven'). When we pray for God's will to be done, we are actually asking for the ability to obey his commands. We are also praying for strength to submit patiently to God's will, if his plan is to test us. God's will is that we should trust in Christ, obey his commands and lead holy lives. We do God's will, as the angels do, when we prefer God's purposes to our own, when we do his will habitually and entirely, and when our actions are without hypocrisy or show. Unlike humans, angels do not wrestle with a weak and sinful nature. They are servants who do the Lord's will and carry out the Lord's commands without hesitation. 'Praise the Lord, all his heavenly hosts, you his servants who do his will' (Ps. 103:21) However, we have the inner struggle with rebellion, pride and a spirit of independence, tempting us to wilfully break God's commandments in thought, word and deed. Yet the Lord calls us to obedience to his will and to the exaltation of his name in the same way as the angels obey and praise him in heaven. Here is our calling: 'If you obey my commands, you will remain in my love, just as I have obeyed my Father's commands and remain in his love' (John 15:10).

SCRIPTURE READING: JOHN 15:1-17

November 27
HEAVEN ON EARTH
(WEEK 48: DAY 2)

The will of God

Westminster Catechism Question #103:

What do we pray for in the third petition? *Answer*: In the third petition (which is 'Your will be done on earth as it is in heaven') we pray that God, by his grace, would make us able and willing to know, obey and submit to his will in all things, as the angels do in heaven.

Theme verse: 'I desire to do your will, O God; your law is within my heart' (Ps. 40:8).

This third petition, 'Your will be done on earth as it is in heaven', is a logical consequence and conclusion from the previous petition, 'Your kingdom come'. God's purposes are being accomplished when his kingdom is advancing on the earth. In heaven the will of God is always being done perfectly. The Scriptures tell us that everyone in heaven offers joyful service to the Lord, anxious to glorify and magnify his name. 'Praise the Lord, you his angels, you mighty ones who do his bidding, who obey his word' (Ps. 103:20). The angels are in flight, all ready and waiting to do the Father's will. The supreme desire of the inhabitants of heaven is to do the will of God, and it should be our desire for everyone on earth to do the same. Of course, this petition will never be fulfilled until the kingdom of God is established here on earth at the end of the age. Only then will the purposes of God be perfectly done on earth as they are in heaven. There will be 'a new heaven and a new earth, the home of righteousness' (2 Peter 3:13). Heaven and earth will become one, the world will be changed, evil will be burned out of it, and the glory of God will shine on us. 'May he strengthen your hearts so that you will be blameless and holy in the presence of our God and Father when our Lord Jesus comes with all his holy ones' (1 Thess. 3:13).

SCRIPTURE READING: 1 THESSALONIANS 3:6-13

November 28
CONTENTMENT AND GOD'S WILL
(WEEK 48: DAY 3)

The will of God

Westminster Catechism Question #103:

What do we pray for in the third petition? *Answer*: In the third petition (which is 'Your will be done on earth as it is in heaven') we pray that God, by his grace, would make us able and willing to know, obey and submit to his will in all things, as the angels do in heaven.

Theme verse: 'I desire to do your will, O God; your law is within my heart' (Ps. 40:8).

It is difficult to do God's will on earth as it is being done in heaven if we lack contentment. So many followers of Christ have such deep-seated resentments about the lives they are leading that it is impossible for them to see the will of God in much of their daily activities. Discontentment has a mixture of anger and grief in it. When God tests us, one response is to become sullen. But murmuring cannot stand side by side with God's will. Murmuring is the height of impatience; it is a kind of mutiny in the soul against God. Although the people of Israel had witnessed the miracle of the dividing of the Red Sea and were fed manna from heaven, when they were tested in the wilderness 'they spoke against God and against Moses, and said, "Why have you brought us up out of Egypt to die in the desert?"' (Num. 21:5). Murmuring and impatience spring from pride. We think we deserve better from God. Murmuring also springs from distrust. We conclude that God cannot bring good out of all our troubles. We refuse to trust in his providence or believe his promises that 'never will I leave you; never will I forsake you' (Heb. 13:5). It is the gracious, humble Christian who can say, 'I have learned to be content whatever the circumstances' (Phil. 4:11). Contentment is essential if God's will is to be done on earth as it is in heaven.

SCRIPTURE READING: NUMBERS 21:1-9

November 29
JOB'S TEST
(WEEK 48: DAY 4)

The will of God

Westminster Catechism Question #103:

What do we pray for in the third petition? *Answer*: In the third petition (which is 'Your will be done on earth as it is in heaven') we pray that God, by his grace, would make us able and willing to know, obey and submit to his will in all things, as the angels do in heaven.

Theme verse: 'I desire to do your will, O God; your law is within my heart' (Ps. 40:8).

Job was a righteous man, described in the Bible as 'the greatest man among all the people of the East' (Job 1:3). The Lord called Job 'my servant' and declared that 'there is no one on earth like him; he is blameless and upright, a man who fears God and shuns evil' (Job 1:8). Job enjoyed a close relationship with God and sought to do his will. But Satan accused Job of being loyal to God purely for reasons of self-interest. If he was severely tested, Satan argued, Job would curse God to his face. God allowed Satan to test the motivation behind Job's loyalty. Did Job perform God's will only because it brought him blessings, or did Job really love God unconditionally and want his will done on earth even if that involved suffering? Despite great trauma: the loss of his wealth, livestock and eventually his entire family, Job proved his sincerity. He made no claims to the blessings that had previously been bestowed on him by God. His response to God's severe testing was one of humble trust in the Lord's sovereign purposes for his life. Though he questioned the Lord's dealings at times, he refused to charge God with wrongdoing. Job's response to this time of testing vindicated the Lord's view of him as a loyal servant. We should pray for the ability to respond to difficulties the way Job did: 'Though he slay me, yet will I hope in him' (Job 13:15).

SCRIPTURE READING: JOB 1:1-22

November 30

The agony of Gethsemane
(week 48: day 5)

The will of God

Westminster Catechism Question #103:

What do we pray for in the third petition? *Answer*: In the third petition (which is 'Your will be done on earth as it is in heaven') we pray that God, by his grace, would make us able and willing to know, obey and submit to his will in all things, as the angels do in heaven.

Theme verse: 'I desire to do your will, O God; your law is within my heart' (Ps. 40:8).

Upon arriving at the Garden of Gethsemane, Jesus entered into his night of anguish: 'My soul is overwhelmed with sorrow to the point of death' (Matt. 26:38). Soon he lay prostrate on the ground, crying out in prayer: 'My Father, if it is possible, may this cup be taken from me. Yet not as I will, but as you will' (Matt. 26:39). Read again the essence of his prayer: 'not as I will, but as you will.' Jesus was embroiled in the titanic struggle between his Father's good and holy purpose and the temptation to run from carrying our sin. The agony suffered in Gethsemane was unimaginably greater than what we face as mere humans because the holy, sinless Son of God was being asked to take sin upon himself. Because he was sinless, he should not die; yet, because he was sinless and holy, he willed to die for our sin. The death of Jesus was far different from that of the courageous martyrs. They died after Jesus' death had removed their sin and guilt, so the fear of judgement after death had been removed through Christ's death. But Jesus died under sin and its curse, and the sting of death tortured him with all its damnable power. Nevertheless, Jesus left the decision entirely up to his Father, in order that the will of the Father might be done on earth as it is in heaven. Our struggle to be faithful in small things seems less impossible when we reflect on Christ's faithfulness in great things.

Scripture reading: Matthew 26:36-46

December 1

The will of God

Westminster Catechism Question #103:

What do we pray for in the third petition? *Answer*: In the third petition (which is 'Your will be done on earth as it is in heaven') we pray that God, by his grace, would make us able and willing to know, obey and submit to his will in all things, as the angels do in heaven.

Theme verse: 'I desire to do your will, O God; your law is within my heart' (Ps. 40:8).

It is only fair that God requires our obedience. After all, he is our Creator and we owe our life and every breath to him. God's great design in the Word of God is to set out his commands and precepts so that we would not merely listen to the word but also 'do what it says' (James 1:22). Why did God need to give us his Ten Commandments and all of his counsel and teaching in both the Old and New Testaments, if it was not his purpose to make us gladly submit to his will in our lives? When Jesus was wrapping up his Sermon on the Mount (Matt. 5–7), he concluded by saying: 'Therefore everyone who hears these words of mine and puts them into practice is like a wise man who built his house on the rock' (Matt. 7:24). Christ's words do not mean that after hearing his divine message to us that we step in with our own natural powers and begin to practise that Word. When it comes to all truly spiritual requirements we are dead and lifeless, unable to respond. The words of Christ meet this situation, however, because they are spirit and life; they carry their own power in them, and are able to move us to do what they say in the power of the Holy Spirit. And his words must increasingly accomplish their purpose because, 'Not everyone who says to me, "Lord, Lord," will enter the kingdom of heaven, but only he who does the will of my Father who is in heaven' (Matt. 7:21).

SCRIPTURE READING: MATTHEW 7:15-29

December 2
Peaceful life, peaceful death
(week 48: day 7)

The will of God

Westminster Catechism Question #103:

What do we pray for in the third petition? *Answer*: In the third petition (which is 'Your will be done on earth as it is in heaven') we pray that God, by his grace, would make us able and willing to know, obey and submit to his will in all things, as the angels do in heaven.

Theme verse: 'I desire to do your will, O God; your law is within my heart' (Ps. 40:8).

Doing God's will on earth brings peace in life and in death. 'The ordinances of the Lord are sure and altogether righteous ... in keeping them there is great reward' (Ps. 19:9,11). When we walk closely with God in obedience there is a secret joy that enters the soul. 'Oh, how I love your law! I meditate on it all day long' (Ps. 119:97). There is also peace when we come to die. When Hezekiah thought he was about to die he was greatly comforted by the remembrance that he had sought to do the will of God on earth. 'Remember, O Lord, how I have walked before you faithfully and with wholehearted devotion and have done what is good in your eyes' (Isa. 38:3). The Apostle Paul enjoyed the same comfort when he realized that he had few remaining days left in this world: 'For I am already being poured out like a drink offering and the time has come for my departure. I have fought the good fight, I have finished the race, I have kept the faith' (2 Tim. 4:6-7). Have you ever heard someone complain at the close of his life that he had done God's will too much? Isn't it always the sad testimony that we have all done too little to honour our Saviour's hallowed name and that his will was not always our chief desire? With this reminder before us, let us pray for fresh obedience today and a deepened longing to do all God's will.

Scripture reading: Psalm 119:97-112

December 3
OUR ATTITUDE TOWARDS POSSESSIONS
(WEEK 49: DAY 1)

Daily Provision

Westminster Catechism Question #104:

What do we pray for in the fourth petition? *Answer*: In the fourth petition (which is 'Give us today our daily bread') we pray that by God's kindness we may receive a portion of the good things of this life, and enjoy his blessing with them.

Theme verse: 'Give me neither poverty nor riches, but give me only my daily bread' (Prov. 30:8).

This petition, which asks God to extend his mercy to us by supplying our daily bread, reminds us that everything we have is a gift sent from God. Our own skills and ingenuity do not bring material blessing. Only our Heavenly Father's delight to provide for his children allows us these gifts. The Lord also teaches us to cast off any care or anxiety about the future. We should not be consumed by the desire or concern to store up material possessions on earth. Instead, we should lay up treasures in heaven (Matt. 6:19-20). The Saviour warns us to live each day as if it was our last. This portion of the Lord's Prayer reminds us to be content with what the Lord gives us. As the Apostle Paul explained to Timothy, 'if we have food and clothing, we will be content with that' (1 Tim. 6:8). We are unbalanced if we crave earthly possessions when the Lord has told us to seek first his kingdom and righteousness. Such a covetous attitude is idolatry. The proper attitude towards material possessions flows out of our theme verse from Proverbs, requesting neither poverty nor riches. Poverty can give rise to the temptation to covet or steal another person's belongings. Riches can tempt a person to forget his dependence on the Lord and lead to the worship of self. Instead, the Christian's focus should be on Christ, the Bread of life and supplier of all our needs.

SCRIPTURE READING: 1 TIMOTHY 6:3-10

December 4
SUSTAINED THROUGH PRAYER
(WEEK 49: DAY 2)

Daily Provision

Westminster Catechism Question #104:

What do we pray for in the fourth petition? *Answer*: In the fourth petition (which is 'Give us today our daily bread') we pray that by God's kindness we may receive a portion of the good things of this life, and enjoy his blessing with them.

Theme verse: 'Give me neither poverty nor riches, but give me only my daily bread' (Prov. 30:8).

The first three petitions of the Lord's Prayer are devoted to God and his glory, and now the remaining three petitions deal with our particular needs and challenges. Our most important necessities are summed up by these three petitions: 'Give us today our daily bread,' 'forgive us our debts as we also have forgiven our debtors,' 'and lead us not into temptation, but deliver us from the evil one,' which cover the whole life of the Christian with respect to our physical needs (sustenance like food, water and shelter), mental and social needs (community), and spiritual needs (salvation). Yet the order of the phrases in the Lord's Prayer reminds us of the importance of starting prayer with praise rather than with personal requests. Even if our difficulties are urgent, whether it is physical illness, war, calamity, or some terrible problem suddenly confronting us, we should first acknowledge God's honour and glory before we ask for help for ourselves or others. If we fail in this, God soon becomes for us just a doting grandparent who hands out goodies irrespective of the attitude of our heart. Because the Lord will provide for us even without our asking, praise him in advance, knowing that all our needs are met according to his glorious riches in Christ Jesus (Phil. 4:19). 'Cast your cares on the Lord and he will sustain you; he will never let the righteous fall' (Ps. 55:22).

SCRIPTURE READING: PSALM 55:1-23

December 5

THE WAY GOD WORKS
(WEEK 49: DAY 3)

Daily Provision

Westminster Catechism Question #104:

What do we pray for in the fourth petition? *Answer*: In the fourth petition (which is 'Give us today our daily bread') we pray that by God's kindness we may receive a portion of the good things of this life, and enjoy his blessing with them.

Theme verse: 'Give me neither poverty nor riches, but give me only my daily bread' (Prov. 30:8).

When Jesus taught us to pray 'Give us today our daily bread,' he was not confining the request merely to food. Jesus meant for this phrase to cover all our material needs, everything that is necessary for us to get along in this world. When we think about this, it is amazing to consider that the Creator and Sustainer of the universe, the God who is forming his eternal kingdom and who will usher it in at the end, the God to whom 'the nations are like a drop in the bucket; they are regarded as dust on the scales' (Isa. 40:15) — is prepared to consider our little needs even down to the most minute details in this matter of daily provision! But this is the consistent teaching of Scripture. The Lord tells us that a sparrow cannot fall to the ground without our Father, and that 'even the very hairs of your head are all numbered' (Matt. 10:30). This means that the smallest and most trivial matters in our lives are known to him and that he knows our needs even before we pray about them. This is the way that God works. 'For this is what the high and lofty One says — he who lives forever, whose name is holy; "I live in a high and holy place, but also with him who is contrite and lowly in spirit"' (Isa. 57:15). In the end, this is the miracle of redemption, which takes hold of us here on earth and links us with the high and holy God of glory.

SCRIPTURE READING: ISAIAH 57:14-21

December 6
Sustained through prayer
(week 49: day 4)

Daily Provision

Westminster Catechism Question #104:

What do we pray for in the fourth petition? *Answer*: In the fourth petition (which is 'Give us today our daily bread') we pray that by God's kindness we may receive a portion of the good things of this life, and enjoy his blessing with them.

Theme verse: 'Give me neither poverty nor riches, but give me only my daily bread' (Prov. 30:8).

There are some people who might see an apparent contradiction with this petition. The Lord Jesus asks us to make requests for our daily provisions, but he has also told us not to babble like pagans, 'For they think they will be heard because of their many words' (Matt. 6:7). Jesus told us: 'Do not be like them, for your Father knows what you need before you ask him' (Matt. 6:8). If God knows what we need before we ask him, why should we express our needs to him? Why tell the Lord about things he knows about already? These questions bring us to the heart of the meaning of prayer. We do not tell God about our daily needs because he is not aware of them. Instead, we must think of prayer more as a relationship between a father and child. The value of prayer is that it keeps us in touch with God. God does not give us one great lump of grace and then, having received it, we live off of God's grace. If the Lord gave us grace in one lump sum we could be tempted to enjoy the gift and forget the Giver. But God is like an earthly father or mother in this respect. The Lord wants our company, he wants us to speak to him, and providing for all our needs is how the Lord accomplishes his desire of intimacy with his children. It is astounding, but the great Jehovah, the God who depends on no one, enjoys having his children come to him with their prayers and requests.

Scripture reading: Revelation 3:14-22

December 7

Daily Provision

Westminster Catechism Question #104:

What do we pray for in the fourth petition? *Answer*: In the fourth petition (which is 'Give us today our daily bread') we pray that by God's kindness we may receive a portion of the good things of this life, and enjoy his blessing with them.

Theme verse: 'Give me neither poverty nor riches, but give me only my daily bread' (Prov. 30:8).

In spite of all the grumbling by the people of Israel in the desert, the Lord provided them with manna. 'I will rain down bread from heaven for you. The people are to go out each day and gather enough for that day' (Exod. 16:4). Everyone gathered enough so that they were completely satisfied. However, when some of the Israelite community attempted to hoard the manna until morning, 'it was full of maggots and began to smell' (Exod. 16:20). There is much that is instructive here. First, without the Lord's merciful provision of daily bread we would all starve. Secondly, he allowed the people to participate in his miracle by gathering up the manna themselves, teaching us that we should be diligent in providing for the physical needs of ourselves and our families. We are to be industrious in order that we 'do not eat the bread of idleness' (Prov. 31:27). Thirdly, the Lord seeks to instil contentment in our lives for his daily provision. 'He who gathered much did not have too much, and he who gathered little did not have too little' (Exod. 16:18). God supplied just enough for each day so that the people would learn to depend on him and trust his loving care to meet all their daily needs. We, too, are not to hoard. Instead, we can trust the Lord to provide us our daily bread, just as he supplies for all our needs.

SCRIPTURE READING: EXODUS 16:13-23

December 8
FEEDING THE MULTITUDE
(WEEK 49: DAY 6)

Daily Provision

Westminster Catechism Question #104:

What do we pray for in the fourth petition? *Answer*: In the fourth petition (which is 'Give us today our daily bread') we pray that by God's kindness we may receive a portion of the good things of this life, and enjoy his blessing with them.

Theme verse: 'Give me neither poverty nor riches, but give me only my daily bread' (Prov. 30:8).

'When Jesus looked up and saw a great crowd coming toward him, he said to Philip, "Where shall we buy bread for these people to eat?"' (John 6:5). The Scriptures tell us that Jesus was testing Philip and all the disciples, hoping to stretch their faith beyond the horizontal and temporal. Unfortunately, the disciples could only see one thing that should be done, namely, that Jesus should send the multitude away at once. The disciples assumed that Jesus had forgotten to think about the physical needs of the multitudes and suggested that it was high time to act if all the people were to reach the neighbouring villages in order to purchase bread. Or perhaps, the disciples reasoned, they could run to a nearby village and buy enough bread so that everyone could have a few bites to stave off their hunger. None of the disciples mustered enough faith to think that Jesus himself intended to abundantly feed the crowd. So Jesus told the disciples to have the people sit down (Matt. 14:19) and, using the disciples as waiters, he performed the great miracle that is recorded in all four gospels. We might chide the disciples for their lack of faith, only seeing things from a worldly viewpoint when Jesus was in their midst. But the application is an obvious one for us as well. Why do we see our little problems as insurmountable when, by faith, we can turn in prayer to the Bread of Life?

SCRIPTURE READING: MATTHEW 14:13-21

December 9
REAL FOOD AND DRINK
(WEEK 49: DAY 7)

Daily Provision

Westminster Catechism Question #104:

What do we pray for in the fourth petition? *Answer*: In the fourth petition (which is 'Give us today our daily bread') we pray that by God's kindness we may receive a portion of the good things of this life, and enjoy his blessing with them.

Theme verse: 'Give me neither poverty nor riches, but give me only my daily bread' (Prov. 30:8).

Jesus declared, 'I am the bread of life. He who comes to me will never go hungry, and he who believes in me will never be thirsty' (John 6:35). Jesus was contrasting the manna that fell in the wilderness to himself. The manna provided physical nourishment, but Christ as the 'Bread of Life' satisfies our spiritual hunger. The Old Testament manna met the people's temporal need for food, but it could not sustain life beyond the grave. But Christ feeds us continuously by his Word and promises eternal life to all who feed on him. 'Your forefathers ate the manna in the desert, yet they died. But here is the bread that came down from heaven, which a man may eat and not die' (John 6:49). There were some similarities between the manna and the Lord Jesus. Both the Lord and the manna came down from heaven and both the Lord and the manna provided the people's daily needs. But of course, with Christ we receive so much more blessing than with temporal food. Jesus invites us to 'eat the flesh of the Son of Man and to drink his blood' (John 6:53). His flesh and blood are real food. There is nothing false or deceptive about the power of his sacrificial death. Jesus alone is able to bestow eternal life for those who are joined to him through faith. He is the vital, living element in which we live, move and have our being spiritually. Eat and drink of Christ and live.

SCRIPTURE READING: JOHN 6:25-59

December 10

Confession

Westminster Catechism Question #105:

What do we pray for in the fifth petition? *Answer*: In the fifth
petition (which is 'Forgive us our debts, as we also have forgiven
our debtors') we pray that God would freely pardon all our sins,
which we are encouraged to ask because by his grace we are
enabled from the heart to forgive others.

Theme verse: 'Have mercy on me, O God, according to your
unfailing love; according to your great compassion blot out
my transgressions' (Ps. 51:1).

In the fifth petition of the Lord's Prayer we ask God to forgive
us our debts. Debt occurs when we do not pay what we owe, and
we owe to God perfect obedience. Since we do not perfectly obey
God, we are debtors to him and it is right for him to judge us. Our
only hope is to plead for mercy and express true sorrow for our
sin. So we pray with sincerity, 'Forgive us our debts.' God requires
true confession for our sins and promises that 'If we confess our
sins, he is faithful and just and will forgive us our sins and purify
us from all unrighteousness' (1 John 1:9). The second part of the
petition requires us to forgive others. When we strive against all
thought of revenge and pray for our enemies, desiring their good
and seeking to be reconciled to them, then we forgive as God has
forgiven us. Only people who experience the grace of God in forgiveness through Christ have this supernatural ability to forgive
others. Unless we are willing to forgive those who have wronged
us, we should not expect God to forgive us the great debt we owe
him. 'For if you forgive men when they sin against you, your heavenly Father will also forgive you. But if you do not forgive men
their sins, your Father will not forgive your sin' (Matt. 6:14-15). So
in this critical matter of confessing sin, God's Word gives us solid
reasons for real encouragement as well as dire warning.

SCRIPTURE READING: 1 JOHN 1:1-10

December 11

Confession

Westminster Catechism Question #105:

What do we pray for in the fifth petition? *Answer*: In the fifth petition (which is 'Forgive us our debts, as we also have forgiven our debtors') we pray that God would freely pardon all our sins, which we are encouraged to ask because by his grace we are enabled from the heart to forgive others.

Theme verse: 'Have mercy on me, O God, according to your unfailing love; according to your great compassion blot out my transgressions' (Ps. 51:1).

As soon as Jesus taught us to say 'Give us today our daily bread,' he quickly added, 'and forgive us our debts, as we also have forgiven our debtors.' There is something strangely macabre about asking a condemned prisoner what meal he would like to eat before he is taken to his execution. A good meal brings little satisfaction without pardon, and receiving our daily provision from the hand of God without cleansing from sin is also joyless (Deut. 8:3). The manna in the wilderness was called 'the food of angels', but it quickly dried up under the scorching sun. Daily bread may satisfy the appetite for a moment but what we all need is forgiveness of sins which satisfies the conscience for all eternity. What every believer in Jesus knows experientially is that the saving of our souls brings meaning to our daily lives, since the Lord is the Lord of eternity as well as the Lord who concerns himself with our daily needs. For the unbeliever, the problem of eating a delicious meal is that there is no one to thank, since their sins remain. But Christians, whose sins are forgiven, eat and drink to the glory of God. Believers pray that God will bless the food to the nourishment of their bodies in order to energize them for service to their Saviour, both now and for eternity. And as much as we all like a good meal, we desire cleansed and forgiven consciences far more.

SCRIPTURE READING: DEUTERONOMY 8:1-20

December 12
ACCUMULATING DEBT
(WEEK 50: DAY 3)

Confession

Westminster Catechism Question #105:

What do we pray for in the fifth petition? *Answer*: In the fifth
petition (which is 'Forgive us our debts, as we also have forgiven
our debtors') we pray that God would freely pardon all our sins,
which we are encouraged to ask because by his grace we are
enabled from the heart to forgive others.

Theme verse: 'Have mercy on me, O God, according to your
unfailing love; according to your great compassion blot out
my transgressions' (Ps. 51:1).

A debt arises due to non-payment and when debts pile up we can
expect a bill collector to come knocking at the door. Hopefully,
even if we have many debts, a way will be found to work ourselves
out from under them. But our debts to the Lord we can never
repay. That is why Jesus taught us to pray 'Forgive us our debts,'
an acknowledgement that we have no means to pay for them. We
are all sinners and spiritually bankrupt. There was a time when
Adam and Eve were perfectly righteous, but they squandered their
original inheritance and were broken by sin. We have been impov-
erished ever since. Our debts are of the worst kind because our
sins are against a perfectly holy and righteous God. An offence
against a king is considered high treason and receives a harsher
penalty, and similarly, sin against God's rule is rebellion which
makes our debt incalculable. To make matters worse, we cannot
number all of our debts. Jeremiah perceived this dilemma when
he wrote, 'The heart is deceitful above all things and beyond cure.
Who can understand it?' (Jer. 17:9). We simply do not know how
much we owe to God. To make matters still worse, we cannot
shift our debt onto another mortal. No, we simply must come
empty-handed and seek mercy. Please, Lord, forgive us our debts,
as we also have forgiven our debtors.

SCRIPTURE READING: JEREMIAH 17:5-18

December 13

Confession

Westminster Catechism Question #105:

What do we pray for in the fifth petition? *Answer*: In the fifth petition (which is 'Forgive us our debts, as we also have forgiven our debtors') we pray that God would freely pardon all our sins, which we are encouraged to ask because by his grace we are enabled from the heart to forgive others.

Theme verse: 'Have mercy on me, O God, according to your unfailing love; according to your great compassion blot out my transgressions' (Ps. 51:1).

What does it mean to be forgiven of our debts? First, it means that God lifts our sins from off our shoulders and takes them away. When the heavy burden of sin is upon us, God, in pardoning, lifts it off of us and lays it on Christ. 'The Lord has laid on him the iniquity of us all' (Isa. 53:6). Secondly, to forgive sin is to cover it. Jesus uses his own blood, poured out for us, to cover over our sins, so that the Father sees us as righteous in his sight. 'You forgave the iniquity of your people and covered all their sins' (Ps. 85:2). Thirdly, to forgive sin is to blot it out. 'I, even I, am he who blots out your transgressions, for my own sake' (Isa. 43:25). The allusion is to a creditor who, when his debtor has paid him, blots out the debt and gives the debtor a receipt that states, 'paid in full'. When God forgives sin he blots out the debt and treats our sin as though it never existed by drawing the red lines of Christ's blood over it. And fourthly, to forgive sin is to have God cast our sins 'into the depths of the sea', that is, burying them and putting them out of sight so that they never come back to haunt us on Judgement Day. 'You will tread our sins underfoot and hurl our iniquities into the depths of the sea' (Micah 7:19). Who is a God like this, who pardons, covers, blots out and buries our sin, and delights to show mercy to sinners? (Micah 7:18).

SCRIPTURE READING: MICAH 7:14-20

December 14
A BROKEN AND CONTRITE HEART
(WEEK 50: DAY 5)

Confession

Westminster Catechism Question #105:

What do we pray for in the fifth petition? *Answer*: In the fifth
petition (which is 'Forgive us our debts, as we also have forgiven
our debtors') we pray that God would freely pardon all our sins,
which we are encouraged to ask because by his grace we are
enabled from the heart to forgive others.

Theme verse: 'Have mercy on me, O God, according to your
unfailing love; according to your great compassion blot out
my transgressions' (Ps. 51:1).

After King David's moral failures he was confronted by the
prophet Nathan, and was devastated by his judgement. Out of
the depths of his repentant heart David sought mercy from God
and desired to be washed clean of his sin. He had lost fellowship
with God and agreed that God was right to judge him for his
sinful behaviour (Ps. 51:1-4). David reflected on how he used to
praise the Lord with a pure heart and longed for the kind of inner strength that would keep him from falling into sin again. He
pleaded for the strong presence of the Holy Spirit in his life who
would fill him with the joy of his salvation and make it possible
for him to live a godly life (Ps. 51:5-12). David then made promises to God, that if the Lord would be merciful and forgive him
of his great transgressions, he would instruct others to avoid the
foolishness and deceitfulness of sin. He even anticipated sinners
turning to God through his evangelistic efforts and such musings
filled him with even deeper longing for God's forgiveness. David
also pledged that if the Lord forgave him he would open his lips
to declare God's praise and hallow his name. David knew that if
the Lord required only an animal sacrifice or a burnt offering he
would gladly offer it, but what the Lord requires of all of us is 'a
broken and contrite heart' (Ps. 51:17).

SCRIPTURE READING: PSALM 51

December 15

Confession

Westminster Catechism Question #105:

What do we pray for in the fifth petition? *Answer*: In the fifth petition (which is 'Forgive us our debts, as we also have forgiven our debtors') we pray that God would freely pardon all our sins, which we are encouraged to ask because by his grace we are enabled from the heart to forgive others.

Theme verse: 'Have mercy on me, O God, according to your unfailing love; according to your great compassion blot out my transgressions' (Ps. 51:1).

The disciples had been arguing about the miserable question of which of them would be greatest in the kingdom of heaven. They turned to the Lord to get a final verdict on the matter and Jesus responded by setting a child in front of them. Jesus was brusque with his rebuke: 'I tell you the truth, unless you change and become like little children, you will never enter the kingdom of heaven. Therefore, whoever humbles himself like this child is the greatest in the kingdom of heaven' (Matt. 18:3-4). It appears that Peter was still smarting from the dispute, having been the object of special envy as well as caustic and hurtful remarks, when he asked Jesus how long he had to put up with the ridicule from his fellow disciples. 'Lord, how many times shall I forgive my brother when he sins against me? Up to seven times?' (Matt. 18:21). Jesus answered Peter, 'I tell you, not seven times, but seventy-seven times' (Matt. 18:22). Under old Jewish teaching a person was called upon to forgive personal wrongs up to three times. Peter had made progress under his Master's teaching and more than doubled the limit. But Jesus takes Peter's breath away by calling for no less than seventy-seven times, a number so great that keeping an account of wrongs is impossible. The Lord is teaching us to forgive all wrongs done to us, no matter how many times we are offended.

SCRIPTURE READING: MATTHEW 18:1-22

December 16

Confession

Westminster Catechism Question #105:

What do we pray for in the fifth petition? *Answer*: In the fifth
petition (which is 'Forgive us our debts, as we also have forgiven
our debtors') we pray that God would freely pardon all our sins,
which we are encouraged to ask because by his grace we are
enabled from the heart to forgive others.

Theme verse: 'Have mercy on me, O God, according to your
unfailing love; according to your great compassion blot out
my transgressions' (Ps. 51:1).

Since it seemed almost unbelievable to Peter that Jesus would require that we always forgive those who have wronged us, Jesus
clarified the matter by means of a parable. The Lord told a story
of a king who wanted to settle accounts with his servants. One of
his servants, who owed him millions of dollars but was hopelessly
unable to repay, begged his master for mercy. And instead of sell-
ing this servant to another, the king took pity on him, cancelled
his huge debt, and let him go. As soon as the servant left, however,
he found one of his fellow servants who owed him just a few dollars. 'He grabbed him and began to choke him, "Pay back what
you owe me!" he demanded' (Matt. 18:28). And although his fellow servant begged for time to repay, this wicked servant refused
to show the forgiveness he had earlier received from his master
and had the poor servant thrown into prison. When the king heard
about this he was enraged, handing over the wicked servant to the
jailers to be tortured until he paid back what he owed. When Jesus
finished his parable he gave an immediate application. 'This is
how my heavenly Father will treat each of you unless you forgive
your brother from your heart' (Matt. 18:35). Offering genuine forgiveness when we are wronged is not optional, not if our massive
debt has been forgiven by a gracious, bleeding Saviour.

SCRIPTURE READING: MATTHEW 18:21-35

December 17
DELIVER US FROM EVIL
(WEEK 51: DAY 1)

Deliverance

Westminster Catechism Question #106:

What do we pray for in the sixth petition? *Answer*: In the sixth petition (which is 'And lead us not into temptation, but deliver us from the evil one') we pray that God would either keep us from being tempted to sin or support and deliver us when we are tempted.

Theme verse: 'Watch and pray so that you will not fall into temptation. The spirit is willing, but the body is weak' (Matt. 26:41).

This final petition of the Lord's Prayer consists of two parts: 'Lead us not into temptation' and 'Deliver us from the evil one.' There are two sources of temptation: internal — our sinful hearts deceive us; and external — Satan tempts us. God never tempts us to sin. He permits sin, but never promotes it. However, God does test us as he tested Abraham when he asked him to offer Isaac as a sacrifice. Testing keeps us from pride, makes us better able to comfort others, and encourages us to long for heaven. God promises to provide a way of escape for tempted souls: 'God is faithful; he will not let you be tempted beyond what you can bear. But when you are tempted, he will also provide a way out so that you can stand up under it' (1 Cor. 10:13). Although Christ never sinned, he sympathizes with our weakness because he was tempted himself while on earth. He warns us to watch and pray. He sends his Spirit to comfort and strengthen us, reminding us that Scripture is our great weapon against the attacks of the evil one. Remember, too, that abstaining from overtly sinful acts is not enough. When we pray 'Deliver us from evil,' we are asking God to enable us to make genuine progress in holiness. We are seeking to live sanctified lives in which we increasingly reflect the image of the perfect Saviour.

SCRIPTURE READING: 1 CORINTHIANS 1:1-13

December 18
TRIALS AND TEMPTATIONS
(WEEK 51: DAY 2)

Deliverance

Westminster Catechism Question #106:

What do we pray for in the sixth petition? *Answer*: In the sixth
petition (which is 'And lead us not into temptation, but deliver us
from the evil one') we pray that God would either keep us from
being tempted to sin or support and deliver us when
we are tempted.

Theme verse: 'Watch and pray so that you will not fall into
temptation. The spirit is willing, but the body is weak'
(Matt. 26:41).

We should differentiate between trials and temptations. Trials are
used by God to perfect us, to develop maturity in us, and to make
us more like Christ. The Apostle James wrote that we are blessed
if we persevere under trials God sends our way. If we see God's
hand in it, and can still 'consider it all joy' (James 1:2) when we
are tested, it proves that we are genuine believers who love the
Lord. God promises to bless such persevering, joyful Christians
with eternal life (James 1:12). Trials may turn into temptations if
we fail to exercise faith in the midst of them, or allow ourselves
to be enticed or discouraged by them, but God never intends for
trials to do anything but grow us in Christ-likeness. Temptations,
on the other hand, are never sent by God. 'When tempted, no one
should say, "God is tempting me"' (James 1:13). We cannot shift
blame to God, although we often try. Adam blamed God for his
original sin: 'the woman you put here with me — she gave me
some fruit from the tree, and I ate it' (Gen. 3:12). Or we blame
God for making us as we are — acting on our lusts or greed. But
the Scriptures are clear: each one of us is tempted by our own evil
desires, when we yield to them we sin, and sin leads to spiritual
death. We are commanded to pray for strength to resist temptation and praise God during trials.

SCRIPTURE READING: JAMES 1:1-18

December 19

Deliverance

Westminster Catechism Question #106:

What do we pray for in the sixth petition? *Answer*: In the sixth petition (which is 'And lead us not into temptation, but deliver us from the evil one') we pray that God would either keep us from being tempted to sin or support and deliver us when we are tempted.

Theme verse: 'Watch and pray so that you will not fall into temptation. The spirit is willing, but the body is weak' (Matt. 26:41).

The Holy Spirit led Jesus into the wilderness to be tempted by the devil (Matt. 4:1). In the wilderness he was 'tempted in every way, just as we are — yet without sin' (Heb. 4:15). This means the Lord did not resort to supernatural powers to resist temptation. Though he did not possess a sinful nature as we do, he used the same weapon that we have at our disposal: the Word of God. He confronted all three temptations that were hurled at him by quoting Scripture from the book of Deuteronomy. Then Jesus, in holy indignation, ordered Satan to depart. The devil realized he was getting nowhere anyway, since Jesus had thwarted his strongest temptations. He departed as a vanquished enemy and Christ was our exalted victor over temptation's power. In a real sense, Jesus was tempted for our sakes. In the Lord's Prayer we ask God to so lead us by his providence as to keep us out of temptation that is too strong for us and to strengthen us in the temptations we do have to face. When God sent Jesus to be tempted by Satan, and when he now lets Satan tempt us, we should not blame God but should remember that God's own Spirit helped Jesus to crush Satan, and that he now helps us to vanquish him. Therefore, part of our calling as believers is to demonstrate the power of Christ in us over the power of the evil one.

SCRIPTURE READING: MATTHEW 4:1-11

December 20
THE SPIRIT IS WILLING
(WEEK 51: DAY 4)

Deliverance

Westminster Catechism Question #106:

What do we pray for in the sixth petition? *Answer*: In the sixth petition (which is 'And lead us not into temptation, but deliver us from the evil one') we pray that God would either keep us from being tempted to sin or support and deliver us when we are tempted.

Theme verse: 'Watch and pray so that you will not fall into temptation. The spirit is willing, but the body is weak' (Matt. 26:41).

Our theme verse comes from the Lord Jesus and was spoken to Peter during those moments of deep agony in the Garden of Gethsemane. Christ's admonition to Peter was to 'watch and pray,' that he not give way to the temptation to be unfaithful in the face of the threatening circumstances that were about to confront him. To watch is to be alert and ready in advance, and to pray is to receive from God the help needed in the critical hour. When Christ saved us we received the spirit of adoption that made us want to please the Lord, ready to respond to his directions and promises. On the other hand, we still have a weak, old nature that clings to our worldly instincts and a proclivity to sin. Our old sinful nature opposes our new spirit (Gal. 5:17); in fact, it would like to regain control of our personality again. The spirit is eager to endure and overcome temptation, but the body is weak and utterly helpless in warding off temptation. So Jesus warned us to be careful that our hearts not be carried away by temptation and anxiety, and to prepare for his return and our future home in his kingdom. In fact, in the Lord's mind, nothing could be more important than victory in this matter: 'Be always on the watch, and pray that you may be able to escape all that is about to happen, and that you may be able to stand before the Son of Man' (Luke 21:36).

SCRIPTURE READING: LUKE 21:29-38

December 21

Deliverance

Westminster Catechism Question #106:

What do we pray for in the sixth petition? *Answer*: In the sixth petition (which is 'And lead us not into temptation, but deliver us from the evil one') we pray that God would either keep us from being tempted to sin or support and deliver us when we are tempted.

Theme verse: 'Watch and pray so that you will not fall into temptation. The spirit is willing, but the body is weak' (Matt. 26:41).

One of the ways to ward off temptation is to have a regular check-up of our spiritual health, and there is no better doctor to examine us than the Lord himself. King David asked the Lord to examine him thoroughly: 'Search me, O God, and know my heart; test me and know my anxious thoughts. See if there is any offensive way in me, and lead me in the way everlasting' (Ps. 139:23-24). David was eager for the Lord to search his heart because he was convinced of the integrity of his devotion, that it was pure and true. We find David asking for regular check-ups: 'Test me, O Lord, and try me, examine my heart and my mind; for your love is ever before me, and I walk continually in your truth' (Ps. 26:2). David refused to settle in or associate himself with the wicked or to give way to the temptation to take advantage of others simply because he was in a position of power (Ps. 26:4-5). David requested in this psalm to have his inmost soul searched by the Lord. He was aware of the deceitfulness of his own heart and his desire was to detect and put to death every sin. He longed for the assurance of his salvation and to worship with a clean heart. With the assurance of God's approval, he could delight in praising the Lord in the congregation on earth and also look forward to joining the great assembly of worshipers in heaven, singing praises to the Lamb for evermore.

SCRIPTURE READING: PSALM 26:1-12

December 22

Deliverance

Westminster Catechism Question #106:

What do we pray for in the sixth petition? *Answer*: In the sixth petition (which is 'And lead us not into temptation, but deliver us from the evil one') we pray that God would either keep us from being tempted to sin or support and deliver us when we are tempted.

Theme verse: 'Watch and pray so that you will not fall into temptation. The spirit is willing, but the body is weak' (Matt. 26:41).

It is sometimes difficult to distinguish between temptations which come from Satan and those that are concocted in our own hearts. But the nature and severity of some temptations serve as indicators as to their source. For instance, most temptations that spring up from our own hearts are more casual. We ponder and reflect on them, then yield to the temporary pleasures without considering the damage they will cause to our soul. But temptations that are satanic in origin are usually quite sudden, and they come on us unexpectedly. In such cases we are admonished to 'take up the shield of faith, with which you can extinguish all the flaming arrows of the evil one' (Eph. 6:16). Again, most temptations that come from within are milder in nature, but satanic influences are often vivid, ghastly and frightening. Nightmares, extreme violence, suicidal or murderous thoughts are demonic in origin. In such cases we call out on God to deliver us. King David had no need to take a military census but the idea suddenly popped into his head. His action was motivated by pride and an attitude of self-reliance that was uncharacteristic of the godly king. The Lord's anger burned against Israel for the census and we know the culprit behind this temptation. 'Satan rose up against Israel and incited David to take a census of Israel' (1 Chr. 21:1).

SCRIPTURE READING: 1 CHRONICLES 21:1-19

December 23

Deliverance

Westminster Catechism Question #106:

What do we pray for in the sixth petition? *Answer*: In the sixth petition (which is 'And lead us not into temptation, but deliver us from the evil one') we pray that God would either keep us from being tempted to sin or support and deliver us when we are tempted.

Theme verse: 'Watch and pray so that you will not fall into temptation. The spirit is willing, but the body is weak' (Matt. 26:41).

The Bible provides plenty of comfort for tempted souls. First, we can take comfort in the fact that we are not alone. All of God's people are tempted. Even Elijah gave way to the temptation of discouragement. In the face of Jezebel's rage he prayed, 'I have had enough, Lord, take my life' (1 Kings 19:4). Job was tempted to curse God. Peter was tempted to deny Christ. Even the Lord Jesus, though free from sin, was not free from temptation. Secondly, when we are burdened by temptations it is evidence of God's grace at work in us. Satan does not tempt God's children because there is sin in us but because there is grace in us. Just as thieves prefer to rob richly-appointed houses rather than empty ones, Satan targets people who are filled with joy and peace. Though temptations are a burden, knowing the reason why we are tempted is a comfort. Thirdly, we have the certainty that Jesus Christ is near at hand and stands by us in all our temptations. 'We do not have a high priest who is unable to sympathize with our weaknesses' (Heb. 4:15). Jesus is like the Good Samaritan, pouring in the wine and oil, supporting and delivering us when we are tempted. 'Because he himself suffered when he was tempted, he is able to help those who are being tempted' (Heb. 2:18). Take comfort that God is able to deliver us in times of temptation.

SCRIPTURE READING: HEBREWS 2:10-18

December 24
DOXOLOGY
(WEEK 52: DAY 1)

Praise

Westminster Catechism Question #107:

What does the conclusion of the Lord's Prayer teach us? *Answer*:
The conclusion of the Lord's Prayer (which is, 'For yours is the
kingdom and the power and the glory forever. Amen') teaches us
to take our encouragement in prayer from God only, and in our
prayers to praise him, and ascribe kingdom, power and glory
to him.

Theme verse: 'To him who sits on the throne and to the Lamb be
praise and honor and glory and power, for ever and ever!'
(Rev. 5:13).

This final phrase of the Lord's Prayer is a doxology, an offering
of praise to God. Several variations of the doxology are recorded in the writings of the early church, so we know that the early
Christians recited these phrases during worship. The doxology,
with its final exclamation of praise, is a fitting conclusion to the
Lord's Prayer, for it is difficult for us to ask the Lord to 'lead us
not into temptation, but deliver us from the evil one,' without
then ascribing power and glory to our victorious King. In fact,
the deliverance we are asking for, while it includes rescue from
wickedness throughout our lives, is deliverance at the end of life
from the world of darkness that we can only find through Christ's
death and resurrection. This is what the final petition is actually
requesting, and we need this final rescue more than anything else
in the world. It is no wonder, then, that the early church erupted in
praise when it concluded the Lord's Prayer. Our great God is holy.
He establishes his kingdom and accomplishes his will among us.
He provides for all our needs, cleansing us from sin by the sacrifice of his own Son, and delivering us from death, hell and coming
wrath. To such a God as this we join the hosts of heaven and proclaim: 'To him who sits on the throne and to the Lamb be praise
and honor and glory and power, for ever and ever!' Amen.

SCRIPTURE READING: JUDE VV. 24-25

December 25

Praise

Westminster Catechism Question #107:

What does the conclusion of the Lord's Prayer teach us? *Answer*: The conclusion of the Lord's Prayer (which is, 'For yours is the kingdom and the power and the glory forever. Amen') teaches us to take our encouragement in prayer from God only, and in our prayers to praise him, and ascribe kingdom, power and glory to him.

Theme verse: 'To him who sits on the throne and to the Lamb be praise and honor and glory and power, for ever and ever!' (Rev. 5:13).

The kingdom of God slipped into our world unannounced and without fanfare. Phillips Brooks penned the words to the hymn 'O Little Town of Bethlehem', and in it, Brooks expresses eloquently those initial moments when the kingdom of God entered our world:

'How silently, how silently, the wondrous gift is given;
So God imparts to human hearts the blessings of his heaven!
No ear may hear his coming, but in this world of sin,
Where meek souls will receive him still the dear Christ enters in.'

Who could imagine, with such an ignominious beginning, that the holy child's entrance into our world would inaugurate a kingdom that has no end? So, what is this kingdom of God like? How do you describe it? 'It is like a mustard seed, which is the smallest seed you plant in the ground. Yet when planted, it grows and becomes the largest of all garden plants' (Mark 4:31-32). This kingdom, with its humble beginnings, has become the glorious kingdom of our God and of his Christ. Every generation of believers is privileged to participate in its growth. Come, let us adore Christ the King!

SCRIPTURE READING: MARK 4:30-41

December 26

Praise

Westminster Catechism Question #107:

What does the conclusion of the Lord's Prayer teach us? *Answer*:
The conclusion of the Lord's Prayer (which is, 'For yours is the
kingdom and the power and the glory forever. Amen') teaches us
to take our encouragement in prayer from God only, and in our
prayers to praise him, and ascribe kingdom, power and glory
to him.

Theme verse: 'To him who sits on the throne and to the Lamb be
praise and honor and glory and power, for ever and ever!'
(Rev. 5:13).

Faith's view of the glory of Christ in this world is dark and hazy.
'Now we see but a poor reflection as in a mirror; then we shall see
face to face' (1 Cor. 13:12). We could never discover Christ at all
if it was not for the gospel; nevertheless, the Bible is still very far
from fully displaying the greatness of his glory. The Bible cannot
tell us everything about the immensity and majesty of our God.
His glory is beyond description, and besides, we are too weak and
imperfect to bear greater demonstrations of his glory now. But
when we are in heaven our sight of him will be immediate, direct and steady. Then we will know the Lord, even as we are fully
known. Our faith will give way to the sight of the Saviour's beauty
and power. Christ with all his glory will be continually with us.
We will no longer have to be satisfied with mere descriptions of
him that we have in the gospel. The sight of Christ is what all his
followers have been longing for. Like Paul, we 'desire to depart
and be with Christ, which is better by far' (Phil. 1:23). For now, let
us weave praise into our prayers, ascribing glory to the Lamb, but
also recognizing that we apprehend only the smallest fraction of
all the effulgence and glory of Christ until that day that we, like
Stephen, will proclaim: 'Look, I see heaven open and the Son of
Man standing at the right hand of God' (Acts 7:56).

SCRIPTURE READING: 1 CORINTHIANS 13:1-13

December 27
CORONATION PSALM
(WEEK 52: DAY 4)

Praise

Westminster Catechism Question #107:

What does the conclusion of the Lord's Prayer teach us? *Answer*:
The conclusion of the Lord's Prayer (which is, 'For yours is the
kingdom and the power and the glory forever. Amen') teaches us
to take our encouragement in prayer from God only, and in our
prayers to praise him, and ascribe kingdom, power and glory
to him.

Theme verse: 'To him who sits on the throne and to the Lamb be
praise and honor and glory and power, for ever and ever!'
(Rev. 5:13).

Psalm 110 is classified as a 'coronation psalm', meaning that it
is an oracle concerning the installation of a great King upon his
throne. It is no wonder, then, that it is so frequently quoted in
the New Testament, either by the author to the Hebrews, Peter
or the Lord Jesus himself. Christians have generally held that this
is the most directly prophetic of all the psalms. In the psalm, David muses upon the stunning truth of the Messiah enthroned as
the supreme Lord of all the earth. In David's theologically-alive
mind, he could picture the Messiah being crowned by his Father,
an act that would frustrate all human rebellion and efforts to in-
stall a different king. This, in fact, would be the most important
divine act of all time; it would dominate and give meaning to all
human history. David reflected on what it would be like when the
King of kings undertook his final triumphant march against his
enemies. He was filled with love towards his future royal Son and
his thoughts led David into worship, praise and a sense of delight
at the exaltation and success of the Lord Jesus. It also brought
him calm in the face of current affairs, patience with the events of
his own life, and expectancy that a glorious future was coming.
We, too, can enjoy the peace that passes understanding because
we know the One who sits upon the throne.

SCRIPTURE READING: PSALM 110

377

December 28
WAITING FOR THE WEDDING
(WEEK 52: DAY 5)

Praise

Westminster Catechism Question #107:

What does the conclusion of the Lord's Prayer teach us? *Answer*: The conclusion of the Lord's Prayer (which is, 'For yours is the kingdom and the power and the glory forever. Amen') teaches us to take our encouragement in prayer from God only, and in our prayers to praise him, and ascribe kingdom, power and glory to him.

Theme verse: 'To him who sits on the throne and to the Lamb be praise and honor and glory and power, for ever and ever!' (Rev. 5:13).

In biblical times marriage was arranged by parents for their children, and betrothal was the first public announcement of the intention of the young people to wed. At the betrothal, God's blessing was pronounced on the union. Between the betrothal and the actual marriage the groom paid a dowry to the father of the bride. When the actual wedding day arrived the bride would adorn herself in her finest clothing. The groom also dressed impressively, and was then led by his attendants to the bride's house. The couple would then be escorted back to the groom's house where a joyful wedding feast was held that would last a week or even two. Psalm 45 describes a wedding procession for a royal couple, one in which the groom has a throne (Ps. 45:6) and lives in palaces adorned with ivory (Ps. 45:8). The verses in this psalm describe the stately spectacle of the king coming for his bride (Ps. 45:2-9), the response of the bride as the king comes into her view (Ps. 45:10-15), and the divine benediction on the marriage as the imperial couple enters the king's palace (Ps. 45:16-17). The king is none other than the Lord Jesus who has come to retrieve his bride, the Church. He has purchased her with a great price and she has prepared herself for his coming and this glad day. Let us join this joyful celebration and praise the young prince, ascribing kingdom, power and glory to him.

SCRIPTURE READING: PSALM 45:1-17

December 29

THE LORD'S RETURN

(WEEK 52: DAY 6)

Praise

Westminster Catechism Question #107:

What does the conclusion of the Lord's Prayer teach us? *Answer*:
The conclusion of the Lord's Prayer (which is, 'For yours is the
kingdom and the power and the glory forever. Amen') teaches us
to take our encouragement in prayer from God only, and in our
prayers to praise him, and ascribe kingdom, power and glory
to him.

Theme verse: 'To him who sits on the throne and to the Lamb be
praise and honor and glory and power, for ever and ever!'
(Rev. 5:13).

The great event of the future is the second coming of the Lord
Jesus. There are a number of things that we know about this event
from Scripture. First, it will be personal. 'The Lord himself will
come down from heaven' (1 Thess. 4:16). Secondly, it will be visible. 'This same Jesus, who has been taken from you into heaven,
will come back in the same way you have seen him go into heaven'
(Acts 1:11). Thirdly, it will be sudden and unexpected. The word
'apocalypse', which means 'revelation', has the idea of sudden-
ness and unexpectedness in it. His coming will be 'as a thief in the
night'. Jesus said that his return would be 'as lightning' (Matt.
24:27). Fourthly, the second coming of Christ will be glorious and
triumphant. When Jesus came into our world the first time he
came as a humble servant. But when he comes again, 'every knee
shall bow' to him (Phil. 2:5-11). He came earlier to be rejected and
killed, but he will come again 'in his glory and in the glory of the
Father and of the holy angels' (Luke 9:26). He came as a child but
he will return as King of kings and Lord of lords, victorious over
every foe. The saints of the Old Testament looked forward to the
Messiah's first coming. Now, the New Testament keeps Christ's
second coming before our minds, and urges us to earnest prayer
and watchfulness for the King's return.

SCRIPTURE READING: MATTHEW 24:1-35

December 30
PRAYER AND PRAISE
(WEEK 52: DAY 7)

Praise

Westminster Catechism Question #107:

What does the conclusion of the Lord's Prayer teach us? *Answer*:
The conclusion of the Lord's Prayer (which is, 'For yours is the
kingdom and the power and the glory forever. Amen') teaches us
to take our encouragement in prayer from God only, and in our
prayers to praise him, and ascribe kingdom, power and glory
to him.

Theme verse: 'To him who sits on the throne and to the Lamb be
praise and honor and glory and power, for ever and ever!'
(Rev. 5:13).

The catechism commends prayer that is praise-centred or Christ-
centred. It states that in our prayers we should praise the Lord,
and ascribe power and glory to him. Such praying will inspire and
express itself in authentic worship, whether individual worship
or in the congregation. In true worship we see the excellence of
our God, and join with David, praying, 'O God, you are my God,
earnestly I seek you; my soul thirsts for you, my body longs for
you, in a dry and weary land where there is no water' (Ps. 63:1).
Jesus gave us the Lord's Prayer to foster not only proper prayer,
but also proper worship. The worst thing we can do is to make the
Lord's Prayer a rote prayer, without feeling or emotion. If we turn
Christ's model prayer into mere duty and mindless recitation, we
have done exactly the opposite of what our Lord sought for his
disciples in prayer. Prayer is the highest form of worship and true
prayer is alive, rejoicing in the relationship we have with Christ.
Prayer and worship require a strong affection for God or else it
is nothing more than hypocrisy. Good preaching should inspire
solid worship. Our hymns and praise songs should do the same.
The psalmists gave us prayers to inspire praise. And the Lord's
Prayer was given to us by Christ to teach us to pray to him only,
with hearts full of praise. 'Let everything that has breath praise
the Lord!' (Psalm 150:6).

SCRIPTURE READING: PSALM 63:1-11

December 31

Abundant life

'I have come that they may have life, and have it to the full'
(John 10:10).

Christ summarized his missionary purpose when he declared that he had come to 'seek and to save what was lost' (Luke 19:10), meaning that in his coming to earth he would redeem the helpless and provide eternal life in his kingdom for his chosen people. The Apostle John, awestruck by the depth of God's love, wrote, 'This is love: not that we loved God, but that he loved us and sent his Son as an atoning sacrifice for our sins' (1 John 4:10).

An example of the depth of Christ's love is the story of Christ's encounter with the Samaritan woman. At that well in Samaria, Jesus demonstrated to his disciples that his Father was interested in turning outcasts, such as the Samaritan woman, into worshipers; seeking them out in order to save them, demonstrating his love towards them, removing their sin and implanting the Holy Spirit and the Word in them. What we notice in the story is the depth of Christ's love and the extent of his grace. The Redeemer's initial words to the woman are direct: 'If you knew the gift of God and who it is that asks you for a drink, you would have asked him and he would have given you living water' (John 4:10). Think of what Christ knew. He had just come from heaven where myriads of angels attended to him. The Saviour's heavenly environment was full of spine-tingling excitement and euphoric praise. He lived where the knowledge of the universe is stored and the galaxies are but a short flight away, where there is sinless perfection and no darkness dwells. And now Jesus was resting at a well in Samaria, bone-weary after a long day's journey. Imagine what the Lord knew and what this woman of Samaria did not know. She knew heartbreak and what it was to be abused. She knew loneliness, sin and desperation. And she knew nothing about eternal life and what is in store for those who repent of their shallow and sinful ways to embrace true life. Then the Lord told her about his mission. He had come from heaven to procure worshipers for his Father, to bring them to heaven where they would sit down at the great banquet hall of God, where they would live for ever.

What is waiting for those who, in simple faith, surrender their lives to Jesus Christ? 'No eye has seen, no ear has heard, no mind has conceived what God has prepared for those who love him' (1 Cor. 2:9). There is no better time to respond to Christ's invitation to worship his Father than today. Christ has come to seek and save what was lost. Jesus offers meaning and purpose for your life today, and unspeakable glory and joy for an eternity of tomorrows.

SCRIPTURE READING: JOHN 4:1-14

Devotional Index

DATE	TITLE	SCRIPTURE
January 18	God's early intention to bless	Genesis 1:1-31
January 19	Squashing misconceptions	Mark 12:28-34
January 20	Power to obey	Romans 8:5-11
January 21	Discussing God's commands	Deuteronomy 6:1-9
January 22	Worshiping in Spirit and truth	John 4:7-26
January 23	The glory of God	Psalm 102:18-28
January 24	Contemplating God's character	Isaiah 6
January 25	The glory of God in the Psalms	Psalm 147
January 26	The Great 'I Am'	Exodus 3:1-15
January 27	The response of worship	Exodus 34:1-9
January 28	Worshiping in heaven	Revelation 5:1-14
January 29	No other God	Romans 1:18-25
January 30	The true God resisted	Acts 19:23-41
January 31	The names of God	Psalm 48:1-14
February 1	Elijah's God	1 Kings 18:16-40
February 2	The temptation of Jesus	Matthew 4:1-11
February 3	The god of materialism	Philippians 3:12-21

DATE	TITLE	SCRIPTURE
February 22	Overruling stubborn servants	*Book of Jonah*
February 23	God's special care	*Acts 23:11-22*
February 24	Who killed the Lord?	*Isaiah 53:1-12*
February 25	Under his control	*Colossians 1:15-23*
February 26	Out of nothing	*Hebrews 11:1-6*
February 27	The heavens declare God's glory	*Psalm 19*
February 28	Caring for God's creation	*Matthew 6:19-34*
February 29	Making reconciliation possible	*Matthew 23:13-26*
March 1	The day of the Lord	*2 Peter 3:8-14*
March 2	A new creation	*2 Corinthians 5:11-21*
March 3	Entering God's rest	*Hebrews 4:1-13*
March 4	God's re-creation	*Revelation 21:1-8*
March 5	The creation of man	*Genesis 2:5-25*
March 6	Image-bearers	*Ephesians 4:17-24*
March 7	Written upon the heart	*Romans 2:5-16*
March 8	Crowned with glory and honour	*Psalm 8*
March 9	Restoring the image of God	*Colossians 3:1-11*
March 10	Work in the garden	*2 Thessalonians 3:6-15*
March 11	No surprises	*Romans 5:12-21*

DATE	TITLE	SCRIPTURE
April 1	Christ's ascension	*Matthew 26:57-68*
April 2	Christ's three offices	*Deuteronomy 18:14-22*
April 3	The prophetic fulfilment	*Acts 3:17-26*
April 4	A better priesthood	*Hebrews 7:23-28*
April 5	The Most Holy Place	*Hebrews 9:11-15*
April 6	Wonderful Counsellor	*Isaiah 9:1-7*
April 7	The rejected king	*Psalm 2*
April 8	The chosen servant	*Matthew 12:15-21*
April 9	Christ's prophetic words	*John 15:9-17*
April 10	The prophetic voice	*Matthew 5:1-12*
April 11	A question of the heart	*Matthew 5:21-32*
April 12	Measuring our faith	*Matthew 6:1-18*
April 13	Where is our treasure?	*Matthew 6:19-34*
April 14	False prophets	*Matthew 7:15-23*
April 15	The authoritative voice	*Luke 6:43-49*
April 16	A sympathetic High Priest	*Hebrews 4:14*
April 17	Daily intercession	*Hebrews 7:23-28*
April 18	The true sanctuary	*Hebrews 9:11-15*
April 19	An offering of praise	*Hebrews 5:1-10*
April 20	Carrying us in his heart	*Exodus 28:15-21; 29-30*

DATE	TITLE	SCRIPTURE
May 9	Transfiguration glory	*Matthew 17:1-9*
May 10	Two hymns in one	*Philippians 2:1-11*
May 11	Spine-tingling worship	*Revelation 5:1-14*
May 12	A reason for encouragement	*1 Thessalonians 4:13-18*
May 13	Watching and waiting	*Matthew 25:1-13*
May 14	Calvary's application to us	*Philippians 1:3-11*
May 15	The test of faith	*Romans 8:5-14*
May 16	The order of salvation	*Ephesians 1:11-14*
May 17	Rebirth by the Holy Spirit	*Titus 3:3-8*
May 18	Written on our hearts	*Ezekiel 36:24-28*
May 19	Two things needful	*2 Thessalonians 2:13-17*
May 20	Spiritual power	*Ephesians 3:14-21*
May 21	Approved by God	*Romans 3:21-26*
May 22	Justified by grace	*Romans 4:1-8*
May 23	The tax collector	*Luke 18:9-14*
May 24	The central doctrine	*Acts 13:13-41*
May 25	Keeping the law	*Romans 6:11-23*
May 26	Legal bondage	*Galatians 3:1-14*
May 27	Imputed righteousness	*Romans 5:1-11*
May 28	No longer foreigners	*Ephesians 2:11-22*

DATE	TITLE	SCRIPTURE
June 18	Strive to enter	*Luke 13:22-30*
June 19	Authentic religion	*Matthew 23*
June 20	King Saul's rebellion	*1 Samuel 15*
June 21	The blessing of obedience	*Genesis 22:1-19*
June 22	Hypocrisy from within	*Acts 5:1-11*
June 23	The all-sufficient Scriptures	*Psalm 19*
June 24	Doing good	*Acts 10:34-48*
June 25	The greatest commandment	*Matthew 22:23-40*
June 26	Not far from the kingdom	*Mark 12:28-34*
June 27	Our moral compass	*Romans 7:7-25*
June 28	The uniqueness of the law	*Exodus 19:16-25*
June 29	Loving our neighbour	*James 2:1-13*
June 30	The Good Samaritan	*Luke 10:25-37*
July 1	Love's direction	*Romans 13:8-14*
July 2	God as our God	*Psalm 89:1-18*
July 3	Joshua's exhortation	*Joshua 24:1-27*
July 4	The fear of the Lord	*Daniel 3:1-30*
July 5	Trusting God	*Habakkuk 3:8-19*
July 6	Hear, O Israel	*Deuteronomy 6:1-25*

DATE	TITLE	SCRIPTURE
July 27	A day of light	*Psalm 118*
July 28	A good habit	*Acts 20:7-12*
July 29	Our use of the Lord's Day	*Matthew 12:1-14*
July 30	Relationships	*Romans 12:9-21*
July 31	Harsh punishment	*1 Samuel 2:12-25*
August 1	Twisting the commandments	*Mark 7:1-22*
August 2	Teaching our children	*Ephesians 6:1-4*
August 3	Equality in marriage	*Ephesians 5:21-33*
August 4	Honouring authority figures	*1 Peter 2:13-25*
August 5	Honour to Christ alone	*Matthew 2:1-12*
August 6	Do not murder	*Galatians 5:13-26*
August 7	Preserving life	*1 Kings 18:1-16*
August 8	Slow to anger	*Matthew 5:21-26*
August 9	Envy's target	*Genesis 4:1-16*
August 10	No place for hatred	*James 3:13 – 4:3*
August 11	Caring for ourselves	*1 Timothy 4:1-16*
August 12	The murder of Jesus	*1 Peter 2:21-25*
August 13	Taking drastic measures	*Matthew 5:27-30*
August 14	David's rebellion	*2 Samuel 11:1-27*
August 15	Consequences for sin	*2 Samuel 12:1-23*

DATE	TITLE	SCRIPTURE
September 4	Simon the sorcerer	*Acts 8:9-24*
September 5	Breaking all ten	*Romans 13:8-14*
September 6	The purpose of the law	*Romans 7:7 – 8:4*
September 7	Overcoming temptations	*2 Timothy 4:6-22*
September 8	Rich fools	*Luke 12:13-34*
September 9	The cure for covetousness	*1 John 5:1-12*
September 10	Justified by grace	*1 John 1:5 – 2:6*
September 11	No one is righteous	*Romans 3:9-20*
September 12	Bible light	*Matthew 9:1-13*
September 13	Partial obedience prohibited	*Galatians 3:1-14*
September 14	Prior knowledge	*John 2:12-25*
September 15	The downward spiral	*Genesis 6:1-8*
September 16	Suddenly perfect	*Isaiah 35:1-10*
September 17	Removing condemnation from us	*John 3:22-36*
September 18	Controlled wrath	*1 John 4:7-21*
September 19	Wheat or chaff	*Matthew 3:1-12*
September 20	Human depravity	*Romans 1:18-32*
September 21	Objects of wrath	*Ephesians 2:1-10*
September 22	Greater warnings	*Hebrews 10:19-39*
September 23	Final judgement	*Revelation 19:11-21*

DATE	TITLE	SCRIPTURE
October 14	The need for preaching	*Matthew 9:35-38; Romans 10:8-18*
October 15	Meditating on the Word	*Psalm 119:1-16*
October 16	A covenant with the Lord	*2 Chronicles 34:14-33*
October 17	The noble Bereans	*Acts 17:1-15*
October 18	Knowing the Bible systematically	*1 Timothy 4:1-16*
October 19	Craving spiritual milk	*1 Peter 1:13 – 2:3*
October 20	The gift of wisdom	*Proverbs 2:1-22*
October 21	Divine revelation	*Psalm 119:17-40*
October 22	Sacrament similarities	*Mark 14:12-26*
October 23	The outward sign	*Ezekiel 36:24-38*
October 24	The necessity of baptism	*Acts 8:26-40*
October 25	A sign of grace	*Romans 6:1-14*
October 26	Not forgetting	*1 Corinthians 11:17-26*
October 27	Who is invited?	*1 Corinthians 11:27-34*
October 28	Benefits of the Supper	*1 Corinthians 10:1-22*
October 29	Communion with God	*James 5:13-20*
October 30	The importance of prayer	*Luke 18:1-8*
October 31	The necessity of prayer	*1 John 5:13-21*
November 1	Joyful in prayer	*John 16:17-33*

Date	Title	Scripture
November 22	Longing for Christ's return	*2 Peter 3:1-18*
November 23	Satan's defeat	*Luke 10:1-24*
November 24	Protective armour	*Ephesians 6:10-20*
November 25	Two kingdoms	*Matthew 13:24-43*
November 26	Angelic obedience	*John 15:1-17*
November 27	Heaven on earth	*1 Thessalonians 3:6-13*
November 28	Contentment and God's will	*Numbers 21:1-9*
November 29	Job's test	*Job 1:1-22*
November 30	The agony of Gethsemane	*Matthew 26:36-46*
December 1	God's great design	*Matthew 7:15-29*
December 2	Peaceful life, peaceful death	*Psalm 119:97-112*
December 3	Our attitude toward possessions	*1 Timothy 6:3-10*
December 4	Sustained through prayer	*Psalm 55:1-23*
December 5	The way God works	*Isaiah 57:14-21*
December 6	Sustained through prayer	*Revelation 3:14-22*
December 7	Bread from heaven	*Exodus 16:13-23*
December 8	Feeding the multitude	*Matthew 14:13-21*
December 9	Real food and drink	*John 6:25-59*

Scripture Index

SCRIPTURE	TITLE	DATE
2 Kings 1:1-17	Communicating the gospel	October 9
2 Kings 19:14-19	God as our God	July 2
1 Chronicles 21:1-19	The sources of temptation	December 22
1 Chronicles 29:10-20	Unrivalled authority	February 15
2 Chronicles 34:14-33	A covenant with the Lord	October 16
Nehemiah 13:15-22	Sabbath reforms	July 26
Job 1:1-22	Job's test	November 29
Job 12:10-23	Job's fresh understanding	February 17
Job 22:19-30	Intimacy with God	July 8
Psalm 2	The great King	April 23
Psalm 8	Crowned with glory and honour	March 8
Psalm 15	Entry requirements	August 31
Psalm 19	The all-sufficient Scriptures	June 23
Psalm 26:1-12	Thorough examination	December 21
Psalm 33:1-22	Hallowing God's name	November 12

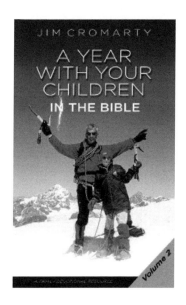

A Year with Your Children in the
Bible, Volume 2
Hardback

Author: Jim Cromarty

Evangelical Press

ISBN-13: 978 0 85234 6 846

This is the second volume in Cromarty's highly acclaimed devotional series *A Year with Your Children in the Bible*.

Parents are encouraged to spend time, on a daily basis, reading with their children from the Bible. This accessible devotional will draw your family into the deep waters of the gospel in a simple and yet profound way. In addition to each day's devotion are thoughts for family discussion. Cromarty concludes each day with a brief meditation and a quote from a trusted source in Christian history.

Let *A Year with Your Children in the Bible, Volume 2*, guide you and your family throughout the year.